ANTISEMITISM
TODAY

How It Is the Same,
How It Is Different, and How to Fight It

Kenneth S. Stern

D1253264

AMERICAN JEWISH COMMITTEE

To Margie, Daniel, and Emily

In memory of James O. Freedman (1935-2006)
A wonderful human being.

Kenneth S. Stern has been the American Jewish Committee's expert on antisemitism since 1989. Mr. Stern, an
attorney, has testified before Congress, argued before the
United States Supreme Court, and was an invited pre-
senter at the White House Conference on Hate Crimes.

Other books by Kenneth S. Stern:
Holocaust Denial (1993)
*Loud Hawk: The United States vs. The American Indian
Movement* (1994)
*A Force Upon the Plain: The American Militia Movement
and the Politics of Hate* (1996)

ISBN 0-87495-140-2

Contents

Foreword   v

Introduction   1

Chapter One: What Is Antisemitism?   7

Chapter Two: An Old Hatred
in New Circumstances   15

Chapter Three: Durban—
Antisemitism as Anti-Racism   23

Chapter Four: 9/11   43

Chapter Five: Antisemitism
in the Arab and Muslim Worlds   55

Chapter Six: Antisemitism in Europe   70

Chapter Seven: Denial of the Holocaust   78

Chapter Eight: Crafting a
Working Definition of Contemporary
Antisemitism for Today's Monitors   96

Chapter Nine: Combating Antisemitism—
The Importance of Strategic,
Venue-Specific Thinking   107

Chapter Ten: United States Campuses   118

Chapter Eleven: The Danger of Relying on Old,
Unproven Gauges and Answers   136

Chapter Twelve: Looking Ahead
in the United States   149

Chapter Thirteen: Conclusion   163

Acknowledgments   170

Notes   172

Index   203

Foreword

In February of 1906, in the aftermath of a series of pogroms in Europe, a group of prominent American Jews met in New York and discussed what they could do about rising antisemitism. From this meeting emerged the American Jewish Committee, America's oldest human-relations organization. While AJC's mission has broadened in its 100 years to include combating all forms of bigotry and promoting democratic values globally, antisemitism has remained one of its core concerns, and I have been honored to be its expert on this subject since 1989.

I grew up in the 1950s and 1960s in New York, where antisemitism was not a major problem that I encountered personally. There were minor irritants, such as the teacher at my private middle school who chastised me for not saying the Lord's Prayer or singing Christian hymns during chapel. But these were years when the evening news showed blacks in the South being doused with fire hoses, beaten, even killed. That was true hatred and bigotry. By comparison, my teacher was merely an annoyance.

I first experienced antisemitism in the late 1970s and 1980s. I was living in Portland, Oregon, working as a trial and appellate attorney. A right-wing group called the Posse Comitatus was particularly active, distributing antisemitic literature (with fraudulent quotations purporting to be from Benjamin Franklin and George Washington) in Portland's Multnomah County Courthouse. While these people seemed like buffoons, they were no laughing matter, as various Posse members from different parts of the country were soon charged with criminal and violent activities.

One April a local neo-Nazi group identified every Jewish family in an Oregon college town and mailed each of them a hateful card on Hitler's birthday. I offered whatever help—legal or otherwise—I could, but I wondered: How should the community respond to such hatred? Ignore it? Program against it? I did not know, but I was certain that the answer from a professional in the Jewish community—telling the people in the small town not to worry because there were fewer card-carrying members of the Ku Klux Klan that year than in the year before—was not sufficient.

More troubling was the antisemitism among my friends in "progressive" circles. After Israel invaded Lebanon in the early 1980s, there were protests by the same people with whom I had worked on a wide range of issues, from combating police brutality and homelessness to promoting tenants' rights and American Indian sovereignty. I too was critical of the Israeli government's actions, but some of the Israel-related literature I saw at the rallies was eerily reminiscent of the material the Posse had been distributing about Jews, with assertions of Jewish power, Jewish conspiracy, and ingrained Jewish venom toward non-Jews. Yet while the Posse would not take offense if someone said they were antisemitic, my friends on the left did not even want to discuss the matter. To do so, they alleged, would be a distraction from the "real" work and would harm the progressive agenda. This reaction bothered me for a number of reasons. First, this refusal to discuss a serious issue came from friends and allies who were eager to discuss just about everything else. Second, it showed that many on the left had a politically driven, as opposed to an analytical, understanding of how bigotry worked. And, third, it proved that combating antisemitism was not easily done.

When I joined the AJC staff a few years later, it was not to bean-count swastikas or dissect the ramblings of the hateful fringe, but rather to focus on how key institutions react to, and can be empowered to counteract, bigotry in general and antisemitism in particular. I had been a lay member of the American Jewish Committee chapter in

Portland and was impressed that AJC was not driven by hysteria about antisemitism or any other issue, but was committed to careful research and honest and respectful debate. I published booklets about and conducted programs on how to combat bigotry on campus, in the media, and in politics. I also wrote in-depth background pieces about the antisemites who were getting some level of traction—people such as David Duke, Louis Farrakhan, and Pat Buchanan, and movements such as skinheads, the militias, and Holocaust deniers.

In the summer of 2000, I decided that it was time to begin a book about contemporary antisemitism. Some well-respected colleagues and pundits had been arguing in the late 1990s that antisemitism was "dead." They asserted that Jews had unprecedented acceptance in American society, with Jews welcomed on boards of major corporations and serving as presidents of Ivy League universities that had, not too many decades ago, used quotas to restrict the number of Jewish students. Further, they pointed to the high rate of Jewish-gentile intermarriage. If Americans were willing to have Jews in their families, so much so that Jews worried about the basics of Jewish continuity, how bad could antisemitism be?

I agreed with their view that we American Jews were in a "golden age," but I thought it dangerous to declare that antisemitism was a thing of the past. It was, rather, a very well-established hatred, and there were new lies—such as Holocaust denial—and recurrent political needs, especially in and related to the Middle East, that were likely to breathe new life into antisemitism in the years ahead. At the least, I thought it only responsible to take advantage of these good times to plan how to counteract antisemitism in the future, rather than to declare victory and ignore a problem with a 2,000-year history.

The collapse of the Israeli-Palestinian peace process in the fall of 2000, sure enough, was followed by increased antisemitism in Europe and an escalation in anti-Israel activity that frequently smelled of antisemitism. There has been much written describing a renewed (some say "new") antisemitism in the last few years, but little about how we must evaluate what should be done about it, and the logical and necessary prior step: whether we need to reevaluate how we think about it.

It is hard to imagine what the group of American Jews, meeting in 1906, would make of the great acceptance of Jews in American society today and the established role of Jewish organizations working to combat antisemitism and bigotry. But the questions they raised 100 years ago—how to gauge the problems, how to respond effectively, how to find allies and really change things for the better—are at least as pressing today as they were then.

This book is an effort, not necessarily to provide the right answers, but more urgently to help ensure that those who care about combating antisemitism are asking intelligent and relevant questions, and not defaulting into comfortable but too often unproved and perhaps ineffective answers.

Kenneth S. Stern
New York, NY
July 19, 2006

The increasing frequency and severity of anti-Semitic incidents since the start of the twenty-first century, particularly in Europe, has compelled the international community to focus on anti-Semitism with renewed vigor.

"Report on Global Anti-Semitism,"
U.S. State Department,
January 5, 2005

Introduction

Despite resistance from some in the United States Department of State, President George W. Bush signed the Global Anti-Semitism* Awareness Act into law on October 16, 2004. For the first time, the United States was obliged to collect and analyze information about, and then issue a report on, antisemitism around the globe. The State Department had to investigate not only what bad things were happening, but also what countries were doing about them.

The report was published in early 2005.[1] The mere appearance of such a document was important, if for no other reason than that the U.S. government could use it in its bilateral relations with many countries to address the problem of antisemitism. It correctly noted, among other things, that many recent incidents in Europe involved members of the Muslim community, and that some antisemitism was sparked by anti-Israel attitudes which "cross[ed] the line," sometimes making comparisons between Israelis and Nazis.

---

* The word "antisemitism" can be spelled with or without a hyphen. Although the *New York Times* and many other publications prefer "anti-Semitism," the trend among experts is toward "antisemitism." Except in quotations or exact references to printed matter that use the spelling anti-Semitism, as in the State Department's "Report on Global Anti-Semitism," this book will use the single-word, lower-case form. While the spelling is a minor point, some try to downplay the significance of Jew-hatred by implying that the word "Semite" has some independent importance, as will be discussed in Chapter 3. Unless the context refers to this particular issue, I use "antisemitism" throughout. See also http://sicsa.huji.ac.il/hyphen.htm.

1

The report not only described the problem, but also offered recommendations for fighting antisemitism around the world. What was its number one and most often repeated suggestion? The development and expansion of "Holocaust education curricular and teacher training programs."[2]

Less than a year earlier, the Organization for Security and Cooperation in Europe (OSCE) held a landmark conference on antisemitism in Berlin. Secretary of State Colin Powell represented the United States at the meeting, hosted at the German Foreign Ministry building. One can but imagine what Adolf Hitler would have thought of the sight: an African-American, representing the United States, speaking at a major government center in the heart of Berlin, protected by German soldiers with guns and tanks, lecturing white Europeans about the need to combat antisemitism.

Increased Holocaust education was among the key recommendations of the conference, proposed and endorsed by nations and nongovernmental organizations (NGOs), including Jewish NGOs—and mentioned by Powell in his speech.

At first blush, this might seem logical. After all, six million Jews died in Europe in the 1940s because Nazi Germany and its allies embraced antisemitism. But despite the undoubtedly true accounts of children and others "learning the lesson of the Holocaust" from books such as *The Diary of Anne Frank* and from interaction with the ever dwindling number of Holocaust survivors, there is simply no research-based proof that Holocaust education is an antidote to antisemitism. This solution is merely asserted and assumed to work. And there is anecdotal evidence that it might actually be counterproductive in some circumstances.

While antisemitism has been around for over 2,000 years, its most recent upsurge began in the fall of 2000, after the collapse of the Israeli-Palestinian peace talks at Camp David and the beginning of the second intifada. Jews and Jewish-linked properties were attacked in Paris, London, New York, and Berlin, and in many other places around the globe. The accepted profile of the likely perpetrator (although many—particularly in Europe—were reluctant to admit it) was a young male Muslim who saw the fighting in the Middle East, wanted somehow to play a part, and assumed that the Jew or Jewish-linked property near him was an acceptable low-risk target upon which to strike a blow.

Such a youngster,[3] learning from his family, imams, and antisemitic satellite television programs, may have been taught that Jews were the descendants of apes and pigs, infidels who have no right to live in—let alone have a claim on—the Arab land of Palestine; Israelis are monsters who are not only oppressing people but also defiling the Holy Land. If he understood the Holocaust at all, he saw it as the justification the Europeans used to rid themselves of the Jews who were not killed in World War II, dumping them onto the land of his Arab brothers. Or perhaps he saw it as the lie the Jews made up to get European acquiescence to their nefarious plot to steal Arab land.

This young man would have come to antisemitism from the teachings of a certain brand of Islam, fueled by another layer of antisemitism having to do with denial of any Jewish connection with the land of Israel, flavored with recycled European conspiracy theories about Jews, and energized by the Arab-Israeli conflict. How exactly would making him understand fully the Nazis, Hitler, Wannsee, Treblinka, Auschwitz, and the *Einsatzgruppen* cure his antisemitism? Even if he believed what he was taught, why should anyone presume that learning about dead Jews from the 1940s would impact his view of live ones—ones he believes are harming his Arab and Muslim brothers today and will tomorrow, while controlling a land to which only Muslims have a claim?

Another catalyst for both the law requiring the State Department report and the holding of the Berlin conference was the UN's 2001 World Conference Against Racism held in Durban, South Africa. Overt antisemitism was articulated and applauded there, so much so that the United States delegation was withdrawn in protest.

Who were the spewers of antisemitism? They were not skinheads and neo-Nazis but representatives of nongovernmental organizations from around the globe, people who were committed to combating racism. Yet they were so blinded by antisemitism that they believed that demonizing the sole Jewish state on the planet, and the Jews within it, was the best way to fight racism. Was their problem really a lack of Holocaust education? Those present at Durban likely had had more Holocaust education than the norm. They certainly equated Ariel Sharon and Adolf Hitler, and Israel and Nazi Germany, with alacrity, all the while using the Holocaust-produced lexicon of genocide— terms such as "ethnic cleansing" and the like—to antisemitic ends.

Holocaust education is certainly not a bad thing. In fact, since the Holocaust was one of the most significant events in recent history, it is important that students learn about it everywhere, particularly in the former Soviet-dominated Eastern European countries, where this history was suppressed. Students can learn valuable lessons from Holocaust curricula. Yet there exists a seemingly ubiquitous yet some- what illogical presumption that Holocaust education is an antidote for antisemitism, and a corresponding willingness of governments and individuals to invest great sums of money in a strategy that no one can show is effective. The purpose of this book is not to prove that Holocaust education does not work, nor is it to denigrate Holocaust education. It is rather to insist that blind faith and wishful thinking have no place in combating something as dangerous as hate, and that therefore a burden of proof must be placed on the proponents of any program against antisemitism to demonstrate that it is effective (espe- cially ones in which millions of dollars are invested).

Part of the reason that too much of the campaign against anti- semitism is based on faith rather than tailored and testable theories is that people do not pause to define what antisemitism actually is. (The next chapter will dissect and identify in detail the component parts of this oldest hatred.) There is little recognition that it is a complex phe- nomenon, with three major strains, and that while Jews and others who care about antisemitism are frequently willing to speak out and "do something" about "it," they too often do the wrong thing, for a number of intellectual and institutional reasons.

Many commentators have likened antisemitism to a "virus." That is an inadequate analogy—there is something just too easy about it: perhaps the suggestion that there is little one can do to stop it from spreading, because it is an unseen germ; or perhaps the converse, the notion that something as simple as a shot or a pill will "cure" it.

If one must analogize, perhaps antisemitism should be considered a rash. While this formulation has its problems too (antisemitism is frequently hidden deep down, and is not apparent on the surface), it is useful in one regard. Not all rashes are the same type. Not all rashes are equally full-blown. In different environments, and on different people, the same rash might be treated differently. One medication does not all rashes cure. And it is important before treating any rash to be sure that the proposed remedy is not likely to make matters worse.

It is strategically vital that governments, and Jewish agencies tasked with countering antisemitism, analyze the antisemitism that they propose to combat. What type is it? What institutions is it impacting? How does it play out within those institutions? How serious is it? Which tools, or combination thereof, are the most likely to have an impact (and how and why is this so)? Are we sure that we are not making matters worse?

This book is designed both for those who have had little experience looking at antisemitism closely, as well as for those whose work touches on this and other forms of hatred, whether in government, law enforcement, civil society, or the academy. From a common understanding of what antisemitism is, we then examine whether there is a "new" antisemitism, as some have alleged, or whether the antisemitism is, in fact, old, but playing out somewhat differently due to new circumstances.

All antisemitism, as we will see, is a form of conspiracy theory about Jews. To understand the way antisemitism works as a self-sustaining system of ideas, regardless of how bizarre and contradictory they are, we will examine one of the more recent strains—Holocaust denial—in some detail.

And just as antisemitism has different types, what can be done about it is also greatly influenced by the different venues and institutions in which it exists. Later chapters will look at antisemitism in Europe, in the Arab and Muslim worlds, and in the United States (with particular emphasis on U.S. college campuses).

While predicting the future is a dangerous thing to do, the final chapters look at some demographic and ideological trends in the United States and Europe, and suggest a methodology for approaching antisemitism in the decades to come.

The common thread throughout this book is an insistence that, regardless of whatever challenges lie ahead, strategies to combat antisemitism—or any form of hatred—must be grounded as much as possible in fact, hard data, and testable theories, not impression or intuition or wishful thinking. The pages ahead lay out the case for a more systematic approach to combating this longstanding hatred.

Antisemitism frequently charges Jews with conspiring to harm humanity, and it is often used to blame Jews for "why things go wrong." It is expressed in speech, writing, visual forms and action, and employs sinister stereotypes and negative character traits.

—European Monitoring Centre on Racism and Xenophobia (EUMC) "Working Definition of Antisemitism"

Chapter One
What Is Antisemitism?

In the summer of 2000 it seemed clear, if it had not before, that Jews had made it. Antisemitism appeared, if not dead, certainly a minor and diminishing phenomenon. After all, Joseph Lieberman, an Orthodox Jew, ran as the vice presidential candidate of the Democratic Party. There was no backlash, aside from a few predictable fringe voices and Internet postings. Lieberman may well have been elected too, if some older Jews in Florida, misdirected by a confusing ballot, had not voted for Pat Buchanan instead of Al Gore.

But in the fall of 2000 the Middle East peace process collapsed and the second intifada began. Whereas weeks before, pundits had been saying antisemitism was a thing of the past, now they claimed it was rampant worldwide. Once the second intifada started, Jews and Jewish-linked property were attacked in the United States, Belgium, Canada, Australia, Germany, England, Argentina, Panama, Bosnia, Italy, Brazil, Greece, Sweden, South Africa, Switzerland, Russia, Austria, the Netherlands, Mexico, Morocco, Spain, and France.[1] And while the attacks shortly stopped in some countries, they continued unabated in others.

Other major antisemitic events would follow in 2001, including the orgy of Jew-hatred at the UN's World Conference Against Racism in Durban, and the claims—articulated and believed in many parts of the world—that Jews/Israelis were behind the attacks of September 11.

No longer was anyone asserting that antisemitism was gone. Now, at the other extreme, there were voices comparing, wrongly, current times to those of the 1930s.

People such as the great human rights lawyer Irwin Cotler and former Israeli Deputy Foreign Minister Michael Melchior began speaking about a "new" antisemitism. Others began to follow their example. Was antisemitism, a 2,000-year-old hatred, now something really "new?" Was antisemitism really like laundry detergent, now perhaps "new and improved?" Back in 1974 Arnold Forster of the Anti-Defamation League of B'nai B'rith (ADL) wrote a book which used the term "new antisemitism." What is new post-2000 is not the antisemitism, which in most regards is very old, but rather the circumstances in which it is playing out.

Religious Antisemitism

Before looking at these circumstances, it is important to understand what antisemitism is. While there is no universally agreed definition,[2] a working one might be:

> Antisemitism is hatred toward Jews and is directed toward the Jewish religion, Jews as a people, or, more recently, the Jewish state. Antisemitism frequently charges Jews with conspiring to harm non-Jews and is often used to give an explanation for why things go wrong. It is expressed in speech, writing, visual forms, and action, and regularly employs stereotypes.

The word itself, by the way, is a misnomer. Coined by Wilhelm Marr in Germany in 1873, it has nothing to do with a prejudice against "Semites." "Semitic" is an adjective that applies to languages, not people. But Marr used it to mean hatred of Jews.

Of course, antisemitism was around for centuries before Marr. It has three distinct strains that sometimes overlap. In order to combat it intelligently, it is important to keep these differences in mind.

For many historians, religious-based antisemitism is the oldest form. Indeed antisemitism (or "Jew-hatred") can be traced back to biblical times. Recall the Book of Esther, with King Ahasuerus's edict to wipe out all the Jews and Haman's insinuation that Jews are "a people apart."[3]

The birth of Christianity saw the rise of some of the most cardinal and long-lasting themes of antisemitism. Christianity and Judaism were competitive faiths in the late Roman Empire. Jesus, of course, was a Jew, as were many of the early Christians. But many Jews refused to join the new faith, and their continued existence had to be explained in light of Christian belief that Christians had made a new covenant that superseded the Jewish covenant with God. Some concluded that God had permitted the Jews to live only as a sign of what would happen if people rejected and denied Jesus. Jews were forced to the fringes of society, and church edicts segregated them into ghettos. Jews were blamed for the death of Jesus, and canards such as "Christ-killers" were leveled against them century after century.

As Christianity became dominant in Europe, Jews were discriminated against through special taxes, special clothing, limited avenues of employment, and periodic expulsions. During the years of the Black Death, Jews were accused of poisoning wells; at other times they were charged with stealing Christian children to use their blood to make Passover matzah (a charge termed the "blood libel"). During the Crusades, Jews were murdered, raped, forced to convert, or expelled from their homes. On the Iberian Peninsula, after the Christian victory over Islam, Jews who did not leave their homes of long duration were subject to the tortures of the Inquisition, which sought to determine whether they were true Christians.

Religious antisemitism defines the common denominator for how all forms of antisemitism work: Jews are seen as a group that conspires to harm non-Jews, and "blaming the Jews" provides a simple explanation for what has gone wrong in life.

In modern times, while religious antisemitism remains a problem, it is less so in the Christian world since the reforms of Vatican II, which both removed the charge of deicide and identified antisemitism as a sin. Where these reforms have been taken to heart, the dialogue between Judaism and Christianity has flourished, and the level of antisemitism has diminished.

In the Muslim world, however, the recent trend has been the other way. While Jews and Muslims lived together on relatively better terms than Jews and Christians did in Europe, Jews never enjoyed full equality under Muslim rule. Islam defines Jews (and Christians) as *dhimmis* ("protected peoples"), meaning tolerated but second-class citizens. In recent years, largely due to the Arab-Israeli conflict as well as to the untenable notion that non-Muslims should never have sovereignty over lands that were once linked with Islam, the Islamic form of religious-based antisemitism has been growing. Religions are usually defined by what their practitioners say they are. Rather than highlight the elements of Islamic teachings that recognize Jews as "people of the book," there have been increased references to Jews as the offspring of apes and pigs and the quotation of Koranic verses calling for the killing of Jews.

While Christian and Muslim antisemitism certainly differ in many ways (and, in fact, there are differences among the various Christian and Muslim antisemites), they share a commonality of belief (to varying degrees among their proponents) that antisemitism either pleases or serves God.

Race-Based Antisemitism

The second form of antisemitism—which builds on the story lines and culture of Christian-based antisemitism—is race-based antisemitism. Following the advent of nineteenth-century science, most especially the evolutionary ideas of Charles Darwin and the writings of people such as Joseph Gobineau, came the notion of distinct races of people. While one could change one's religion, one could not change one's race.

Jews, of course, are not a "race." Jews are a people and are of all races. But the notion became popularized that Jews were, indeed, a distinct race. Conversion, therefore, was no longer a life-saving option. Nazi Germany represented the extreme application of this type of antisemitism: Even someone who did not consider himself Jewish but had Jewish grandparents could be sent to the death camps.[4] On the other hand, this form of antisemitism worked just like the older religious-based hatred had: demonizing Jews, identifying them as "the problem," and suggesting that they exercised secret power.

Race-based antisemitism has its own literature. A czarist forgery, the *Protocols of the Elders of Zion*, argues that Jews meet secretly to control the world. This document, translated into various languages, was used to propel many pogroms (violent attacks) against Jews in Europe in the early 1900s. It was popularized in the United States in the 1920s by automaker Henry Ford. While the book continues to be a staple of white supremacist groups today, it is also promoted by other groups, showing how easily antisemitic conspiracy theories can be recast for different audiences, expressing different types of anti-Semitism.[5] (For example, the *Protocols* is also readily available and promoted among the Arab and Muslim countries of the Middle East and was even popularized into a TV series in Egypt. In the United States the Nation of Islam not only sells the book, it peddles its own version, *The Secret Relationship between Blacks and Jews*, which is a functional rewrite designed to paint the history of slavery as a Jewish operation against black people.)

Today's main practitioners of race-based antisemitism in the U.S. are neo-Nazis, skinheads, Christian Identity adherents (who believe that people of color are subhuman and that Jews are the offspring of Satan), and various other white supremacists and white nationalists.[6] While there are important ideological and theological differences among these groups, they all hate nonwhites. They also see Jews as responsible for opening the door to equal rights and opportunity for nonwhites, as part of a nefarious plot to destroy "white America" through immigration, affirmative action, control of the media, and other alleged schemes. While we think of white supremacists as essentially anti-people-of-color with some antisemitism thrown in, antisemitism is actually the ideological (as opposed to emotional) anchor for their movement. If blacks and other minorities are, in their view, unquestionably inferior, how could the superior whites be "losing" the battle? The white supremacists believe it is because of the secret, cabalistic hand of the Jew, pulling the strings behind the scenes. It is because of ZOG (the Zionist Occupied Government).

While race-based antisemitism is at a low point, and has been for many decades, there are reasons to be concerned about its possible growth in the decades to come, particularly because demographic projections indicate that the United States will be a majority nonwhite country by the middle of this century. The race-based antisemitism which is at the core of white supremacy may prove an ideological magnet for people who fear this change. (See further discussion in Chapter 12.)

Political Antisemitism (Anti-Zionism)

The third form of antisemitism is political antisemitism (or anti-Zionism*). It is the most recent and least understood form of this prejudice. While all forms of antisemitism serve political purposes, the reestablishment of the State of Israel in 1948 after a 2,000-year exile of the Jewish people was the occasion for the birth of this most modern variant.[7] Abba Eban, the quintessential Israeli diplomat, noted: "Classical antisemitism denies the rights of Jews as citizens within society. Anti-Zionism denies the equal rights of the Jewish people to its lawful sovereignty within the community of nations.... All that has happened is that the discriminatory principle has been transferred from the realm of individual rights to the domain of collective identity."[8]

---

* Zionism is the belief that Israel has the right to exist as a homeland for Jews. It says nothing about the policies or programs of the state, merely that it has a right to exist. There are left-wing Zionists and right-wing Zionists, and many in between. Some Zionists are harsh critics of Israeli policies; others are supportive. Anti-Zionists, on the other hand, treat Israel more harshly and by a different standard than they would treat any other state on the globe. They frequently demonize it and essentially believe that Israel has no right to exist as a Jewish state, regardless of its policies, its leaders, or how the society is run.

Of course, one can—and should—criticize Israel, just as one would be critical of the United States, France, Egypt, or any other nation. There is no antisemitism in honestly disapproving of a party, a program, a policy, or a political leader. But when Israel is expected to live up to standards not applied to any other nation, or when the perceived deficiencies of Israeli society are used to attack its basic legitimacy, that is a problem. In the current context, if one supports the right of the Palestinian people to self-determination in a land of their own, but would deny the Jews the same right in their historic homeland, that is antisemitism.[9]

While the religious or racial-based antisemite would generally not want to associate with Jews (although there are many instances when such people point to a "good Jew" they know, just as some would point to the "good black" or "good Latino"), the political antisemite likely has no problem with an individual Jew. It is the collective identity of Jews—expressed in the existence of the modern State of Israel—which animates him. Not surprisingly, the myths that fuel the older types of antisemitism are recycled here: Jews are seen as secretly influencing or controlling U.S. policy or public attitudes.

Political antisemitism can be found on both the far right and the far left, with many of the same canards. But whereas most racial and religious-based antisemites would not deny their prejudice (or, if they did, their denials would be seen as transparent), political antisemites generally deny their bigotry.

In practice, the three different strains of antisemitism—religious, racial, and political—are not so pristinely isolated from each other. Since they rely on the same structure—seeing Jews as conspiring to harm non-Jews—the tropes that help dehumanize Jews to one type of antisemite frequently are adopted by the others, although with limitations. For example, Holocaust denial—the brainchild of the white supremacist/neo-Nazi crowd (i.e., race-based antisemites) is a growth industry in the Arab and Muslim world (i.e., among religious and political antisemites), but is relatively rare among nonethnic purely political antisemites (those on the extreme left, who might not care too much if the Jews in present-day Israel were slaughtered, but would not do anything to minimize the perception of the crimes of the fascists during World War II).

As we shall see later, the first question which one should be asking when figuring out a strategy to combat a problem of antisemitism is: "Which type of antisemitism is it?"

In addition to distinguishing the three basic types of antisemitism, it is also important to understand the environment and institutions in which it is being expressed. One can, for example, look at antisemitism by venue: on campus, in Europe, in the Arab and Muslim worlds, in the media, etc. Each setting is its own universe with unique rules and pressure points and interests.

It is also important to identify the strain of antisemitic ideas and story lines that are most in play in any particular situation. Denial of the Holocaust, the claim that Zionism is racism, the charge that Jews secretly control the United States government (or the media, or the entertainment industry), that they are more loyal to Israel than to their home country, or that they were responsible for 9/11 are each systems of ideas which, while integrally related, also have distinct characteristics.

Finally, antisemitism of every type treats Jews, either individually or collectively, as an "other." It ascribes pernicious motives to them and frequently recycles and updates old canards painting the Jew as plotting to harm non-Jews, often in order to provide an explanation for world events. Despite this commonality, however, many people tend to care more about one type of antisemitism than another. There were people in Durban who would have condemned the peddling of *Mein Kampf* there if the promoters had been neo-Nazis, yet they were conspicuously silent when it was being hawked in an Arabic edition. Antisemitism of all types is dangerous, and not only to Jews. History has repeatedly shown that antisemitism is the miner's canary for a society's health. It always starts with the Jews, but it never ends there. And it is always dangerous to democracy, human rights, and freedom.

*Israel must be wiped off the map.... The establishment of a
Zionist regime was a move by the world oppressor against the
Islamic world.... The skirmishes in the occupied land are
part of the war of destiny. The outcome of hundreds of years
of war will be defined in Palestinian land.*

—Iranian President Mahmoud Ahmadinejad, October 26, 2005[1]

*If international finance Jewry inside and outside of Europe
should succeed once more in plunging nations into another
world war, the consequence will not be the Bolshevization of
the earth and thereby the victory of Jewry, but the annihilation of the Jewish race in Europe.*

—Adolf Hitler, January 30, 1939[2]

Chapter Two
An Old Hatred in New Circumstances

A century ago memories were fresh of antisemitic political agitating in
pre-World War I Germany, of pogroms in Russia, of the Dreyfus
Affair in France. Yet the author of the entry on antisemitism in the
1910 edition of the *Encyclopedia Britannica* saw it as "exclusively a
question of European politics, and its origin is [not] to be found ... in
the long struggle between the Church and the Synagogue ... but in the
social conditions resulting from the emancipation of the Jews in the
middle of the nineteenth century."[3]

Jews, he believed, were well prepared by their European ghetto
history to thrive in the growing economic, urban, and democratic
ways of early twentieth-century Europe. Antisemitism, it seemed to
him, was not a matter of old hatreds, but rather political machinations linked to the last gasps of feudalism and the growth of the bourgeoisie. He argued that since Jews—unlike their Christian counter-
parts—were likely to be part of the growing industrial middle class,
they were therefore heavily represented in the new societal leadership.

15

Antisemitism, then, was not a problem in and of itself, but something promoted for political ends by the bourgeoisie's "enemies among the vanquished reactionaries on the one hand, and by the extreme Radicals on the other."[4]

Consider the implication of this 1910 analysis. The Russian Revolution of 1905 had failed, but few would have wagered on the survival of the last vestiges of feudal institutions. The industrial revolution was thriving, and as it consolidated its hold on world institutions, the "vanquished reactionaries" and the "extreme radicals" would surely become weaker, thereby diminishing antisemitism and making it a thing of the past.

While this view might have been abstractly logical in 1910, it was embarrassingly wrong. Clearly modern European social and economic changes did not make antisemitism wither away in the twentieth century, as witnessed both by Nazi Germany and her allies, and by the Soviet Union under Stalin and others.

Yet, the 1910 analysis was also perceptive in seeing antisemitism as having a political function, and its expression being influenced by political events. The encyclopedia's failure was that while it recognized that people would use antisemitism for cynical political purposes, it did not sufficiently understand that these political movements actually drew upon, incorporated, and invigorated classic antisemitism. It also failed to anticipate that new and changing political realities would find ways of using antisemitism as well.

In some important ways the 1910 *Encyclopedia Britannica* analysis, while breathtakingly wrong in its predictive powers, was superior to some analyses today, which treat antisemitism as detached from the social and political environment in which it functions. In fact, there are three major new circumstances (addressed in this chapter) and two new events (treated in the next two chapters) that impact the way antisemitism is playing out today as compared to the postwar period.

New Circumstance #1:
Fall of the Soviet Union

The first changed circumstance is the fall of the Soviet Union.[5] For most of the last half of the twentieth century, the world was divided into two ideological camps. People in Europe and elsewhere gravitated toward one side or the other. Now, with only one superpower, it is only human nature that some level of resentment would be felt toward the United States, the strongest and richest country on earth. During the Cold War there may have been reasons to downplay the demerits of the superpower with which you were ideologically aligned, because those of the other were seen as worse. Now there is no such counterbalance.

While anti-Americanism is not directly related to antisemitism, it does have connections. For example, some in the anti-globalist left define the U.S. as a capitalist-imperialist exploiter of people of color around the world. In their view, Israel is America's client state and its lapdog in the Middle East.

But the collapse of the Soviet Union also changed the relations and blurred the distinctions between the political extremes, and antisemitism plays an important role here.[6] For instance, in the days leading up to the second Iraq war, there was a seeming flirtation between left and right. Alexander Cockburn, writing for the *Nation*, advocated reaching out to the "populist" (read Buchanan-backing, racist-tinged) right, to form a larger antiwar coalition. And the antisemitic *American Free Press* (formerly the *Spotlight*) reprinted antiwar articles by figures such as Gore Vidal. There was a clear subtext to this interaction, a "debate" between the left and right having to do with Jews and Israel. The underlying question was: Who was correct, the left, which generally saw the U.S. imperialist dog wagging the Israeli tail, or the right, which posited a secret "Zionist Occupied Government" that ruled Washington and used the American government to do its bidding?[7] While they did not agree about the scope and purpose of the disagreeable actions of Israel and Jewish figures, both extremes found ways to blame Israel and people whose Jewishness they noted for why things were going wrong—a classic antisemitic trope.

But it was not only American and European leftists and rightists whose political groundings and antisemitic activities were impacted by the fall of the Soviet Union. More important was the impact on Islamists—the people who believe in a politicized, anti-Western, anti-Christian, and vehemently antisemitic version of Islam. With the collapse of the Soviet Union, they saw themselves newly empowered.

In Iran in 1979 and 1980 they had held off one superpower—the United States. In the late 1980s they actually defeated the other superpower in Afghanistan. They envision themselves (falsely) as representing "true" Islam, and thus some one billion Muslims around the globe. They also see themselves as the rightful successor to the Soviet Union, as the new superpower opposing the "Great Satan," the United States.

Certainly, many of the conflicts since the early 1990s—from Chechnya to Afghanistan to Iraq—have come about in large measure because of the combination of the aspirations of the Islamists and the political and military void left by the collapse of the Soviet Union. What does this have to do with antisemitism? These Islamists are anti-semitic to the core, and their increased influence clearly poses a challenge in the fight against antisemitism. This is doubly true because some appeasers will think they can protect themselves by "blaming" the Jews for Islamist acts of terror, by expressing sympathy for some of the terrorists' agenda, or by making antisemitic statements, thereby showing that they and those whom they fear might attack them actually have a common enemy.

While the full fallout from the collapse of the Soviet Union is yet to be determined, three things seem clear: It has emboldened the Islamists (who are anti-West and antisemitic); it has created an environment for increased anti-Americanism, which is correlated with opposition to Israel; and it has blurred distinctions between and increased affection among people of the extreme right and left who, while still quite far apart on many issues, share important elements of a similar vision and common vocabulary when it comes to Jews and Israel.

New Circumstance #2:
Collapse of the Israeli-Palestinian Peace Process
in Late 2000

The second changed circumstance is the collapse of the Israeli-Palestinian peace process in 2000.

The background to the collapse is also related to the fall of the Soviet Union. During much of the Cold War, Israel was seen as aligned with the United States, and the Arab world with the Soviet Union. It was no coincidence that with the Soviet Union gone and the United States the only superpower, there was some movement forward toward a peace process with the Oslo Accords in the early 1990s.

While the Oslo process had many problems, it did diminish some expression of left-wing and Arab vitriol toward Israel. Holocaust denial, while still to be found in the Palestinian and Arab press, was at a much lower level than in the years leading up to the 1993 handshake on the White House lawn. And the left's demonization of Israel as a white, European, racist colonizer of people of color was also lowered a few notches—for who were white progressives to demonize Israel while the Palestinians, it appeared, were ready to make a deal with the "Zionists?"

When the peace process collapsed in the fall of 2000, any restraint about expressing antisemitism seemingly evaporated. Holocaust denial, accusations of Jews stealing non-Jewish children and draining their blood to make pastries, and other such credulity-straining canards became frequent front-page news in much of the Arab media.[8] And those on the left who saw the Israeli-Palestinian conflict as black and white (everything the Israelis did was for the purpose of suppressing the Palestinians; everything the Palestinians did was for the noble purpose of liberation), felt a renewed license to vent.

In Europe in particular, where a French official termed Israel a "shitty little country," and where Israel was pictured in newspaper cartoons as eagerly killing Palestinian children (much as the classic Jew was pictured as killing Jesus or Christian children in the blood libel), demonizing Israel—as opposed to careful, balanced criticism of Israeli policy—became a regular and unremarkable event, perhaps even sport.

Frequently, the parallel was made between the supposed evil agenda of Israel and that of the Nazis, the alleged evil deeds of Ariel Sharon and those of Adolf Hitler, and the claimed oppression of present-day Palestinians and that suffered by European Jews in the 1940s. Some portion of this grotesque equation no doubt comes from an ignorance of the details of the Holocaust and the seeming equation of it with undifferentiated racism. (Where, one might ask, are the Israeli gas chambers?) But there is also the sense that some, perhaps many, Europeans have a psychological post-Holocaust need to demonize Israel. For if Israel is depicted as doing to the Palestinians what Europeans did to Jews in the last century, then European guilt associated with the Holocaust can be expiated.

European racism also has had an impact on European antisemitism. Recall that for good parts of the nineteenth and twentieth centuries, Europeans actively engaged in colonialism and the suppression of people of color. In the past decades, following the liberation movements of the 1960s and thereafter, many people from the former colonies moved to Western Europe. France took in great numbers of immigrants from North Africa, for example. Even before the widespread riots in France in the fall of 2005, immigrants were never fully absorbed into the societal mainstream and were always viewed—and viewed themselves—as somehow not fully part of general French society.

Many white Christian Europeans feel guilty for their colonial history and for the poverty, separateness, and environment of bigotry in which many immigrants live. However the psychology of this guilt works, two things seem clear: First, antisemitism from young Muslims is treated as less serious than that from others. For example, where British leftists would have been quick to denounce teenage skinheads marching with a banner denying the Holocaust, they have made excuses for teenage Muslims doing the same thing.

Second, there seems to be an inability to denounce both Islamaphobia and antisemitism simultaneously, at least when the starting point of the conversation is antisemitism. Yes, an antisemitic attack will be bemoaned, but the conversation will soon turn to the "worse" conditions Muslims suffer from Islamophobia in Europe, as if that somehow were an explanation for attacks on Jews or a reason that they should be seen as less serious.

Certainly all forms of bigotry must be combated, but the willingness to downplay antisemitism from Muslims in Europe reflects both a problem with antisemitism and also with racism—expecting less of Muslims than of others.

New Circumstance #3:
Demographic Changes and the Rise of Islamism

The third new circumstance—and probably the most significant—is the demographic change in Europe. That the French were slow in addressing the attacks on Jews after the collapse of the peace process, only taking action after the election of Jacques Chirac in 2002, reflects in part a growing political calculus. Whereas France has the largest Jewish population in Europe (approximately 500,000 to 600,000), it has about ten times as large a number of Muslims. The Muslim population is growing; the Jewish population will certainly shrink.

While each country in Western Europe is different, there are similar challenges among many. Large numbers of immigrants from Asia, the Middle East, and Africa—and their descendants, many of whom are Muslim—are a growing demographic force. Unlike the United States, which has a unique and generally successful history of absorbing people of all backgrounds and making them part of the larger social compact, there is a large divide between those who trace their lineage to the various European countries for centuries and those for whom the connection is more recent.

This demographic shift has many implications for antisemitism. First, as mentioned, is the political calculus. If every eligible Jew voted in France, and only a ten or eleven percent of Muslims did so, there would still be more Muslim votes than Jewish ones. Aware of this in the time leading up to the 2002 elections, politicians were reluctant to speak out about antisemitic outrages, for fear of alienating potential Muslim and Arab voters.

Second, as noted above, is the growth of the Islamist movement, for which antisemitism and anti-Christianity are a given, and which is finding a receptive audience among many of the increasing numbers of young Muslims in Europe.

And third is the impact of this demographic change on white nationalists, white supremacists, neo-Nazis, and racists. Traditionally, these groups were seen as the main instigators of postwar antisemitism in Europe, and indeed they still play a significant role.[9] But as the immigrant population has continued to grow, there has been increased, albeit uneven, support for such far-right racist politicians as Jörg Haider in Austria, Jean-Marie Le Pen in France, candidates of the British Nationalist Party in the UK, and others. None have yet achieved their goal of full access to power, but each has engaged in a largely racially-based antisemitism. It is small consolation that the main attention of these racists has lately turned to the question of immigration. With antisemitism as a core value, any ascendancy of people who see themselves in white supremacist terms can only further antisemitism.

In short, antisemitism always plays out on a field defined by politics, and although the *Encyclopedia Britannica* of 1910 reminds us that it is treacherous to predict how social and political circumstances will impact this hatred, recent changes provide at least some cause for concern.

*[The NGO Declaration at Durban] took the vision of
universal human rights standards applicable to all races,
nationalities, and religions in the words of the Universal
Declaration of Human Rights and excluded the Jew.
It took the vision of the equality of all nations large and
small in the words of the United Nations Charter and
barred the State of Israel.*

—Statement of the Jewish Caucus at the World Conference Against Racism,
September 1, 2001[1]

Chapter Three
Durban: Antisemitism as Antiracism

To recap, antisemitism is a multifaceted phenomenon, with three
main strains (which sometimes overlap): religious-based, race-based,
and political.

To counteract antisemitism, it is important to keep these distinctions in mind, as well as to understand the environments and
institutions in which antisemitism plays out.

Contemporary antisemitism is not "new." What is new are the
circumstances in which it appears. The fall of the Soviet Union
changed the political stage and empowered the Islamists. The collapse
of the peace process seemingly gave new license to express vitriol
against the sole Jewish state on the planet, without much fear of
breaking taboos. And the demographic changes within Europe have
made combating antisemitism much more of an uphill battle.

Two other relatively recent events have had an impact on contemporary antisemitism. It is worthwhile to examine them in detail,
since they are models of how antisemitism can quickly come to the
fore as part of, or in reaction to, major events. The first is the UN's
World Conference Against Racism, Racial Discrimination, Xenophobia and Related Intolerance, held in Durban, South Africa, in the
summer of 2001. The second is the attacks of September 11, 2001.

Setting the Stage:
UN General Assembly Resolution 3379

While the human rights community sees national rights of self-determination as an important principle, the UN had, at times in its history, an entirely different standard toward the Jewish national movement of self-determination known as Zionism. In 1975, the UN adopted General Assembly Resolution 3379, which declared Zionism—the basic idea that Israel had a right to exist—as a form of "racism."

That awful canard was used as justification for attacks on Israel by terrorists. Three days after the passage of the resolution, a bomb killed six teenagers in Zion Square in Jerusalem. Radio Damascus broadcast: "The fedayeen take one copy of the resolutions adopted at the UN, mix them with TNT and blow up Zion Square!"

The resolution also promoted antisemitism around the world. As the Rev. Martin Luther King, Jr., observed, "When people criticize Zionists, they mean Jews."[2] And as the UN's definition played out in the 1970s and 1980s, a more pernicious derivative equation came to the fore: Jew equals Zionist, Zionist equals racist, therefore Jew equals racist. Some Jewish student groups in Britain were even barred on the basis of this principle. A professor at the State University of New York at Stony Brook asked students to write a paper on the topic that "Zionism is as much racism as Nazism."[3] A frequent speaker at college campuses during that period—Kwame Ture (aka Stokely Carmichael)—said "the only good Zionist is a dead Zionist."[4]

The repeal in 1991 of this 1975 resolution was one of the first direct results of the collapse of the Soviet Union. Many of its former client states that had voted for the resolution in 1975 now voted for repeal. As the late Senator Daniel Patrick Moynihan opined, "What immoral regimes create, moral regimes instantly repudiate."[5]

I had the privilege of sitting in the UN General Assembly Hall, watching the 1991 session that erased the equation. But I was wrong to think that the battle against this particular canard had been won. Ten years later, Arab and Muslim groups went to the UN Conference in Durban, wanting to reinstate the equation, despite UN Secretary-General Kofi Annan's pointed reference to Resolution 3379 as a "low point"[6] in UN history.

Early Warning Signs

The stated purpose of the World Conference Against Racism was to move closer to the "dream of a world free of racial hatred and bias."[7] But signs that it would actually become a nightmarish forum for promoting hatred were clear, even at the preparatory events held months beforehand.

A meeting of the Interministerial Committee on Human Rights had been scheduled for a Saturday, thereby excluding Jewish organizations. When these groups asked that the meeting be held some other day so that they might be included, they were told by representatives of other NGOs, "Here we go again with the Jewish lobby." "Why should we accord special privileges to Jews?" "Have the rabbi give you special dispensation!" "Enough of Auschwitz," and "Jews always put on their victim act."[8]

A preparatory meeting in Tehran, of all places (at which, reportedly, "it was made impossible for a UN accredited Jewish [NGO] to participate"[9]) produced a draft document accusing Israel of "ethnic cleansing of the Arab population of historic Palestine," and said that Israel practices a "new kind of Apartheid, a crime against humanity." It condemned "Zionist practices against Semitism," and referred to "the increase of racist practices of Zionism and anti-Semitism in various parts of the world, as well as the emergence of racist and violent movements based on racist and discriminatory ideas, in particular the Zionist movement, which is based on race superiority." It also deferred a decision on whether "Holocaust" should have an upper or lower case "h," with some countries arguing that Jews had made up the whole thing.[10]

The debate seemed surreal—determining whether denial of the Holocaust, or merely demeaning it, was the better way to refer to it in a document intended to fight racism in the twenty-first century!

The real agenda, of course, was an all-out assault not only on "Zionism," but also on anything having to do with Jews. The Holocaust, with a capital H, defining as it always has the Nazi genocide in World War II, now might become a word of common usage, with a lower case, and pluralized, thus making it synonymous with "genocide" and robbing it of its meaning. The irony is that such a formulation not only does harm to Jews, but also to other victims of genocide. Which is the more precise and evocative term to teach people the horrors of slavery: the "African holocaust," or the "transatlantic slave trade" and "the horrors of the Middle Passage"?

But "Zionism" and the "Holocaust" were not the only Jewish-related terms under attack. "Antisemitism" was, too. Iran would later argue that it should not even be mentioned in a document about world racism, because it was not a "contemporary form of racism."[11] Others were intent to rob the term of its meaning by a disingenuous semantic game.

The term "anti-Semitism," as mentioned on page 8 was coined by a German, Wilhelm Marr, in 1873. He used it to vilify Jews, not Arabs, in a book called *The Victory of Judaism over Germanism*. Since then, and especially in the context of the Holocaust, it has always—and only—meant Jew-hatred. (When Arabs are victims of hate crimes, Arab groups do not put out press releases using the word "anti-semitism" to describe the attack.) Yet some Arabs, to suggest that they are somehow genetically incapable of antisemitism, have said that they are "Semites" too. Aside from the fact that the word refers to a family of languages, not a "race" of people, the implication that Arabs are incapable of antisemitism is bizarre. This would imply that a copy of the notorious czarist forgery the *Protocols of the Elders of Zion* in Russian would be antisemitic, but an Arabic edition not. Employing this semantic sleight of hand, the full assault on Jews was on, even on the accepted name of Jew-hatred, so the draft that emerged from the meeting in Tehran lamented "Zionist practices against Semitism." As Israeli Deputy Foreign Minister Michael Melchior explained, the draft statement that came out of Tehran was even worse than had the 1975 equation been reaffirmed word for word, because the language earmarked for Durban was

> ... much more sophisticated, much more serious than the equation. It includes the equation implicitly, but is on a much broader aspect of issues. What it is really saying is that everything that has to do with the birth of the State of Israel, with Zionism, with Israeli government policy, and in general with the Jewish people, its past, its suffering, and its future, is not legitimate. It's a total delegitimization of the State of Israel and the Jewish people. And that is why it is in many aspects much more serious than the Zionism=racism equation.[12]

Actually, it was worse than that. It was not only a demonization of Jews and a delegitimization of Israel, but also an implicit statement that attacks on Israel's right to exist have a moral foundation in the fight for human rights and against racism. At the conference itself, the philosophical context for this assault on Zionism would become explicit: It was both modeled on and promoted as the current-day successor to the worldwide fight against South African apartheid.

Obviously, this was not antisemitism for the hell of it. It had a political agenda, with ominous implications for the peace process, as Melchior also noted:

> [Y]ou can only find a compromise if you keep and stick to the conflict being a ... national conflict, as a territorial conflict. Then you can sit around the table and divide territory. But if you take it out of that framework ... [and put] it into an existential framework, then [you define the conflict as one with] no possibility [of] negotiating.
>
> You don't negotiate with the devil; he can't be a half-devil. You don't negotiate with apartheid. If the whole of the being and existence of Israel is apartheid, racism, is the devil, is the anti-Christ,

is ethnic cleansing and genocide, if that is our whole being in existence, not only in the territories but as the beginning and the creation of the State of Israel, then there can be no negotiations with that entity, there can only be a justification for violence and terror and eventually to wipe out this entity from the face of the Earth, because that is what you do with apartheid and racism and the absolute evils of the Earth.[13]

The NGO Forum

The Durban gathering in late August and early September actually had three parts: a youth summit, a meeting of nongovernmental organizations (NGOs), and then the UN conference itself. The tone was set early.

Just before the conference opened, the *Jordan Times* wrote that Israel's "racist activities against the Palestinians [have] surpassed the Holocaust in horror."[14]

The Arab Lawyers Union distributed a tract entitled "That is the fact ... Racism of zionism & 'Israel,'" which sported on its cover a swastika superimposed on a Star of David. It went downhill from there, defaming and distorting the Jewish religion, calling Zionism "a system based on the worst form of apartheid, even worse than that of South Africa," and concluding that Zionism harms the Jew too, because it "distorts his humanity and turns him into aggressive [sic], racial and destructive entity."[15]

The same group also distributed a collection of cartoons reminiscent of the Nazi era. It showed Jews as sadistic, obsessed with money, with large hooked noses and fangs dripping blood.[16]

As Australian Jeremy Jones described it, "All around Kingsmead Stadium posters and banners comparing Israel to Nazi Germany and to apartheid South Africa were prominently displayed."[17] One such poster reportedly said: "Hitler should have finished the job."[18]

These were the themes in the literature that was distributed at Durban, too. One tract claimed "Zionism has remained conspicuously akin to Pan-Germanism. They both believed in racial theories and presumptions on matters such as 'national character' and 'exclusiveness.'"[19] Another was entitled "Occupied Jerusalem: A New Soweto?"[20]

Given this environment, it was not surprising that thousands of demonstrators marched, calling for an end to the Jewish state,[21] or that at a rally someone shouted, "Kill the Jews."[22]

Remember, however, that this was not a neo-Nazi skinhead rally. It was an international meeting, under UN auspices, convening human rights activists from around the world to combat racism. As such, it offered an exhibition tent for distribution of literature to help the world combat the scourge of racism. Yet it was no doubt easier to obtain the *Protocols of the Elders of Zion* here than in czarist Russia in the early twentieth century.[23]

A leaflet was circulated claiming:

Zionism and Apartheid represent two sides of the same coin. Apartheid enslaved Black people in South Africa, Zionism enslaves Palestinians in the land of Palestine.... The children of the victims of the Holocaust are now perpetrating the same heinous crime on another people. The world can no longer stand aside. The World stopped Nazism! The World stopped Apartheid! The World must stop Zionism![24]

Another brochure said:

We call on all the international institutions, all states, all human rights and democratic organizations and all honest women and men to take an active part in insolating [sic] and boycotting the Israeli Apartheid, on all levels. Expel Israel from all the international institutions, block economic cooperation, prosecute Israeli war criminals. This is the only way to stop the bloodshed in Palestine and ensure a democratic solution.[25]

Another leaflet had a picture of Hitler with the caption: "What if I had won? The good things: there would be NO Israel and NO Palestinians' blood shed. The bad things: I wouldn't have allowed the making of the new Beetle."[26]

The problem was not only what was going on outside. Jeffrey Weill of the Jacob Blaustein Institute for the Advancement of Human Rights, who was present at Durban, commented that it was "incredible, the disproportionate number of thematic commissions that were focused on Israel."[27] Jewish students who attended the WCAR Youth Summit complained of intense "intimidation and hostility" and walked out in protest. They were said to be "astonished" that a proposal calling for "a cessation of violence in the Middle East on all sides of the conflict" was rejected and that the Summit "would opt to issue a declaration that sanctions rather than rejects violence as a means to resolve political conflicts."[28] There seemed a common belief that any violence committed by Palestinians against Israelis—even against Israeli children—was reasonable resistance, no matter what, and that no Israeli action negatively impacting any Palestinian could be justifiable.

Human rights activists from around the world witnessed antisemitism firsthand. Their almost uniform response was either to encourage it or to let it pass without speaking out. Had nothing been learned from the many twentieth-century battles against hatred? Almost everyone seemed to be ignoring the basic principle that, no matter what other political considerations there may be, if a group is being dehumanized, others need to speak up for them. Regardless of individual human rights activists' views on the Arab-Israeli conflict, Jews were being dehumanized at a UN forum, and their response, at best, was silence.[29]

The intimidation of Jews was so extreme that some hid their name tags, and some males concealed their yarmulkes under caps.[30]

Some of the personal remarks directed at Jews by other delegates at this antiracism conference demonstrated that once antisemitism—in the guise of anti-Zionism—was given license, other, more traditional forms of antisemitism quickly come to the fore. The entire repertoire was used. Comments heard included:

— You don't belong to the human race! "Chosen people?" You are cursed people!

— I won't talk to you until you take off that thing. [Referring to a yarmulke]

— Why haven't the Jews taken responsibility for killing Jesus?

— Arabs are Semites, too, and should be listed as victims of the Holocaust and be compensated.

— They've sucked our blood all these years.

— We don't want you here. Jews don't belong in Jordan. Jews don't belong in Israel.

— You are killers! You are killers![31]

— Jews are not members of the human race!

— I believe in a Jewish state ... on Mars.[32]

The same abuse was heard at the NGO forum. In a session about hate crimes, a speaker called the existence of Israel a "hate crime." At the same meeting, a person raised a question of procedure and, reportedly, was shouted at "Jew, Jew, Jew, Jew." Another woman was heckled as an "Israeli dog."[33] A Jew from Uruguay was cut off by the Palestinian chairperson, who said, "This is a discussion about victims, and you are not a victim."[34]

The demonstrations were so intense that people were chanting, "Hitler didn't finish the job" as they distributed copies of the *Protocols of the Elders of Zion.* The Jewish Center was closed as a precaution.[35]

A session on Holocaust denial had to be cancelled because of security concerns.[36]

A press conference called by Jewish NGOs was "invaded," and journalists were unable to ask questions over the loud chants of "Zionism is racism."[37] An Iranian woman screamed, "Six million dead and you're holding the world hostage!"[38]

Karen Pollock, a representative of British Jewry at the conference, said that she had to explain "why I have the right to exist."[39]

NGOs put forth statements that would make Nazis, neo- and the original brand, proud. "The Revolutionary Committees Movement in Libya" proclaimed:

> Anti-Semitism is by definition a racist concept, because it stands
> for superiority on the basis of religion and national grounds.
> Adherents of all religions, not only a specific one, face intolerance
> in certain parts of the world. Similarly, different peoples and
> nationalities face discriminatory practices in specific regions the
> world over. Why should the grievances of the followers of a specific
> religion or national origin be singled out in the Conference? Must
> the whole world bear the burden of the third Riche [sic] (Hitler)?[40]

An Iranian group put out a two-page leaflet that was a model of
conciseness in an avalanche of verbose, hateful documents. In two
pages, it captured just about every contemporary antisemitic canard,
not only denying the Holocaust and accusing Zionism of racism, but
also (copying the Nation of Islam) Jews of responsibility for slavery.

Some church groups tried to have it both ways, by calling Zionism racism, but not in so many words. For example, the Ecumenical
Caucus (which includes representatives of the World Council of
Churches, the Presbyterian Church USA, the Lutheran World Federation, and many others) issued a statement that termed colonialism
one of the "manifestations and historical expressions" of racism in one
part, and then referred to the "Israeli colonialist occupation in the
occupied Palestinian territories" in another.[41]

This was all the more outrageous given the ubiquitous antisemitic material around the NGO forum, including a banner which
advocated violence: "For the liberation of Quds [Jerusalem], machine
guns based on faith and Islam must be used."[42] The argument was
clearly being advanced that violence against Jews in Israel will help aid
the worldwide fight against racism. In this environment, was this all
the Ecumenical Caucus could say?

The document on "Palestine" that emerged from the NGO
forum was outrageous. It accused Israel of "systemic perpetration of
racist crimes ... war crimes ... genocide ... ethnic cleansing ... and state
terrorism" and that was only in the opening paragraph. Other para-
graphs accused Israel of "settler colonialism," being "a racist, apartheid

state in which Israel's brand of apartheid [is] a crime against humanity," and conducting a "war on civilians."

The document also called for the reinstatement of Resolution 3379 (equating Zionism with racism) and the creation of educational materials for schools to teach Israel's "racist" nature, how it is an "apartheid state."[43] It asked for the prosecution of Israeli "war crimes." And it called for "mandatory and comprehensive sanctions and embargoes, the full cessation of all links (diplomatic, economic, social, aid, military cooperation and training) between all states and Israel [and the] launch of an international anti-Israel apartheid movement."[44] As eminent human rights lawyer Irwin Cotler noted, "In a world in which human rights has emerged as the secular religion of our time, Israel, portrayed as the worst of human rights violators, is the new anti-Christ."[45]

Perhaps the most disingenuous assault on Jews and Israel was the condemnation of Israel's Law of Return as "racist," and the endorsement of the right of return of Palestinian refugees to Israel proper. The Israeli Law of Return[46] provides the right of any Jew (with the exception of criminals and other undesirables) to move to Israel and receive Israeli citizenship. The Law of Return provides security for Jews (who, of course, come in all races)—a need that no one of goodwill would question in the aftermath of the Holocaust. That state in the Jews' historic homeland is tiny, the size of New Jersey, in a miniscule portion of a huge region. As of 2005, 5,237,600 Jews live in Israel,[47] surrounded by about 300 million Arabs living in 22 Arab countries.[48] Why is this somehow unjust, especially in a world that does not complain about other countries having similar provisions for their diasporas, such as, among many others, the ethnic Russians who have been allowed to return from the former Soviet republics, or the ethnic Germans who were absorbed into Germany following 1945?[49]

All the peoples in the world have a recognized international right to "self-determination," yet the antisemitic voices in Durban attempted to make Jews the only people in the world who do not have such a right. Or, as a Jewish group in Durban noted: "If Palestinians are entitled to a Palestine, why are Jews not entitled to an Israel?"[50]

Conversely, Palestinians themselves seek a "right of return," not to the eventual state of Palestine, but to Israel itself. This is not a simple matter of justice, because the refugees created by the war of 1948 were not only Arabs; the number of Jews who were displaced from Arab states[51] starting in 1948 also numbered in the hundreds of thousands, and they have never been compensated for their misfortune or for what many were forced to leave behind. (In fact, the majority of Jews in Israel are now those who fled from Arab countries and their descendents.[52]) The desire is to outnumber Jews in Israel and thus to eliminate the State of Israel as a Jewish state.

Jewish groups walked out of the meeting at which the NGOs adopted resolutions stating their venom toward Israel. The final straw was when it was suggested that language complaining about anti-Jewish bias be removed from the document.[53]

Neither Amnesty International nor Human Rights Watch acted heroically, or in consonance with their mission. (In fact, Human Rights Watch acted particularly badly—its advocacy director announced that a representative of a group would not be allowed to participate in a caucus of human rights NGOs to which it belonged because, as a Jewish group, it allegedly could not be objective about the draft statement.[54]) While neither AI nor HRW signed onto the NGO statement (how could they stomach the misuse of the word "genocide," one of the terms of art of their trade?), neither criticized the declaration as hatred.[55]

They were not confused, just unwilling to speak out. After all, the difference between justifiable criticism of Israel and antisemitism is not complex. If the criticism is the same as that by which one would judge any other country—complaining about a policy, a program, a plan or a party—that is fine. But if the perceived deficiencies of a society are used to attack its basic legitimacy, then something else is going on. (We would never say that the U.S. or Egypt should not exist, no matter what the policy criticism.) As the Jewish caucus said, not only was Israel singled out for criticism not leveled at any other country (even the Taliban in Afghanistan), but the attacks fit into the historic construct of antisemitic canards. As the concluding Statement of the Jewish Caucus reported:

> The accusations made against Israel are accusations made against the state and not individuals. They are a form of collective accusation of guilt, rather than individual accusations of crime. The Jewish community is well familiar with collective accusations of guilt, having been told for centuries that the Jewish community, as a community, killed Jesus Christ. The accusations made against the Jewish state of colonialism, war crimes, crimes against humanity, genocide, ethnic cleansing and apartheid are of the same nature, blaming a whole community for the most heinous crimes.

> Insofar as any Israeli policy or practice is racist, that policy or practice should be criticized in terms that are specific to the wrong.... Any wrongs that have been inflicted are wildly inflated to justify the starting position of the critics, that the State of Israel should not exist....

> [The NGO Declaration at Durban] took the vision of universal human rights standards applicable to all races, nationalities, and religions in the words of the Universal Declaration of Human Rights and excluded the Jew. It took the vision of the equality of all nations large and small in the words of the United Nations Charter and barred the State of Israel.[56]

The Main Conference

The main conference, comprised of representatives of states, followed the NGO meeting. As the delegates met, the Tehran language had not been removed, despite the best efforts of many countries. Both the United States and Israel sent midlevel delegations, which must have been a huge disappointment for Secretary of State Colin Powell, who certainly recognized both the symbolic and substantial contribution his presence at the conference would have made. But he understood even more the danger of giving legitimacy to bigotry.

The Draft Declaration still stated:

> We express our deep concern about practices of racial discrimination against the Palestinians as well as other inhabitants of the Arab occupied territories, which have an impact on all aspects of their daily existence such that they prevent the enjoyment of fundamental rights, and call for the cessation of all the practices of racial discrimination to which the Palestinians and the other inhabitants of the Arab territories occupied by Israel are subjected.

> We are convinced that combating anti-Semitism, Islamophobia and Zionist practices against Semitism is integral and intrinsic to opposing all forms of racism and stress the necessity for effective measures to address the issue of anti-Semitism, Islamophobia and Zionist practices against Semitism today in order to counter all manifestations of these phenomena.

> The World Conference recognizes with deep concern the increase of racist practices of Zionism and anti-Semitism in various parts of the world, as well as the emergence of racial and violent movements based on racism and discriminatory ideas, in particular the Zionist movement, which is based on racial superiority.[57]

If it was not changed, it was clear the U.S. and Israel would leave. The language spoken at the Conference, however, was little different from the draft.

"Most peoples of the world have been liberated from colonialism," said Syrian Foreign Minister Farouk Al-Shara. "Zimbabwe, Namibia and South Africa have gotten rid of racism, of which Zionist Israel was the closest ally. Hence the world no longer accepts occupation, colonialism and racism. Only Israel, the last bastion of racism, has failed to recognize this very fact."[58]

Rev. Jesse Jackson was obviously concerned that Durban was heading toward a train wreck over Zionism and Israel, and would derail attention from the slavery issue, also on the conference agenda. Rev. Jackson announced that he had met with Yasir Arafat, who, he said, had agreed to moderate his language. But when Arafat took the podium, he not only accused Israel of a "supremacist mentality, a mentality of racial discrimination," but also spoke about Israel as a practitioner of "settler colonialism and racial discrimination." And, as if that were not enough, he added that Israel shot Palestinians with bullets laced with depleted uranium.[59]

Israel's representative, Mordechai Yedid, said (reading a speech in place of Israeli Deputy Foreign Minister Michael Melchior, who, in protest, refused to attend personally):

> [A]nti-Zionism, the denial of Jews the basic right to a home, is nothing but antisemitism, pure and simple. The venal hatred of Jews that has taken the form of anti-Zionism, and which has surfaced at this conference, is different in one crucial way from the antisemitism of the past. Today, it is being deliberately propagated and manipulated for political ends.

> Racism, in all its forms, is one of the most widespread and pernicious evils, depriving millions of hope and fundamental rights. It may have been hoped that this first conference of the twenty-first century would have taken up the challenge of, if not eradicating racism, at least disarming it. But instead humanity is being sacrificed to a political agenda.

> [Barely a decade after the UN equation of Zionism with racism was repealed] a group of states for whom the terms "racism," "discrimination," and even "human rights" simply do not appear in their domestic lexicon have hijacked this conference and plunged us to even greater depths. Can there be a greater irony than the fact that a conference convened to combat the scourge of racism should give rise to the most racist declaration in a major international organization since World War II?

> Despite the vicious antisemitism we have heard here, I do not fear for the Jewish people, which has learned to be resilient and to hold fast to its faith. Despite the virulent incitement against my country, I do not fear for Israel, which has the strength not just of courage, but also of conviction.

But I do fear, deeply, for the victims of racism, for the slaves, the disenfranchised, the oppressed, the inexplicably hated, the impoverished, the despised, the millions who turn their eyes to this hall in the frail hope that it may address their suffering, who see instead that a blind and venal hatred of the Jews has turned their hopes into a farce. For them I fear.[60]

A last-minute attempt to find acceptable substitute language, offered by the Norwegians, collapsed. Reportedly, "the Egyptians insisted that Israel be termed a racist state; the Syrians repeated Holocaust-denial statements; and the Iranians declared that antisemitism was not a form of contemporary racism that should be dealt with at the conference."[61]

The United States and Israel pulled their midlevel delegations and left. U.S. Secretary of State Colin Powell said:

I have taken this decision with great regret, because of the importance of the international fight against racism and the contribution that the conference could have made to it. But following discussions today by our team in Durban and others who are working for a successful conference, I am convinced that will not be possible....

You do not combat racism by conferences that produce declarations containing hateful language, some of which is a throwback to the days of "Zionism equals racism," or supports the idea that we have made too much of the Holocaust, or suggests that apartheid exists in Israel, or that singles out only one country in the world, Israel, for censure and abuse.[62]

As Charles Krauthammer noted:

This was a universal conference whose overriding objective was to brand one country and one people as uniquely, transcendently evil. The whole point was to rekindle the Arab campaign to delegitimize the planet's single Jewish state—and thus prepare the psychological and political ground for its extinction.[63]

The Islamic tabloid *Al-Hujjat*, distributed in Durban, made the point more directly: "When you see the blood of your innocent brothers and sisters shed on the holy soil of Palestine, and when you observe our lands being destroyed by the criminal Zionist, there remains NO way BUT JIHAD.... Neither the Muslim nation of Iran nor any Muslim—basically no free person—RECOGNIZES Israel, and as for us, we shall ALWAYS defend our Palestinian and ARAB brothers."[64]

The Hijacking of Language

The Israelis seemed happy that the final resolution (ratified a day after the conference was supposed to have ended) had language that was not as bad as had been expected all along. But it was bad enough.[65] Durban effectively recast the canards of antisemitism into the lexicon of human rights and antiracism.

How had such a farce occurred in the country that had defeated apartheid? It happened partly because the Arab countries felt they could get away with it. American Jewish Committee Executive Director David Harris did the math: "Start with the twenty-two-member Arab League.... The fifty-seven-member Organization of the Islamic Conference (OIC) usually follows the Arab lead; and the 113-member Nonaligned Movement, which includes the Arab League and Islamic Conference nations, does as well—so an automatic majority is created. What chance does Israel have in such an imbalanced setting?"[66]

But what happened in Durban was more than the hijacking of a conference; it was the hijacking of language. U.S. history offers examples of those who sought to shroud bigotry in the terminology of rights and liberties. Those who remember the civil rights battles of the 1960s recall the segregationist leaders speaking of "states' rights," rather than oppression of dark-skinned people. And in the 1990s the militias tried describing their agenda of hate as "defending the Constitution." To oppress well, haters need to articulate loftier goals, the best of which are freedom and liberty.

The difference this time: Human rights activists in the 1960s and 1990s saw through these transparent shams and exposed them. In Durban, the human rights community, with only a very few exceptions, either ignored or adopted them. In fact, the Ford Foundation actually helped fund some of the worst offenders in Durban.[67]

Troubling Responses to Durban

How powerful was this renewed antisemitism, targeting Israel and everything Jewish in its wake, distorting Judaism, minimizing or denying the Holocaust, even attempting to deny to Jews the modern word linked to the prejudice against them?

It is not surprising that white supremacists liked what they heard at Durban, nor that the Nation of Islam's paper *The Final Call* lambasted Jesse Jackson for his attempted intercession with Arafat, claiming that he went "on a mission to appease the Zionists who control the American media, and to serve the imperialist interests of the United States government."[68]

What was more alarming was the reportage of some human rights institutions. Political Research Associates (PRA), for example, is an organization that for many years followed far-right groups in America, and noted their racism and antisemitism.

Its fall 2001 newsletter, *The Public Eye*, contained three pages on the World Conference Against Racism. Incredibly, there was no mention of the antisemitism that was so thick in the air in Durban. Worse, the article criticized the "international media" for "reproduc[ing] the official U.S. position [sic] labeling any criticism of Israel's actions toward Palestine as being antisemitic."[69] The PRA was not alone in its treatment of Durban.

Perhaps we are living in a world in which the perceived character of the *Protocols* and other antisemitic literature is determined by the language in which it is written, who is quoting it, and for what purpose. If so, it is a very dangerous world indeed. It is especially dangerous for Jews, for it means that manifestations of antisemitism will be fought by non-Jews when to do so is politically expedient and, at best, ignored when it is not.[70]

That is why the United Nations and most human rights organizations that seek to protect children worldwide from exploitation were mute when Palestinian children were put in front of armed men in order to draw Israeli fire, or were encouraged to become suicide bombers.

That is why the United Nations and most human rights organizations stood mute when Saddam Hussein announced that he was upping his payment to $25,000 to families of suicide bombers who attack Israel.[71] Would the UN have silently acquiesced if, for example, the leader of India offered a functional bounty for the blowing up of civilian Pakistanis, or vice versa?

That is why, following suicide attack after suicide attack against Israeli civilians, including children, the UN Human Rights Commission in Geneva in April 2002 approved a resolution (by a 40-5 vote, with seven abstentions) declaring that in order to establish a Palestinian state it supported the use of "all available means, including armed struggle," which was clearly understood to be a euphemism for terrorism.[72]

Antisemitic double standards clearly have less to do with who the supposed "victims" are and everything to do with who the perceived "victimizer" is.

As Deputy Foreign Minister Melchior's words at Durban underscored, Jews have learned how to survive in such an unfair and bigoted environment. It is unclear, however, how world bodies and groups that exist to promote "human rights" can do so effectively when they increasingly have one standard for most countries and peoples, and another for Israelis and Jews.

Mostly, the example of Durban—to which we will return in the chapters addressing what is to be done—best shows three things. First, it shows how easy it is for one form of antisemitism—anti-Zionism—to open the floodgates for expressions of the other strains, tarring Judaism as a religion and Jews as a people. Second, it demonstrates how easily language can be turned on its head. The bulk of the vocabulary of human rights and antiracism is associated with lessons supposedly learned from the Holocaust. Yet Durban instructed that to be a good antiracist, one had to be an anti-Zionist. Third, despite the exposé of this conference as bigoted to its core, it could still have long-term programmatic effects—namely (as will be addressed in Chapter 10), the efforts on some U.S. campuses to equate Israel with apartheid-era South Africa, and to use against Israel the tools that had helped dismantle apartheid.

Syria has documented proof of the Zionist regime's involvement in the September 11 terror attacks on the U.S.... [That] 4,000 Jews employed at the WTC did not show up for work before the attack clearly attests to Zionist involvement in these attacks.

—Turky Muhammad Saqr, Syrian ambassador to Tehran[1]

Chapter Four
9/11

Antisemitic myths, positing Jews or Israelis secretly working to harm non-Jews, are the streams through which much antisemitism flows. A recent charge—that Jews and/or Israelis were secretly behind the attacks of September 11, 2001—is a good example of how such myths unfold and why they work.

Antisemites, by definition, blame Jews for things that go wrong in the world. And so they did following September 11.

Matt Hale, then head of the World Church of the Creator[2] (a white supremacist and antisemitic group that preached the need for "Rahowa," short for "racial holy war"), said predictably:

> We blame the American government for the tragedy of today.... The tragedy we have witnessed is the inevitable and ultimate result of a foreign policy that has been slavishly pro-Israel in its aggression against its neighbors.... This is why Arab terrorists have launched their "Jihad" against targets in this country.... We call upon all White people to demand that aid to Israel end. We call for the liberation of this land from the manipulations of the Jews that have had such terrible consequences.[3]

Neo-Nazi and former Ku Klux Klan leader David Duke wrote an open letter to President Bush: "[T]hose who attacked us ... did not attack us because they hate our democracy or our freedoms.... It was purely in response to America's foreign policy, and it was primarily about our monetary and military support of Israel."[4] Duke also posted antisemitica on the Internet, railing about "the Jewish-dominated media," "Jewish bosses of American foreign policy," "world-wide Jewish Supremacism," and the "Zionist criminal actions [that] led to this terror."[5]

Tom Metzger of White Aryan Resistance said, "September 11 is the anniversary of the Camp David Accords [and] the Peace Treaty between Israel and Egypt [sic].[6] The white worker and others paid for this phony peace.... Intervention and international policing to protect transnational corporations, banking and Jew intrigue are the causes.... This operation took some long-term planning, and, throughout the entire time, these soldiers were aware that their lives would be sacrificed for their cause. If an Aryan wants an example of 'Victory or Vahalla,' look no further."[7]

William Pierce, late head of the neo-Nazi National Alliance and author of the *Turner Diaries*,[8] said at the time, "Is it any wonder then, that when people are driven into a corner—as the non-Jewish people of the Middle East have been—that sometimes they will fight back.... When someone from the Middle East who has given up all hope of justice for his people pops a biological grenade in a New York subway tunnel or on the grounds of the Washington Monument or somewhere else in the United States, and thousands of our people start dying, some of those who have been too complacent and too tolerant will begin to change their attitudes."[9]

August Kries of the Posse Comitatus wrote, "May the WAR be started.... DEATH to His [God's] enemies.... We can blame no others than ourselves for our problems due to the fact that we allow Satan's children, called Jews today, to have dominion over our lives."[10]

Some admiration for the attackers was inevitable among such hate groups, since neo-Nazis see New York as "Jew York,"[11] but with a degree of caution, since white supremacists may like what antisemitic Arabs do, but they do not like non-whites. Thus, a National Alliance member commented, "The enemy of our enemy is, for now at least, our friend. We may not want them marrying our daughters, just as they would not want us marrying theirs. We may not want them in our societies, just as they would not want us in theirs. But anyone who is willing to drive a plane into a building to kill Jews is all right by me. I wish our members had half as much testicular fortitude."[12]

Or, as Rocky Suhayda, the American Nazi Party chairman from Eastpointe, Michigan, wrote, "It's a DISGRACE that in a population of at least 150 MILLION White/Aryan Americans, we provide so FEW that are willing to do the same. [A] bunch of towel head/sand niggers put our great White movement to SHAME."[13]

Reaction from the Left

Reaction on the left was more complex, generally less vitriolic, but also frequently finding ways to bring Jews and Israel into the mix. *Resist*, a self-styled "progressive" newsletter, said that America has been "seen by an increasing number of people the world over as the enemy." It cited a writer who delineated the places: "in Vietnam ... Chile and El Salvador ... in Iraq ... and perhaps most important for understanding the current situation, in the occupied territories of the West Bank and Gaza.... [C]ontinued unqualified support by the United States for the Israelis in their war against the Palestinians, and military overflights and economic sanctions against the Iraqis will not serve the causes of freedom, democracy and justice."[14]

On a listserv dedicated to fighting the far right, comments suggested that the attack was because the United States had walked out of the World Conference Against Racism in Durban the week before, in protest over language equating Zionism with racism. Another comment raised the question of whether CNN had used old Gulf War film footage to defame Palestinians who were shown celebrating the terrorist attack.

There were, of course, some legitimate issues raised by the American left.[15] The concern that Muslims and Arabs (or those who might be mistaken for them) might become victims of hate crimes was real (and one the Jewish community shared and spoke out about), but, in contrast, there was silence when Jews, here and abroad, were targeted for attack after the collapse of the peace process. For example, Human Rights Watch announced the creation of a position for a researcher to investigate hate crimes against "Muslims, Sikhs and people of Middle Eastern and South Asian descent in the United States since the September 11 attacks," at just about the same time that the FBI's statistics on hate crimes in 2000 were released. In 2000 there were 28 attacks directed against Muslims and 1,119 against Jews. Although Jews make up only about 2.5 percent of the U.S. population, almost 14 percent of all hate crimes, and over 75 percent of hate crimes that were religion-based, were directed against Jews in that year.[16]

The left also expressed a legitimate concern about civil liberties, examining whether or how they should be recalibrated in the aftermath of September 11. It was fair enough that none of us wants to give the terrorists the victory of stealing our freedoms. More problematic, however, was the question of "racial profiling" and the failure to see any fundamental difference between the notion of "driving while black" and the idea that it makes sense to pay closer attention to a Middle Eastern man traveling by air with no baggage than a white-haired grandmother. But fundamentally there was something about the fact that "they're trying to kill us all" that the left simply did not get. This was not an abstract, ideologically driven, new round of repressive legislation to fight. This was Islamic terrorists flying planes into office buildings, the Pentagon, and maybe the White House. This was an attack on America, a war. The significance of that fact seemed outside the left's radar.

There was not only unreality here: There was antisemitism—and it was reflected in some of the punditry, and even reportage, by suggestions that American support for Israel was somehow at the root of the attacks.

First, that claim is not true. Osama bin Ladin and the movement to which he belongs are not basically or primarily anti-American because the U.S. supports Israel. President Bush's statement that Bin Ladin hates our "freedoms" might sound simplistic, but it is actually very close to the truth. Look at the freedoms women enjoy here, and look at their lives under the Taliban, where women are not only forced to cover themselves from head to foot, but also are denied the right to go to school or get a job. These Islamists are not pluralists—you do your thing; we do ours. They see only one proper way, and any other way they define as a threat that needs to be eliminated. Their greatest concern is the U.S. presence in the Middle East, and particularly in Saudi Arabia.[17] That the U.S. helped liberate Kuwait during the first Gulf War did not matter any more than that American troops had been invited into Saudi Arabia by the Saudi rulers. Islamists see the mere presence of Americans in the region as blasphemy and desecration of holy soil. And it is not just that our troops pollute Muslim soil, but also that our basic values are theologically toxic. As Paul Berman makes clear in his excellent book *Terror and Liberalism*, Islamists will continue to target liberal societies since they "put religion in one corner, and the state in a different corner," and thus "den[y] or suspend ... God's sovereignty on earth."[18] For sure, the Islamist movement would cheer and celebrate if Israel were destroyed tomorrow, but that would not stop it from targeting terror against the United States and its inhabitants.

Second, it was immediately clear that the September 11 operation was carefully thought out and very well planned and executed. Such an operation did not happen overnight, and, as it turned out, Muhammad Atta and the other hijackers were taking flight lessons and making preparations more than a year in advance.[19] In other words, this terrorist plot started back in the period following the Oslo Accords and was in full swing during the heady time of Camp David, when it seemed that a negotiated peace in the Middle East, acceptable to the Palestinians and Israelis alike, was indeed possible.

What the left, and some journalists, refused (or were unable) to see was that a peace settlement was much more disturbing to the Islamists than anything else. It would mean that Israel would continue to exist and that infidels—Jews and Christians—would continue to live on "holy soil."

This blindness was the result of antisemitism—maybe not the bone-chilling antisemitism of David Duke and Durban—but antisemitism nonetheless. That may seem like a harsh statement, but consider the test for discerning bigotry: Take a scenario, change a basic characteristic of the "players" (their race, sex, religion, sexual orientation, etc.) and see if the same rules apply.

What if the terrorists in the cockpits had been white supremacists with "testicular fortitude" who had targeted America because it had become a multiracial society? Would the left have had similar difficulty identifying the specifics of the ideology that drove those planes into those buildings? Probably not.

Carry the analogy further. Certainly, under such a scenario, the far right would say that America has to look more closely at the policies that are going to lead this country to become majority nonwhite. But the left, instead of echoing those sentiments, would have condemned the racism inherent in them.

Much of the left's response—"explaining" the attacks as a result of U.S. policy on Israel—was like those who, hearing of a woman who was raped, fault the "provocative" clothing she was wearing. If actions are informed by an ideology of hate, what the victim did or did not do is irrelevant. As veteran human rights activist Dan Levitas noted, would the left have explained away the racist murder of James Byrd, who was torn apart while being dragged behind a truck in Texas, because his white killers were upset with "black crime"? Or the homophobic and horrific slaying of Matthew Shepard—beaten, tortured, and left to die tied up to a Wyoming fence—because the "gay lifestyle" makes some people uncomfortable?[20]

Arab and Muslim Reaction

As troubling as the reaction to 9/11 was, on both America's right and left, what was truly startling was the reaction in the Arab and Muslim worlds.

Soon after the attacks, there was a report in the Israeli media that perhaps 4,000 Israelis normally worked in the World Trade Center. Like the proverbial game of telephone, but amplified at warp speed due to the Internet's ability to spread rumors, this was recast as 4,000 (or 5,000) Israelis (or Jews) who were warned not to go to work that fateful day.

This was a replay of the far-right rumor after the Oklahoma City bombing that government officials had been warned not to go to work on April 19, 1995. The explanation? The government was behind the Oklahoma City bombing as a plot to allow the federal government to crack down on "loyal patriots," such as the militia movement and white supremacists.

The September 11 version of this charge was that Israelis (or Jews) had been told to stay away, so they obviously were behind the attacks. One major and disturbing difference between the 1995 conspiracy theory and its rehash in 2001: Only the extreme fringe had believed this nonsense in 1995; but huge numbers in the Muslim and Arab worlds, including many of its leaders, have adopted "the Jews did it" story line.

Syrian Foreign Minister Mustafa Tlass claimed that the Mossad, an Israeli intelligence service, planned the attack.[21] Likewise, the Syrian ambassador to Tehran, Turky Muhammad Saqr, said, "Syria has documented proof of the Zionist regime's involvement in the September 11 terror attacks on the U.S.," and that "4,000 Jews employed at the WTC did not show up for work before the attack clearly attests to Zionist involvement in these attacks."[22]

In Qatar, a government-sponsored Web site posted an article entitled, "Zionists Could Be Behind Attack on WTC and Pentagon." It began:

> The September 11 terrorist attacks on [the] World Trade Centre (WTC) in New York and Pentagon in Washington were masterminded by an international Zionist organization, "The Elders of Zion."[23]

Columnists and clerics in the Arab and Islamic worlds echoed these antisemitic conspiracy theories, interpreting September 11 as a plot by Israel and Jews. Here are some comments that appeared in the Arab press:

> What happened is the work of Jewish-Israeli-American Zionism, and the act of the large Zionist Jewish mind controlling the world economically, politically, and through the media.[24]

> It is obvious that Israel is the one to gain greatly from this bloody, loathsome, and terrible terror operation, and it seeks to gain further by accusing the Arabs and Muslims of carrying it out.... Only Israel does not fear that the Jews will be discovered to be behind this operation—who inside or outside the U.S. would dare to accuse them, as any harm to them means talk of a new Holocaust? They, more than anyone, are capable of hiding a crime they carry out, and they can be certain that no one will ask them what they have done.[25]

> The investigation of these attacks did not begin from the proper starting point; rather, it was swept away by public opinion, shaped by the American media which is controlled by the Jews.... Why did they inform the Jews that there was no further need for their services only three days before the attacks? Why did they announce huge losses in the technology sector, in which most of the employees are Jews, with offices in the trade building [WTC]—which made the Jews leave the place? Why did rumors spread among the Jews that the "appointed time for the execution of the attack was a day off work?"[26]

Some Islamic leaders in the U.S. made similar claims. Sheikh Muhammad Gamei'a of the Islamic Cultural Center in New York said that "only the Jews" could have destroyed the WTC and that "if it became known to the American people, they would have done to Jews what Hitler did." [27] The sheikh is now in Egypt.[28]

Salam Al-Marayati, executive director of the Muslim Public Affairs Council, said, "If we're going to look at suspects, we should look to the groups that benefit the most from these kind of incidents. And I think we should put the State of Israel on the suspects list, because I think this diverts attention from what is happening in the Palestinian territories, so that they can go on with their aggression and occupation and apartheid policies."[29]

Literally scores of such statements were replayed in the press, in mosques, on the Internet, on television. This conspiracy theory of the Jewish 9/11 worked just like Holocaust denial: Paint Jews as committing the "crime," ascribe to them a "motive," use antisemitic myths to explain the "opportunity," and dismiss inconsistent evidence as either unreliable or manufactured by Jews. A tall order? Not if people want to be convinced. After all, Holocaust deniers (including, it seems, the leaders of the current Syrian and Iranian governments) can explain away a six-year war with millions dead and mountains of evidence. How hard is it to paint a morning's events into such an antisemitic picture?

Taking the various accusations and combining them into a narrative, it goes something like this:

The Jews did it. They did it by the Mossad recruiting the Arabs who went on the plane.[30] Or alternatively, as Orkhan Muhammad Ali, alleged in *Saut Al-Haqq Wa-Al-Hurriyya,* "the planes were not hijacked; they were remotely controlled.... The president of [the companies responsible for this technology] is Jewish."[31]

What about the evidence that Arabs were involved? The Mossad is so powerful that any evidence pointing to an Arab's hand is obviously a forgery; in fact, the manifests of the planes show that of the 600 people on the planes, "there were no Arabic sounding names."[32] And Atta's suicide note? It "was obviously forged," opined Khalil Al-Sawahri. "[H]ow can a man planning to blow himself up ...

focus his will on the handling of his body ... when he knows that his body will turn to ashes and be scattered all over?"[33]

The Jews did it. They did it to manipulate the stock market, because Jews are greedy, and since, as Dr. Gamal Zahran of the Suez Canal University wrote, they "were huge stockholders in the airlines and insurance companies, [they] sold their stocks at the highest possible prices in Europe some 10 days before the attacks on America."[34] Mostly, as Ahmad Abu Zayid offered, they did it to "divert attention [from] the war of annihilation [Israel] wages against the Palestinian people" and the beating they took in Durban. They did it to get the United States even more active on their side, having the United States now wage war against Muslims and Arabs on their behalf. They did it to shift "world public opinion against the Arabs and Muslims and in favor of Israel."[35]

The Jews did it. We know, because as Sheikh Gamei'a alleged, "only the Jews are capable of planning such an incident, because it was planned with great precision of which Osama bin Laden or any other Islamic organization or intelligence apparatus is incapable."[36] Indeed, as Hilmi Al-Asmar wrote, "Israel was the only one who could have broken into the American security apparatus. Since its past is rife with operations and crimes [that are] far from moral, it is willing to carry out the most monstrous crime in human history even if the victims would be Jews."[37] And history is full of examples of Jews trying to control the world. We have the blueprint: the *Protocols,*[38] and the evidence. Jews were arrested after September 11, and not only Jews who were celebrating the attacks, but Jews with photos of an atomic reactor and of the Alaska oil pipeline. In fact, according to an Egyptian paper, "American security forces burst into the home of seven Israelis from Florida, arresting them and finding in their possession large quantities of anthrax microbes and some 15 maps of the WTC, eight maps of the Pentagon, and six maps of the White House."[39]

But, of course, no one knows about this. Or about the "twenty Jews [who] came from outside the U.S., entered the WTC on the morning of the event, and left before the attack." Or about the Jews who "set up video cameras on the roof of one of the Israeli companies across from the WTC a little while before the incident, in order to film the moment of the explosions."[40] Why does no one know? Because, as Ahmad Al-Musallah explained, "the large Zionist Jewish mind control[s] the world economically, politically, and through the media."[41]

The Jews did it. Want more proof? Turky Muhammad Saqr, the Syrian ambassador to Tehran, explained that Prime Minister Ariel Sharon's postponement of a scheduled visit to the United States at the beginning of September was "additional proof linking the Zionists with this tragedy."[42] What's more, Syrian columnist Mu'-taz Al-Khatib asserted that former Israeli Prime Minister Ehud Barak's "presence in the BBC's head office minutes after the explosion, at a meeting set in advance, to speak ... of the danger of terrorism and chastise the 'rogue states,' particularly the Arabs ... " was more proof of the Israeli plot.

The biggest smoking gun, of course, was that 4,000 Jews were tipped off NOT to show up at work that day. As Dr. Gamal Zahran wrote, "At the WTC, thousands of Jews worked in finance and the stock market, but none of them was there on the day of the incident. Out of 6,000 killed, of 65 nationalities from 60 countries, not one was a Jew!"[43]

Think about it. Not one Jew was harmed. Could this be coincidence, that 4,000 don't show up on one day?[44]

There are no coincidences when it comes to the nefarious plots of Jews. Indeed, as Saudi Prince Mamdouh bin Abd Al-Aziz wrote, after citing the *Protocols* and other proofs of a "Zionist conspiracy," "Objectivity demands that we ask whether the disasters that have struck at the heart of the Arab and Islamic world over many long years were mere coincidence, or were the result of a conspiracy."[45]

And, what about Osama bin Ladin's confession? Any entity sophisticated enough to coordinate an attack on America and conceal all the evidence can easily doctor one videotape.[46]

This is quite a story, but it fits classically into the mold of traditional antisemitic myth: Jews conspiring to harm non-Jews. In fact, this one is exceedingly clever, because it makes Jews even more nefarious than poisoners of wells or kidnappers of Christian children. This is double-whammy antisemitism: Jews harming predominately Christian Americans so that Arabs and Muslims would be blamed and, therefore, harmed in response.

Many intelligent people cannot fathom how huge numbers can believe such blatant and obvious lies about Jews. But hate has little to do with truth or accuracy; it is a belief system that dehumanizes and demonizes its target, and thus is actually empowered by the lies. For if you believe Jews are devil-like, then otherwise bizarre allegations of their power and abilities only help substantiate the a priori belief. What is most alarming is that the 9/11 antisemitic myth seemingly has mainstream currency in the Middle East and in Islamic countries. For when leaders say it, and academics, clerics, and the media repeat it, what is fantastic seems credible. How did such hateful and conspiratorial beliefs, which we associate with fringe groups elsewhere in the world, become so institutionalized and unremarkable in the Arab and Muslim worlds?

Thanks to Hitler, of blessed memory, who on behalf of the Palestinians took revenge in advance, against the most vile criminals on the face of the Earth. Although we do have a complaint against him, for his revenge was not enough.

—Ahmad Ragab (Egypt)1

The Jews are portrayed in Arab cartoons as demons and murderers, as a hateful, loathsome people to be feared and avoided. They are invariably seen as the origin of all evil and corruption, authors of a dark, unrelenting conspiracy to infiltrate and destroy Muslim society in order to eventually take over the world.... Judaism ... is presented as a sinister and immoral religion, based on cabals and blood rituals, while Zionists [are called] ... racists or Nazis. The aim is not simply to morally delegitimize Israel as a Jewish state and a national entity in the Middle East but to dehumanize Judaism and the Jewish people as such.

—Robert Wistrich[2]

Chapter Five
Antisemitism in the Arab and Muslim Worlds

Historically, Jews and Christians were designated by the Islamic world as "people of the book," but both were also treated as "infidels" who rejected the Islamic "ultimate revelation of God."[3] Jews in Islamic countries were not allowed to bear arms or ride horses, and the yellow badge on clothing to single out the Jew had its origin in Baghdad, not Berlin.[4]

While Jews were slaughtered from time to time (for example, 6,000 in Fez, Morocco, in 1033), they were massacred less frequently under Islam during premodern times than in Christian societies. At times, relative to Jews in Europe, Jews in Islamic societies prospered.[5]

Yet the infrastructure of antisemitism was fully present in Islam. The Koran paints Jews as wretched and base prophet-slayers, and mandates their "abasement and poverty." They are infidels who have merited God's "wrath" and whom God has "cursed" and of whom he has required a "painful punishment." God turned them into apes and pigs.[6] Even harsher are the *Hadith* (sayings of the Prophet Muhammad and his companions and traditions related to these statements) that paint Jews as cursed liars who are unclean, cheats, and traitors who are incapable of repentance and can never be forgiven.[7]

The *dhimmi* system allowed Jews to live and to pray under a protective status that was below that of a full Muslim citizen, in return for the payment of special taxes. But there was systematic humiliation, degradation, and, at times, violence against Jews. Edward William Lane, a British man who lived in Egypt in the 1820s and 1830s, wrote that Jews were "held in the utmost contempt and abhorrence by Muslims in general."[8] The *dhimmi* system not only oppressed Jews, but it kept the larger Muslim population believing they were kept safe from these infidels. But the birth of the State of Israel turned the dangerous but isolated Jew into a dangerous and newly powerful foe. While the birth of the State of Israel could be seen as a temporary revolt by the *dhimmis*, which would ultimately, of necessity, be turned back, the Israeli victory in the 1967 war seemed incomprehensible.

Not only was the general order of things challenged in terms of Muslim dominance and Jewish submission, but it was also upended on the more tangible level of the land. The often-debated questions of how many Palestinians there were in Mandatory Palestine in 1948, or today, and what has and will happen to them, are to those so religiously driven, hardly relevant. For many Muslims it is the fact of Jews ruling any of the land Muslims view as their own that is theologically impossible.

Historical Background

Indeed, since Jews began moving to join their kinsmen in their home-land and reestablished the State of Israel in 1948, Arab governments and Islamic leaders—even some of the "moderates," who are them-selves targets of the Islamists*—have incorporated a whole panoply of antisemitic myths that fueled attacks on Jews throughout history into their view of the world.

The process had its roots in the Muslim Ottoman Empire, when Christians in the Arab world helped propel these myths into Arab consciousness. The accusation of the blood libel—the ancient Christ-ian charge that Jews use the blood of non-Jews to make Passover matzah—was made against a group of Jews in Damascus in 1840 and became the fuel for many attacks on Jews, well before anyone coined the term "Zionism" or "antisemitism." This classical Christian-based European Jew-hatred was the foundation of myths not only believed, but endorsed by Arab rulers.[9] You might think these absurd claims would have been dismissed, and they have been in most of the world,

---

* By Islamism, and its adherents (Islamists), I do not mean Islam the religion as a whole, but the violent, extremist version of Islam that has caused so much carnage in the last decade around the world. (Some have referred to this movement as "Islamo-fascism," and there is much logic to this formulation as well. See also the first definition under http://www.thefreedictionary.com/Islamism, which gives an indication of Islamism's disdain for any role for a state not in the service of Islam.)

As much as it may seem politically incorrect to say so, Islamism is based on elements of Islam, just as Jewish extremism, such as that of Meir Kahane and Baruch Goldstein, was based on some teachings of Judaism, and just as the anti-abortion bombers draw their justification from parts of Christianity. Religious ideas that serve as the foundation for hateful ideologies are powerful, having both "truth" and "God" on their side. The religious foundations that ideological edifices were built upon—distorted to us, truthful to them—are political to the core and violent in the extreme.

While some have asserted that Islamism is primarily a reaction against Arab autocrats, it is, in fact, not an ideology that seeks to reform bad governments, but rather a revolutionary, violent, intolerant, and utopian worldview that seeks to impose its truth on everyone.

but in the 1970s King Faisal of Saudia Arabia said that Jews "have a certain day on which they mix the blood of non-Jews into their bread and eat it."[10] And, in 1983 Syrian Defense Minister Mustafa Tlass— the same defense minister who later blamed the September 11 attacks on Jews—wrote a book entitled *The Matzah of Zion*, in which he asserted that the blood libel was true.[11] In 1997, in a modern twist on this old lie, Ambassador Nabil Ramlawi, the Palestinian observer to the UN Human Rights Commission, claimed: "The Israeli authorities have infected by injection 300 Palestinian children with the HIV virus during the years of the intifada."[12] In October 2000, both the Qatari- based Arabic cable news channel, Al-Jazeera, and the Egyptian gov- ernment-sponsored daily, *Al-Ahram*, repeated accusations that Jews use the blood of Arabs for religious purposes.[13] In 2001, an Abu Dhabi tel- evision station broadcast a "comedy" in which Israeli Prime Minister Ariel Sharon was shown marketing a drink made from the blood of Arabs. And, also in 2001, the Egypt-based Arab radio and television produced a multimillion-dollar thirty-part series "dramatiz[ing]" the *Protocols* with a cast of 400. An Egyptian publication remarked that now Arabs could see the strategy "that to this very day, dominates Israel's policy, political aspirations, and racism."[14]

Whereas the neo-Nazi crowd cites the *Protocols* as almost abstract proof to paint Jews as conspirators, Arab antisemites seem to have actually paid attention to the text. Mainstream articles in the Arab press, echoing the *Protocols*, claim that Jews use alcohol and prostitu- tion to harm gentiles.[15] Think about Islam's idealized view of the veiled woman in contrast with the images of American MTV, Madonna, and Britney Spears. Combine that with the belief that Jews have a plot to seize world control by corrupting the morals of non-Jews. You can eas- ily see why the *Protocols* would seem not only relevant, but also instructive—and frightening.

Given this longtime view of Jews as not only infidels but people who conspire to harm Arabs, the Arab world reacted to Hitler and Nazism favorably, both in the 1940s and today. Author Robert S.

Wistrich noted, "[t]he Arabs ... evidently rejoiced that a great European power was putting the Jews in their place."[16] During World War II, Haj Amin al-Husseini, the grand mufti of Jerusalem, not only supported the Nazis but even moved to Berlin, met with Hitler, said that Arabs were "natural allies of Germany,"[17] and asserted that as "the Germans know how to get rid of the Jews" and have "solved the Jewish problem." The friendship between Arabs and Nazis, in his words, should not be "a provisional one, dependent on circumstances, but a permanent and lasting friendship based on mutual interest."[18]

When Israel survived the Arab attack in 1948, the *Protocols* were again a useful tool for explaining the loss to the Arab masses. "[T]hey need not feel humiliated," wrote Y. Harkabi, "because they had to confront, not only the Jews of Palestine, but a satanic organization of worldwide scope: 'Israel and all that stands behind her'—a phrase very commonly used."[19]

After the 1967 Six-Day War[20]—when the Arab masses were sorely disappointed that their combined armies could not finish off Israel—there was again reliance on European and white-supremacist antisemitica in the Arab world to "explain" their loss. In fact, this material was used during the war itself: Egyptian soldiers carried pocket-sized editions of an Arabic translation of *Mein Kampf.*[21]

By 1974, the year following the Yom Kippur War, when the combined Arab armies attacked Israel on the holiest day in the Jewish calendar, there were more editions of the *Protocols* published in Arabic than in any other language. As the American Jewish Committee noted in a report that year, there was an ongoing "perversion of religious thought to political ends" in Muslim countries. "Although Islamic tradition holds Judaism to be a religion of true revelation, and the Bible a holy book for both Jews and Christians," the report noted, "Muslim scholars have recently misrepresented and slandered the Hebrew Scriptures and attributed all manner of crimes to the innate depravity of Jews and their religion."[22]

The details of these "crimes," including the nefarious *Protocols*, distortions of the Talmud, and claims that Jews advocate sex with children and conspire against Islam were plagiarisms from old Christian attempts to paint Jews as satanic. As Abdel Halim Mahoud, then rector of Al-Azhar University in Cairo, said at the time, "Satan's best friends today are the Jews. They have prepared a plan for the religious and moral subversion of humanity."[23]

By the late 1980s, the claims of the *Protocols* were so implanted in the Arab world that this book was even referred to by name in the charter of the terrorist group Hamas.[24] In the United States and Europe, the *Protocols* was literature sold by hate groups; in Jordan it was available to guests at the bookstore in the posh Intercontinental-Jordan hotel in Amman.[25]

By the mid-1990s, Arab and Muslim extremists had mined the treasure trove of old-time European-based antisemitica and posted huge chunks of it on the Internet. Radio Islam, an Internet site from Sweden that openly supports terror groups such as Islamic Jihad, Hamas and Hezbollah, offered the *Protocols* online in eleven different languages, as well as material from neo-Nazis and white supremacists from around the world.[26]

Today, Saudi Arabian textbooks teach about the *Protocols* as truth to Saudi schoolchildren.[27] Not surprisingly, author Kenneth Timmerman wrote that when he asked his intellectual friends in the Middle East about the *Protocols*, they were not only familiar with it, they pulled down the volume from their bookshelves. They could also describe in detail this Jewish scheme against humanity and bemoan that too few knew about it, because Jewish control was so powerful.[28]

As Norman Cohn noted, the *Protocols* not only merges "the medieval with the modern," but it also paints the demonology of Jews as operating on a larger and more ongoing scale. "[W]hereas ritual murder was imagined as happening from time to time, now here, now there, the Elders of Zion are imagined as an international government whose machinations constantly affect the whole world.... Instead of muttering spells, these sorcerers place articles in the press; instead of poisoning wells, they plunge whole countries into slumps and wars and revolutions."[29]

This hatred of Jews was so ubiquitous in the Islamic world that it was freely expressed even by the political leadership in Turkey (which has good relations with Israel). For example, Prime Minister Necmettin Erbakan, speaking in Libya in 1996, said that Jews had a 3,000-year-old secret organization that controlled the world; his Welfare Party's campaign manifesto vowed to eliminate "world imperialism and Zionism as well as Israel and a handful of champagne-drinking collaborators in the holding companies that feed it"; and his party-controlled paper, *Milli Gazete*, ran an article entitled "Spoil the Jew and See What Happens," which said:

> When you treat [Jews] humanly, you have to expect them to act like an animal. And history is the witness to this fact.... You can't expect from the Jews the things that are against their nature. Because a snake is assigned to market its poison, just in the same way a Jew is assigned to create mischief. Especially when we make agreements with and spoil them![30]

Demonizing Israel

If the individual Jew is seen as demonic, then, of course, the self-governing collective of Jews is a dangerous powerbase of the devil. That such an organized evil enterprise, existing in the middle of Arab and Muslim states, is considered a full partner among the family of nations is clearly a disquieting thought. No wonder Iranian President Mahmoud Ahmadinejad said Israel must be wiped off the map.

The antisemitism learned from the *Protocols* is seemingly so ingrained in parts of the Muslim world that even before Ahmadinejad's statements, when Malaysian Prime Minister Mahathir Mohamad spoke to the Organization of the Islamic Conference on October 16, 2003, he received "unanimous applause" when he said that the "Jews rule the world by proxy." His words were even called "a very, very wise assessment" by Egyptian Foreign Minister Ahmed Maher and "very correct" by Afghan President Hamid Karzai.[31] (The beauty of this canard is that it is self-authenticating: If the United States protests, it is seen as further proof of Jewish control.)

Old myths never die; they just get recycled and recast. If you believe the premise of the *Protocols*—that Jews secretly conspire to control the world in order to hurt non-Jews—then it is not a huge leap to adopt another antisemitic lie: denial of the Holocaust. This libel began with the Nazis, who carried out their murderous program to wipe out European Jewry in secret, and was popularized in the decades thereafter by white supremacists around the world. (See Chapter 7 for further discussion.)

Neo-Nazis saw Holocaust denial not only as a means of defaming Jews, but also as a necessary precondition to the political rehabilitation of fascism.[32] While American and European white supremacists were the main engine of the denial movement, many Arab groups saw another antisemitic story line they liked. If the Holocaust had never happened, then not only was the "need" for an Israel undercut, but also the Jews could be painted as even more Satanic: Why else would they concoct a horrible story of mass murder that was a lie? This argument was so ubiquitous in the Arab press that it was stated as truth by leaders of the Syrian government and others at Durban.[33] It was even articulated in 2005 by Iranian President Mahmoud Ahmadinejad, who not only denied the Holocaust, but said that if there was to be a Jewish state, it should be in Europe.[34]

Robert Wistrich summarizes the picture of Israel portrayed in the Arab world by much of its media and many of its leaders and clerics as a country that "deliberately spread[s] drugs, vice and prostitution into the Arab world and gasses the Palestinians or deliberately poisons their food and water. This is a criminal nation led by a bloodthirsty cannibalistic ogre who devours Palestinian children every morning for breakfast."[35]

On May 5, 2001, Pope John Paul II came to Damascus and visited Syrian President Bashar Assad, who told the pope:

[T]here are those who invariably attempt to subject all people once and again to the journey of ailments and agony. Therefore, our brethren in Palestine are being murdered and tortured, justice is being violated, and as a result territories in Lebanon, the Golan and Palestine have been occupied by those who even killed the principle of equality when they claimed that God created a people distinguished above all other peoples. We notice them aggressing against Muslim and Christian Holy Sites in Palestine, violating the sanctity of the Holy Mosque (Al-Aqsa), or the Church of the Holy Sepulcher in Jerusalem and of the Church of the Nativity in Bethlehem. They try to kill all the principles of divine faiths with the same mentality of betraying Jesus Christ and torturing Him, and in the same way that they tried to commit treachery against Prophet Muhammad (peace be upon Him).[36]

The pope's silence in reply was of deep concern to Jews around the world.

In August 2001 an Egyptian columnist wrote, "Thanks to Hitler, of blessed memory, who on behalf of the Palestinians took revenge in advance, against the most vile criminals on the face of the Earth. Although we do have a complaint against him, for his revenge was not enough."[37]

And on May 15, 2002, the *Arab News*, a Saudi English-language daily, printed a transcript of a broadcast by neo-Nazi David Duke, who claimed that America is hated because "traitors" in the U.S. support Israel. He said:

As a loyal and patriotic American, my heart grieves at the support given by American traitors to the world's worst mass murderer and war criminal Ariel Sharon. Sharon has killed, maimed and tortured more people than Osama Bin Laden could only fantasize about. In fact, I will present to you compelling evidence that Sharon and the Mossad aided and abetted the horrible terrorist attack on the World Trade Center. By supporting Sharon and his criminal government in Israel, American traitors have not only supported Sharon's crimes against the Palestinian people, and have become accomplices in mass murder and torture, but they directly aided terrorists who have inflicted terrorism on America.[38]

Jews conspiring to harm non-Jews. This is foundational, every-day antisemitism promoted, not only by two-bit bigots such as Duke, but more importantly by leaders in the Arab and Muslim world. When such hatred becomes mainstream, extremists, such as radical Islamists, can more easily draw support and recruits.

How does this view of the Jew as a global devil-like figure impact how the Palestinian-Israeli conflict is seen? Interestingly, Bin Ladin never talked much about the Palestinians because he saw them as a minor skirmish in the larger world struggle. But in the late 1990s, and certainly after the September 11 attacks, he did, much for the same reason Nation of Islam leader Louis Farrakhan harped on Jews in the United States. While Bin Ladin undoubtedly believes his hatred of Jews, to express it will gain him attention, and perhaps some support. How it must rankle many ordinary Muslims that, while their numbers are well over one billion worldwide, approximately 13 million Jews, of whom 5.25 million live in Israel,[39] have not only been able to survive, but seemingly have the upper hand. No wonder the idea of an "evil conspiracy" that is at the heart of antisemitic beliefs is so rampant there; no wonder the mainstream belief that these evil people were behind the carnage on September 11.

Implications for America

The incredibly high mainstream level of antisemitism in the Arab and Muslim worlds is reminiscent of the Nazi era, when many sectors of society mouthed the lies with little contradiction, and with much official support. While there are, of course, fundamental differences between the 1930s and today (there is no operating government-sponsored genocide of Jews), the rhetorical animus is uncomfortably similar. This is clearly a problem for Jews worldwide, but it is also a problem for America.

Antisemitism will strengthen those who view, in former Israeli Deputy Foreign Minister Michael Melchior's words at Durban, the struggle against Israel as "existential" rather than territorial or political.

If Israel is the devil, and Jews defile the Holy Land, then war is forever ordained. This is not a question about settlements, the "occupation" or closures of Palestinian towns, or concerns about the impact of a particular policy or program. It is a "good or evil" question—and the presence of any organized and self-governing Jewish entity in even a thimbleful of the land is evil.

While, as noted elsewhere (see Chapter 4), anti-Americanism would exist in the Arab and Muslim worlds even if Jews and Israel did not, there is also a relationship between anti-Americanism and the demonization of Jews and Israel. While some see the United States as the "Great Satan," others who oppose America do so in more political terms—viewing it as an exploiter, an entity that has undue influence over the sovereignty of the Arab states, and a colonialist and imperialist power. If those in that latter camp view Israel's actions as unfair, even its creation unjust, that is bad enough and fuel for their "anti-colonialist" fire. But if they begin to understand Israel instead in devil imagery, that makes it much more likely that America—which is committed to the continued existence of Israel as a Jewish state—will be seen in much more ominous terms: as working with, if not for, demonic Jews.

Consider how such antisemitic imagery works on the American political fringe and reshapes the views of those who subscribe to it vis-à-vis the United States. One of the basic beliefs of U.S. white supremacists is that the American government is "Zionist Occupied Government." Just as, during the McCarthy era, many conspiracy theorists believed that Communists were secretly in control of the federal government, white supremacists today believe that Jews fulfill that role.

Some of this "ZOG" language has appeared in Arab and Muslim presses, playing to the mainstream in those societies. There is a fundamental difference between seeing the United States as having "wrong" policies regarding Jews on one hand, and being secretly ruled by Jews on the other.[40] Again, the remedy for the former problem is a change of policy; the remedy for the latter is an inevitable war between good (them) and evil (us).

There is precedence for this type of language. It should be remembered that right before the passage of the Zionism=racism equation in 1975, Ugandan President Idi Amin was cheered at the UN General Assembly when he said:

> [T]he United States of America has been colonized by the Zionists who hold all the tools of development and power. They own virtually all the banking institutions, the major manufacturing and processing industries, and the major means of communication; and have so much infiltrated the CIA that they are posing a great threat to nations and peoples which may be opposed to the atrocious Zionist movement.[41]

The more the United States is understood in these existential terms, the greater the support for Islamist movements, the more likely that moderate Arab regimes will fall, and the greater the possibility of terrorist attacks against the United States (and the other Western democracies, such as Great Britain,[42] which are seen, correctly, as allied with America).

Indeed, in September 2001, following the attack on the United States, the mufti of Jerusalem gave his sermon from the Al-Asqa Mosque. "Oh Allah," he prayed, "destroy America, for she is ruled by Zionist Jews.... Allah will paint the White House black!"[43]

Praise for Weapons of Mass Destruction, Terrorism, and Genocide

There have even been open discussions in the Arab press about whether weapons of mass destruction should be used against Israel. Issam Al-Ghazi, editor of the Egyptian paper *Al-Maydan*, wrote:

> The Palestinian Resistance can obtain such weapons for its battle against the enemy at minimal cost.... One hundred mice with the "Super Plague" virus ... could be released in the streets of Tel Aviv. Likewise, a small bottle of plague-infected mosquitoes can be used to destroy entire Israeli cities.[44]

If one believes in ZOG, that Jews secretly control the world, then why stop with biological weapons on the streets of Tel Aviv? Why not target New York or, for that matter, Paris or London too? A Hamas publication, commenting on the post-9/11 outbreak of anthrax in the United States, wrote:

"To Anthrax:" Oh Anthrax, despite your wretchedness, you have sown horror in the hearts of the lady of arrogance, of tyranny, of boastfulness! Your gentle touch has made the U.S.'s life rough and pointless. You have filled the lady who horrifies and terrorizes the world with fear, and her feet almost afraid to bear [her weight] in horror and fear of you.... In sound mind, I thank you and confess that I like you, I like you very much. May you continue to advance, to permeate, and to spread. If I may give you a word of advice, enter the air of those "symbols," the water faucets from which they drink and the pens with which they draft their traps and conspiracies against the wretched peoples.[45]

Another lesson from the American experience with the militia movement applies here. Ground zero for the militias was Montana, home of the Militia of Montana, the Freemen, and other such groups. During the militias' peak in the mid-1990s, hundreds of local townspeople came to their meetings and supported many of their ideas.

Asked to describe the militia movement, Ken Toole, head of the Montana Human Rights Network (and now a Montana state senator), said it was a "funnel moving through space." At the large end of the funnel were those who were supporters of or who agreed with parts of the ideology. At the middle of the funnel were those who became animated by the movement's conspiracy theories in general and antisemitic conspiracy theories in particular. Those who were pulled all the way through and popped out of the short end of the funnel—such as Oklahoma City bomber Timothy McVeigh—were people who were willing to wage war based on these ideas.

Toole's metaphor was useful because it described the movement as a system and defined its various parts. When greater numbers of ordinary people were sucked into the lip of the funnel, more warriors were plunged out of the small end. Conversely, when community leaders spoke out about the hatred in, and dangers of, these groups, fewer people were pulled into the funnel, and thus fewer emerged from the tip. Groups such as Toole's Human Rights Network exposed the militias' leaders as white supremacists and Christian Identity adherents and forced community leaders to speak out. Their work helped undercut the militias and, in a few short years, helped make them nearly irrelevant.

But the antisemitic funnel in the Arab and Islamic world is supersized, and its leaders, even many "moderate" ones, are using the institutions of society to push people into the funnel rather than to warn them away. And not only do the leaders try to get people into the funnel, but to plunge as many as possible out of the small end, to have an endless supply of suicide bombers and other terrorists. It is no coincidence that sheikhs such as Ibrahim Mahdi bless "whoever has put a belt of explosives on his body or his sons and plunged them into the midst of the Jews," that Palestinian Authority television broadcasts such incantations, that Palestinian leaders and columnists praise such violence, that, as Palestinian pollster Ghassan Khatib found, three-quarters of the Palestinians support such terror,[46] that more suicide bombers are in training every day, and that when the Palestinian people in 2006 voted in parliamentary elections, they cast their ballots for Hamas, a terrorist organization.[47] Even Palestinian Authority President Mahmoud Abbas, who has condemned these attacks as counterproductive and "idiotic," has never sufficiently articulated that they are morally wrong.

When a suicide bomber blew himself and others up in Netanya, Israel, in July 2005, the bomber's mother not only praised her son as a hero, but also said she wished her next oldest son, fourteen years of age, would become a martyr too.[48] If a suicide bomber blew himself up in New York, and his mother made such a statement, government officials would immediately remove the child from this home. It is difficult to imagine a clearer case of child abuse than the intentional grooming of a young teenager to become a mass murderer and suicide victim. Yet, by failing to use the instruments of state to condemn such actions, the Palestinian Authority is helping sustain a culture in which terrorism in furtherance of antisemitism (and other hatreds) is held out to youngsters as a commendable life aspiration.

Unlike the militia funnel, which was confined to the United States, this Islamic and Arab funnel is fully transportable. It functions in countries around the world, partly financed by the Saudis and Iranians. It is on display not only in the Palestinian Authority and Syria, but also in countries such as Jordan and Egypt, which have signed peace treaties with Israel, but whose news services have both accused Israel of distributing drug-laced gum and candy to kill children and harm women.[49] This funnel is in England, France, Sweden, Australia, Canada, the United States, and elsewhere. And it is responsible for the rash of hate crimes against Jews worldwide after the collapse of the peace process.

As some commentators have noted, when the Nazis attempted global domination in the 1930s and 1940s, they posited themselves in a life-and-death struggle against Jews, who were seen as pursuing the same goal. Today Islamists—who see themselves aligned against Jews/infidels/America—view the world in much the same way.

*"Why is an Israeli a legitimate target, for example,
in Palestine and not elsewhere? These people need
to be eradicated."*

—Anjem Choudary, British leader of Al-Muhajiroun[1]

Chapter Six
Antisemitism in Europe

The organized presence of Islamist extremists and their sympathizers is
also a problem for Europe. Coupled with a significant far-right fringe,
a left that demonizes Israel in the media, and a reservoir of historic
antisemitism, this relatively new element presents a real danger to
Jews. Much has been written chronicling the details of the upsurge of
European antisemitism in recent years.[2] The scope of this chapter is
not to review what has been published elsewhere, nor to look in depth
at countries in which antisemitism has been a recurrent historical
problem (such as Russia), but rather to define the nature of the challenge, particularly in Western Europe.

While the situation has somewhat improved in many European
countries in the last few years, revisiting a list of incidents from March
and April 2002, outlined in a speech to the American Jewish Committee by Israeli Deputy Foreign Minister Michael Melchior in May
2002, will help illuminate the problems:

— Spain, burning of a synagogue in Seotta.

— France, windows smashed in a synagogue in the town of Erstein.

— France, burning of a synagogue in Lyon by means of two cars.

— France, attempt to set fire to a synagogue in Strasbourg.

— France, break into a Jewish school in Paris, destroyed all the equip-
ment.

— France, attempt to break into a Jewish kindergarten in Marseilles.

— France, burning down a synagogue in Marseilles.

— France, shots fired at a Jewish butcher shop in Toulouse.

— Germany, beating of two Jews just outside the synagogue in Berlin.

— France, Molotov cocktail thrown at a synagogue in Nice.

— Ukraine, Jews stabbed in synagogue in Lutsk.

— France, Molotov cocktail thrown at a synagogue in Lyon.

— Britain, windows smashed at the synagogue in Manchester.

— Switzerland, Jew attacked in a street in Lausanne.

— Belgium, Molotov cocktails thrown at a synagogue in Antwerp.

— Britain, attempt to run down an Orthodox Jew in North London.

— France, Molotov cocktails thrown at a synagogue in Montpelier.

— Ukraine, attack on Jews in the great synagogue of Kiev.

— France, torching of buses used to transport children, near a Jewish school in Paris.

— France, attempt to torch the Jewish school in Nice.

— France, Molotov cocktail thrown at a synagogue in Nice.

— France, stones and Molotov cocktails thrown at the police near the synagogue in Marseilles.

— France, attempt to torch synagogue in Paris.

— Belgium, attack on Jewish-owned travel agency in Brussels.

— Belgium, Molotov cocktail thrown at the old synagogue in Antwerp.

— France, Molotov cocktails torch the Maccabi Club House in Toulouse.

— Belgium, attack on Jews in Antwerp.

— France, school in Marseilles torched.

— France, attack on a Jewish soccer team in Paris.

Melchior's speech contained additional incidents from the end of March and the beginning of April 2002, and was hardly a complete catalogue of the attacks on Jews and Jewish-linked property.[3] Other such incidents took place in Canada, Australia, Morocco, the

U.S., Tunisia, and elsewhere during this time period. But the list from Europe, of numerous attacks on Jews and synagogues, was startling.

Four Factors Combine

These hate crimes were a result of a combination of four factors. First, they were largely taking place in countries that have a significant Muslim and Arab population, who have been fed a steady stream of antisemitism in the media they read and listen to, and in their mosques. Just as Aryan Nation hanger-on Buford Furrow did not see little Jewish children, but little devils, when he shot up the Los Angeles JCC in 1999, this community has been taught to see Jews in devil imagery too: Israelis as Nazis; Sharon as Hitler; the *Protocols* as the plan. Kill them or be killed. (And, thus, Jew-hatred is seen as self-defense.)

But while the Buford Furrows of the world are a distinct fringe, the Arab and Muslim populations in many Western European countries are significant enough to form a political bloc. A year of attacks on Jews occurred before the first significant statement of French leadership against the violence. For a year, if French leaders addressed the issue at all, they either insisted on calling the problem "hooliganism" (if these were hooligans, why were only synagogues, but not churches or mosques, burned?), or claimed that the incidents would stop if the problems in the Middle East were solved (thus defining the situation as a dispute over politics, rather than an antisemitic crime wave). The French leadership at this time was not willing to act decisively, partly because politicians, by nature, count, and Muslims in France outnumber Jews tenfold. It should be noted, however, that Jacques Chirac, president of the French Republic, and French Prime Minister Dominique Villepin, subsequently acknowledged the problem.

Second, these attacks occurred in countries such as France and Germany where there is a tradition of far-right activism. Certainly, some of the growing strength of the far right is directly related to the perceived problems of integrating foreigners, most prominently Arabs and Muslims, into society, but the far right has a rich history of antisemitism, too. While the collapse of the peace process unleashed a flood of antisemitic hate crimes largely committed by Arabs and Muslims, these countries had already been used to a lower-level, but still significant and consistent, quantity of antisemitic hate crimes.

Third is the phenomenon of the "blow back" of some classical, familiar-sounding European antisemitism, adopted in the Middle East, then re-exported to Muslims and Arabs in Europe.[4] As Robert S. Rifkind, chair of the Jacob Blaustein Institute for the Advancement of Human Rights, so eloquently noted in his remarks to the April 2004 NGO conference preceding the OSCE meeting on antisemitism in Berlin:

> Very serious thought must be given to the question of whether Arabs and, more generally, Islamic states are selling antisemitism precisely because they have found willing and eager buyers in the West, because they have found that they could bond with Europe on this front, as the Grand Mufti of Jerusalem found in Berlin some 65 years ago. It is certainly worth noting that when Islamic spokesmen talk of a new crucifixion, when they circulate that old czarist forgery, the *Protocols of the Elders of Zion*, when they invoke the images of the swastika, the SS and the Holocaust, they are not invoking images from deep within Islamic culture. They are dealing in European tropes meant to resonate with European audiences.[5]

Fourth, these attacks took place in countries where the media, largely influenced by the political left, have created a popular image in which the Palestinians are heroes fighting off colonial oppression, and Israelis are the oppressor. Thus Jews in France and elsewhere, who support Israel's fight against terror, are defined instead as supporters of oppression.

In this simplified worldview, the organized presence of white people in Africa and Asia is understood as a manifestation of colonialism and imperialism. Against this background, Jews are seen as little different from British or French or Dutch or Germans who colonized parts of Africa, and who were responsible for oppressing the indigenous population. The fact that the Jewish historic homeland is in Israel, that Jews have always continued to live in the land, and that there was no clamoring for a Palestinian state when the West Bank and Gaza were under Jordanian and Egyptian control, respectively, are somehow lost.[6]

Such ahistoric myopia need not necessarily be antisemitic—it might be the normal problem with dogmatism, blinding adherence to facts that do not necessarily fit the preconceived formula. Nor is it antisemitic for the left to be anti-Israel because Israel is seen as an ally of the United States, and the U.S. is perceived as the key imperialist country on the globe. But on other levels, the left's view, pounded repeatedly in the press and in intellectual discourse, is clearly a manifestation of bigotry and antisemitism.

First, there is the inordinate attention given to Jews and Israel. If the left were really concerned about occupation of Arab land, then why was it so quiet for so many years about the Syrian occupation of the country of Lebanon?[7] Or if it is concerned about human rights, why was it so quiet about the Chinese actions in Tibet, or about the enslavement of people and now genocide in Sudan?

Second, there is the caliber of the attention. It is not Israel's particular programs, policies, or political parties that are criticized, but too frequently the basic legitimacy of the state. To the extent that the policies or personages are questioned, these criticisms are turned into weapons to attack Israel's right to organize itself as a Jewish national homeland.

Defective or Nonexistent Capacity for Empathy with Jews

Just look at the European media's treatment of the Israeli incursion into the West Bank after a series of suicide bombings in 2002. Few had the capacity to put themselves in the place of Israelis and ask what they would want their government to do if they were in a similar situation, facing regular suicide attacks. Rather, they painted the incursion as naked aggression and had sympathy only for the Palestinians. Worse, by and large, they were quick to believe the lies of the Palestinian Authority, which portrayed the Israeli operation in the Jenin refugee camp as a "massacre," when in fact the Israeli forces put themselves in jeopardy and took casualties by going house to house to find terrorists, rather than doing what the Americans did in Afghanistan, dropping bombs from on high. In other words, they were quick to paint Israel's self-defense as aggression and a battle as a massacre. Jews, again, were portrayed as organizing to inflict harm on non-Jews.

This may also be a pathology of the left that simultaneously practices and blinds itself toward racism. Just as American society is generally less critical of black racists than of white ones, could it be that many on the left have defaulted to seeing people of color as always right, and whites (in this case, Jews) as therefore always wrong? Clearly, the ability to have empathy for Palestinians but not for Israelis is a form of bigotry, but it is hard to say what percentage is classic antisemitism and what part is racism.[8]

And is there also a general discomfort among some Europeans, who have a rich tradition of local antisemitism, at seeing Jews defending themselves in Israel? Are they more comfortable understanding Jews in the imagery of the Holocaust, as victims who deserve sympathy, rather than as soldiers defending their society with guns? Perhaps.

Certainly, there is a reluctance to identify antisemitism squarely, and too often an eagerness to explain it away. As Robert Rifkind noted:

> In every age hatred of Jews has been explained in terms that made perfect sense to the populace of the time. We have been told that antisemitism was understandable by reason of Jewish responsibility for the death of God, or for the ritual murder of Christian youth, or for the poisoning of wells. Hatred of Jews has been ascribed to the perception that Jews are rich, blood-sucking, money lenders or miserably poor rag pickers, that they are arrogant separatists or pushy assimilationists, that they are capitalists or communists, that they are historical fossils or the avatars of

unwelcome modernity, that they are timid, unmanly weaklings or storm troopers, that they are landless cosmopolitans or—now— Jewish nationalists. Such supposed explanations, however fervently believed, however obvious they may have seemed, are symptoms of antisemitism and not its cause. They explain nothing except the credulity of the antisemite. In my view, the attempt to explain antisemitism in terms of the behavior of Jews in Jenin, or in Har Homa, or in Wall Street, or in Washington is likewise a manifestation of antisemitism and not an explanation of it.... [T]he challenge of antisemitism in Europe will not be met until it is clearly understood that we are no longer talking about what was once called the Jewish Question. We are talking about the European Question.[9]

Another observation: Western European countries, by and large, have had more Holocaust education than Eastern European countries, and also more antisemitic outbursts. Is there a correlation? Certainly there are a variety of factors involved, including who the perpetrators are. But is it also possible that the wrong lessons have been learned from Holocaust education? That the understanding about the dangers of genocide was wide but not deep, so that people understood the vocabulary, but not fully the details or their importance? The Swedish government, for example, has taken great steps to popularize knowledge about the Holocaust,[10] but there is frequent media bias against Israel, using blatantly bigoted terms, and little recognition of the contradiction.[11]

Is this the functional parallel of Holocaust denial? Holocaust deniers twist the facts of the Holocaust to deny the Nazi genocide. Are contemporary events being twisted so that the obvious antisemitism in synagogue burnings and incitements to violence and dehumanizing caricatures in newspapers is rendered less than fully visible?

As Israeli Deputy Foreign Minister Michael Melchior noted, "There is a clear process from allegations, insinuations, to accusations, to delegitimization, to dehumanization and finally to demonization."[12]

The antisemitic attacks, coupled with the dehumanization of Jews and the attempt to delegitimize Israel, especially when not sufficiently met by condemnation from political leaders, raise the bar. Those who commit crimes of hate, including terror, act like classical bullies. Appeasement only encourages them to do more, more violently and with more deadly results.

Fortunately, as we will examine in Chapter 13, after a miserable start, there are some positive and promising initiatives taking place in Europe to combat antisemitism. But whatever enthusiasm these positive steps produce, there is still great reason to be concerned about the future in Europe. While all problems have possible abstract solutions, those pertaining to demographic realities and their implications are more intractable.

When a young Jew named Ilan Halimi was kidnapped, tortured, mutilated, and murdered in France in early 2006, it was bad enough that some in French society did not understand that this was a crime of hate. (The kidnappers apparently believed that Jews were rich, and on this basis, selected their target.) After a large protest march in response to this brutal deed, two fourteen-year-old students in a leading Paris school explained to their classmates that the reaction to this crime showed that Jews had an unfair place in French society because the killings of Arabs and Muslims and others were not treated with the same fanfare. When the few Jewish students tried to point out that the rally and statements of leaders were not because a Jew was murdered, but because of how and why he was murdered, their teacher refused to let them speak.[13]

It is certainly not clear that this one story is representative of how antisemitism plays out on a daily basis in people's lives in Europe. But it is an indication that Jews are again being seen by many as a people apart from the general social contract, and that taboos that have inhibited expressions of antisemitism continue to weaken.

One atomic bomb would wipe out Israel without a trace while the Islamic world would only be damaged rather than destroyed by Israeli nuclear retaliation.

—Ali Akbar Hashemi Rafsanjani, former president of Iran, 1989-97[1]

Hitler had only killed 20,000 Jews and not six million.

—Ali Akbar Hashemi Rafsanjani[2]

It is all too characteristic of this fanatical mind-set that the real Nazi Holocaust inflicted upon the Jews should be so strenuously denied by those who would repeat it.

—Robert Wistrich[3]

Chapter Seven
Denial of the Holocaust

One of the brightest insights into antisemitism came from Judge Hadassa Ben-Itto, the president of the International Association of Jewish Lawyers and Jurists, 1988-2004. Speaking at a 1990 American Jewish Committee symposium launching what would be a successful effort to repeal the United Nation's 1975 equation of Zionism with racism, she said:

> It behooves us to remember that antisemitism throughout the ages has always rested on labels and on lies. We are not the only people in the world who are victims of racism, but I think that if there was a prize for a group of people about whom the most lies were told, I think we would take that prize. I, representing Israel in many international forums, was called again and again—not me, my people—"Christ killers," "poisoners of wells," "perpetrators of ritual murder with blood," all these things. They don't replace each other, these lies; the list becomes longer all the time.[4]

While antisemitism is, at heart, hatred, it is also a self-sustaining system of belief. Part of the problem in combating it is that people think antisemitism is stupid, so therefore it can be dismissed as something engaged in only by dull or uneducated or demented people. But as any student of history knows, hatred has been indulged, propagated, believed, and exploited by educated and intelligent people too. One need not look further than the civil rights struggle in the United States for an example: While the image of the bigot is that of the hooded Klansman, the leading citizens of the South, through such organizations as white citizens councils, were also fully engaged in bigotry.

Further, in order to understand how best to counteract antisemitism, it has to be understood as a system of ideas. The ideas may seem illogical to the outside viewer, but to the believer they are not only internally logical, they are self-sustaining and—like most conspiracy theories—define attempted refutations as further evidence that the adherents have indeed stumbled onto an important "suppressed truth."

While there are many antisemitic myths that can serve as an example, the best contemporary one for this purpose is denial of the Holocaust. The in-depth examination given here is not meant to suggest that Holocaust denial is the most extreme form of antisemitism, but rather that it is probably the best window on how a system of antisemitic ideas functions.

Holocaust Denial Is Not about the Holocaust, But about Jews

Holocaust denial fits into the pattern of classical antisemitism. It is like a prosecutor's dream: crime, motive, opportunity. Jews made up the Holocaust, it is alleged. Why? For financial gain (reparations), and also to justify the birth of the State of Israel.[5] How? By Jewish "control" over Hollywood and the media. If you see the world through antisemitic lenses, Holocaust denial is a no-brainer. Conversely, if you are an innocent caught in the web of the lies the deniers spin, you inevitably are exposed to antisemitism.

In other words, Holocaust denial is about Jews, not about the Holocaust. It has no more to do with the history of the Holocaust than the medieval charge that Jews poisoned wells has to do with the science of water quality.

Holocaust denial began shortly after the Holocaust—the extermination of approximately six million Jews by the Nazis during World War II, many in purpose-built gas chambers. A few former Nazis in South America and elsewhere—remaining loyal to the cause—denied the Nazis' crimes, despite the overwhelming evidence from perpetrators, survivors, liberators, and bystanders.[6]

By the late 1970s neo-Nazis seemed to figure out that they were not getting much traction from saying that Hitler should have done a "better" job. Willis Carto, then head of the American racist and antisemitic group Liberty Lobby, created a new organization called the Institute for Historical Review. It presented itself as a credible historical group, but, in fact, it was made up of and supported by white supremacists and neo-Nazis from around the world. Its mission—to deny the Holocaust. Its tools—distortion, misquotation, and falsification. The deniers were clever. For the most part, they avoided the gutter language and vile stereotypes that people would expect from neo-Nazis. Their key audience was young people who had no memory of the war. Their aim was not necessarily to convince, but to suggest doubt, to hint that there are "two sides" to the "debate," schools that they labeled "exterminationist" and "revisionist."

For example, deniers would claim that Anne Frank's diary—one of the best-known pieces of Holocaust literature—was a forgery. Why? Because there were markings on a copy of the manuscript in ballpoint pen, and the ballpoint pen was, they said, a 1951 invention. (They did not mention that the writing was emendations made on the manuscript by Anne Frank's father, Otto, and that the diary was first published in 1947.)[7]

They claim that modern crematoria require about five hours to consume one body, so how could the number of crematoria at the death camps possibly account for hundreds of thousands dead? (Unlike modern morticians who use crematoria, the Nazis had no desire to keep the ashes segregated, and the volume of bodies burned kept the furnaces in ongoing use, so that there was no need to restart the fires for each corpse, and the bodies even served as fuel. In fact, at Auschwitz alone there were forty-six ovens, and at peak times fifty-two, that were in operation from ten to twelve hours a day, with a potential burning capacity in the millions.)[8]

The deniers would claim that Zyklon B was not used for killing people, but for helping the inmates by controlling lice; that the number of Jews killed was much smaller than generally accepted; that there were no gas chambers; that the Nuremberg trials were a fraud.

The purpose of all this, of course, was not only to promote anti-semitism, but also to rehabilitate fascism, for the Holocaust was the moral albatross around the image of Nazi Germany. Remove it and the Nazi regime could be portrayed as just another political system, with major warts certainly, but perhaps not so different from any other.

Remove the Holocaust and you remove the lessons of the Holocaust too: foremost, the need to give asylum to those fleeing political, racial, and religious persecution. In fact, remove the Holocaust and the entire history of the second half of the twentieth century would have to be rewritten. Jews would no longer be victims, but the victimizers of Germans and others who had to pay reparations for something they did not do. Remove the Holocaust and the Nazi collaborators who lead many of the Eastern European governments that later fell under the yolk of the Soviet Union could be rehabilitated (as many have been) as "patriots" and "national heroes."

And if Jews complain about this, it is because Jews conspire to harm non-Jews, and, of course, they would complain if their evil plot were exposed.

If you think all this is silly and does not touch an important cord for some, contemplate why neo-Nazis and other white supremacists put so much energy into proclaiming the Holocaust did not happen. Is it because they have a passion about changing a few pages of high school history books about the twentieth century? Or it is because they want power, and Holocaust denial is integral to their identity, their sense that Jews and the West have conspired to harm Aryans with a "big lie"?

David Irving and Friends

To believe in Holocaust denial, you have to believe that historians worldwide—American, German, British, French, Israeli—are either part of a conspiracy to hide the truth, incompetent, or both. While there may be an instructor popping up here or there who dabbles in denial, there are no tenured professors of history who teach this drivel.

Deniers, however, were able to point to a few academics in other fields who shared their viewpoint, most noticeably Arthur Butz, a professor of electrical engineering at Northwestern University, who wrote *The Hoax of the Twentieth Century*. But most of all they coveted having British author David Irving among their crowd, for Irving was a prolific writer whose books, including *Hitler's War* and *The Destruction of Dresden*, were widely circulated.

Irving danced around the edge of denial for many years. Then came the Ernst Zündel case. Zündel was a German national living in Canada in the 1980s, best known as coauthor of the book *The Hitler We Loved and Why*. He was prosecuted under Canadian law for publishing "false news" about the Holocaust, first in 1985, and, after his conviction was overturned, again in 1987-88. Unlike the United States, Canada has no First Amendment. There, and in other democratic countries such as France, Germany, and Australia, denying the Holocaust can lead to prosecution. (In fact, years later—in 2005—Zündel was deported from Canada to Germany to face trial for his Internet-related Holocaust denial activities.[9])

At the suggestion of French denier Robert Faurrison, Zündel began searching for an American expert on gas chambers, someone whom he could send to examine the Auschwitz gas chambers and testify, as Zündel asserted, that no one was killed there. He found an

American named Fred Leuchter who had worked with various state prisons on their methods of capital punishment, but who, as it later turned out, had only a B.A. in history, and was later convicted in Massachusetts of practicing engineering without a license.[10]

Zündel sent Leuchter to Auschwitz, where he illegally hammered some chunks off walls, sent them to a lab, and wrote a report that concluded that there were no gas chambers at Auschwitz. Of course, the report was seriously flawed. It argued that since there was more Zyklon B residue on chambers in Auschwitz dedicated to killing lice than on those "allegedly" dedicated to killing people, and since people were bigger than lice, the result should have been the other way around were people really being killed. But aside from poor sampling methods and poor testing procedures (Zyklon B residue, if present after fifty years, would be likely to be found on the surface, but the lab that tested the chunks of walls ground them up, thereby diluting any residue), the results actually confirmed what we already knew about how the chambers worked. While clothes were deloused at a lower concentration of the gas than people, they were exposed for a much longer period—hours as opposed to the minutes required to kill people—thereby giving the chemical a longer period of exposure to the walls.

Leuchter's flawed report was not allowed as evidence in the case, but it had one immediate convert—David Irving—who was attending the Zündel trial. Irving, claiming that Leuchter's report, unlike historical writings, was based on "exact science," issued a copy of the report under his own imprint, with his own foreword.

Before the Zündel trial, Irving had tried to keep a foot in two worlds—that of neo-Nazis and that of respectability. He was known as a prolific writer and an industrious researcher who had tracked down not only documents, but also many of Hitler's former adjutants. He did not exactly deny the Holocaust—rather he minimized it, suggesting that the numbers of Jews killed were much smaller than commonly believed, while, he asserted, the number of German civilians killed by the Allies was greater than acknowledged. To the extent there was a Holocaust, he argued, it was not the handiwork of Hitler, whom he believed to be the Jews' "best friend" among the Nazis, but that of Heinrich Himmler and others.

Irving's exposure to Leuchter changed all that. Irving, speaking to like-minded audiences in the United States and Canada, began saying outrageous things such as:

> I don't see any reason to be tasteful about Auschwitz. It's baloney. It's a legend. Once we admit the fact that it was a brutal slave labor camp and large numbers of people did die, as large numbers of innocent people died elsewhere in the war, why believe the rest of the baloney? I say quite tastelessly in fact that more women died on the back seat of Edward Kennedy's car at Chappaquiddick than ever died in a gas chamber in Auschwitz. Oh, you think that's tasteless. How about this? There are so many Auschwitz survivors going around, in fact the number increases as the years go past, which is biologically very odd to say the least, because I am going to form an Association of Auschwitz survivors, survivors of the Holocaust and other liars or the A-S-S-H-O-L-S.[11]

In 1993 Emory Professor Deborah Lipstadt wrote a book entitled *Denying the Holocaust: The Growing Assault on Truth and Memory*. She called David Irving, among other things, "one of the most dangerous spokespersons for Holocaust denial." Her book was also published in Great Britain the following year by Penguin, Ltd.

Irving, who was now finding it difficult to persuade major publishers to print his work, sued Lipstadt in London for libel. He could not have done so in the United States since libel laws make it very difficult for plaintiffs—especially public figures—to prevail in the United States. But in Great Britain, once the plaintiff shows that a published book was defamatory, the burden shifts to the defendant, under the assumption that "you wrote it, now back it up."

Between January and April 2000, the trial of *Irving v. Penguin and Lipstadt* was held before Sir Charles Gray at the High Court of Justice in London. In the months leading up to the trial, defense experts poured over Irving's books, tracking his footnotes back to the sources, something that had not been done before. What emerged was a pattern of distortion that was always in one direction—to exonerate the Nazis in general, and Hitler in particular. Of course, everyone makes mistakes, but, as the defense asserted, if they were honestly made, they would not always be in one direction.

While Irving as the plaintiff (representing himself) wanted to put the Holocaust on trial, the defense argued that the case was really about Irving and what a credible historian would have done with the evidence before him. This was not only good trial strategy, but also the proper approach to combating Irving's antisemitism, by recasting the dynamic to put him on the defensive and using the opportunities the trial offered to unmask him and his agenda.

Consider the following example. Irving frequently said that Hitler was the "best friend" that the Jews had in the Third Reich; that, in fact, he had issued an order not to kill Jews. Where was his evidence?

In 1941 there were approximately 146,000 Jews living in Germany under very repressive and difficult conditions. About 76,000 of these German Jews lived in Berlin. After the invasion of the Soviet Union in 1941, Jews were killed in the newly occupied lands by the roving killing groups, the *Einsatzgruppen*. Shortly thereafter, Jews from Germany were deported east, to Poland.

On November 30, 1941, at 1:30 P.M., Heinrich Himmler and Reinhard Heydrich, two high-ranking Nazi officials, spoke by phone. Himmler's handwritten note of that discussion reads: "Judentransport aus Berlin. Keine liquidierung." ("Jew-transport from Berlin. No liquidation.")

What was Irving's take on this? He wrote that Himmler "was summoned to the Wolf's Lair [Hitler's headquarters] for a secret conference with Hitler, at which the fate of Berlin's Jews was clearly raised. At 1:30 P.M. Himmler was obliged to telephone from Hitler's bunker to Heydrich the explicit order that Jews were not to be liquidated; and the next day Himmler telephoned SS General Oswald Pohl, overall chief of the concentration camp system, with the order: 'Jews are to stay where they are.'"

In reality, as the defense showed at trial, Himmler was never "summoned" to see Hitler that day, nor "obliged" to issue an order. In fact, when the two met, it was for lunch at 2:30 P.M., an hour after Himmler's instruction to Heydrich.

The order, as was clear from the context, was not a general order about all Jews, but about a specific trainload of Jews—not Jews captured from Poland, but Germany's own "Berlin Jews."[12]

And what about Irving's assertion that Himmler called SS General Pohl and told him, "Jews are to stay where they are"? The phone log read *"Verwaltungsfuhrer der SS haben zu bleiben,"* meaning, "Administrative leaders of the SS have to stay." The order had nothing to do with Jews.

In any event, once this trainload arrived at Riga, they were nonetheless killed, as described by a German court in 1973:

> In the ditches, the Jews had to lie down next to one another with their faces downturned. They were killed at close range ... by being shot in the back of the neck by Russian machine pistols which had been set to fire individual shots. The victims who came after them had to use the space available and ... lie on top of those who had just been shot. The old, children, and those who had difficulty in walking, were led to the ditches by the stronger Jews, placed by them on top of the corpses, and shot by the marksmen who were standing on the dead in the big ditch. In this way the ditches gradually filled up.[13]

In example after example, the defense showed how Irving had distorted history by mistranslation (as in the Himmler phone call, where he said he had misread *"haben"* as *"Juden"*), manipulation, and distortion.

But it was not enough that the defense exposed how deniers distort history and science; it also had to provide an explanation. Why would someone of Irving's stature lie about history? The answer lay in his antisemitic politics and his connections with like-minded people around the world.[14]

Irving's diaries (to which the defense was given access) gave proof positive of his close association with a far-flung network of far-right racist and antisemitic parties and figures, including nearly two decades of involvement with the major figures at the California-based Institute for Historical Review (Willis Carto, Mark Weber, Tom Marcellus, Greg Raven, and others); American Arthur Butz; American neo-Nazi David Duke; the British National Party, the [British] Clarendon Club; and many German Nazis and neo-Nazis.[15] To document these connections, hundreds of pages of excerpts from Irving's diaries and correspondence, in two huge volumes, were entered into evidence at the trial.[16]

During closing arguments, Irving had a great challenge explaining away the mountains of damning material the defense had introduced. One piece was a video of Irving addressing a group of neo-Nazis at Halle, Germany. While speaking (in German) his arm was resting on what appeared to be a pipe, straight out, reminiscent of a Hitler salute. Two minutes into his presentation, the audience was chanting "Sieg heil!"

Irving, reading from his closing argument, looked up to expand upon what he had written and to explain. Pausing to address the judge, who is called "my Lord" in England, as in America we call a judge "your honor," Irving mistakenly called Judge Gray "Mein Führer," with all the dripping obsequiousness as if he were addressing Hitler himself.

On April 11, 2000, Judge Gray issued a 349-page decision, declaring victory for Dr. Lipstadt and her publisher. He cited example after example where Irving "significantly misrepresented ... the evidence ... pervert[ed] the evidence ... [and where he was guilty of] misrepresentation ... misconstruction ... omission ... mistranslation ... misreading ... double standards." The judge found Irving's explanations for what he wrote "tendentious ... unjustified ... specious ... distorted ... fanciful ... hopeless ... disingenuous ... [and] a travesty."

"It appears to me," Justice Gray wrote, "that Irving qualifies as a Holocaust denier.... Irving is anti-Semitic.... Irving is a racist.... Irving [is] a right-wing pro-Nazi polemicist."

The irony is that Justice Gray's findings were even stronger than the words Dr. Lipstadt had written. He concluded that Irving's distortion of the historical record was "deliberate" and "borne of his own ideological beliefs to present Hitler in a favourable light."

While the verdict was a complete demolition of Irving as well as an exposé of the lies upon which Holocaust denial is so carefully crafted, it did not end denial. It could not, because denial has nothing to do with truth and everything to do with the politics of anti-semitism.

Irving's German activities show how inherently political Holocaust denial is. This is white supremacy at its core, a belief—just as with Nazism—that white "Aryans" are threatened by extinction due to race mixing and other evils, all being orchestrated by Jews. White supremacists see themselves in a war for survival and, not surprisingly, are anti-immigrant. They believe that Turks and others can never be "real" Germans (just as Irving apparently believes that blacks cannot be "real" Englishmen), and that the notion of providing asylum, allowing immigration, and creating a nonracial definition of citizenship is not only suicide, but a legacy left from "the lessons of the Holocaust."

Neo-Nazi-Based Antisemitism Finds a New Audience in the Arab World

The politics of Holocaust denial are also evident in the Arab world. One of Irving's contacts, evidenced from his diary, was Ahmed Rami, the head of Radio Islam. Rami is a key promoter of antisemitism, having a Web site in many languages that is a treasure trove of antisemitica (including the *Protocols* and speeches by Louis Farrakhan and Holocaust denial). But Rami is not alone. The Palestinian Authority, the Syrian government,[17] and others in the Arab world[18] have taken the handiwork of white supremacists and refashioned it for their own interests, to undermine the legitimacy of Israel.[19]

In the early part of 2001, the Institute for Historical Review, which has a close relationship with Irving, was scheduled to hold its conference in Beirut in conjunction with a Swiss Holocaust denier named Jürgen Graf, who was living in Iran. Lebanese authorities, responding to international pressure, ordered the meeting cancelled. And in 2006, when Iranian President Mahmoud Ahmadinejad announced plans to hold a conference promoting denial, the German government actually invalidated the passport of right-wing attorney Horst Mahler, for fear he would attend such a conclave.[20]

Herein lies a source of concern about antisemitism in the decades to come. The engine of Holocaust denial has been the far right, which seeks to promote fascism and antisemitism as basic parts of its core identity. From time to time, it has been aided by the political left, which is anti-fascist, but which tends to be anti-Israel (the most famous example being Professor Noam Chomsky[21]). But Holocaust denial is now a growth industry in the Arab world (coincidently, just when some of the white supremacist groups, such as the IHR, as well as their leading lights, such as David Irving and Ernst Zündel, are respectively in organizational or legal difficulties[22]).

Years ago, before they began denying the Holocaust, some Arab propagandists (who routinely ignored the historic Jewish connections with the Land of Israel) argued that it was unfair to Arabs that after Jews were murdered in Europe, their remnants had to be absorbed in the Middle East. But just as neo-Nazis saw Holocaust denial as a win-win (it defames Jews, and if believed, helps remove the tarnish from fascism), some Arab groups saw in Holocaust denial another antisemitic story line they could not resist. Now they could claim that the Holocaust was a myth that the Jews had made up. By the late 1980s and early 1990s, articles began to appear with titles such as "Burning of the Jews in the Nazi Chambers Is the Lie of the 20th Century in

Order to Legitimize the New Nazism."[23] (Of course, a "soft-core" form of denial has long been in play in the Arab media, comparing Israeli treatment of Palestinians to Nazi treatment of Jews, thereby totally distorting the horrors of the Holocaust. Whatever one thinks about Israeli policies vis-à-vis the Palestinians, they cannot be compared with what the Nazis did, killing all the Jews they could, many in gas chambers built as factories of death.)

Some of this type of propaganda seemed to have quieted down—although it surely did not disappear[24]—during the time following the Oslo Accords, from 1993 until the collapse of the peace process in the fall of 2000.[25] Denial appeared full-throttle again when the peace talks foundered. When the Beirut meeting organized by American Holocaust deniers was cancelled in the spring of 2001, the Jordanian Writers Association set up another meeting to promote denial in the Arab world.[26] Palestinian schoolbooks (some published with United Nations funds) denied the Holocaust (and also referred to Jews as the enemy of God and Islam).[27] And as we saw in Chapter 3, Holocaust denial was repeatedly voiced at the United Nations World Conference on Racism, Racial Discrimination, Xenophobia, and Related Intolerance in Durban in the summer of 2001.

It should also be remembered that Palestinian President Mahmoud Abbas wrote his doctoral thesis asserting that not only had the Holocaust not occurred, but that it was a "Zionist fantasy." He claimed that only about 890,000 Jews were killed by Hitler, and that Zionists were also culpable for these deaths.[28] Despite the clear benefit it would have had toward promoting peace, Abbas never publicly retracted and repudiated his thesis. And with Hamas having won the 2006 Palestinian parliamentary elections, denial of the Holocaust will likely become more routine in Palestinian discourse, since Hamas—which even cites the *Protocols* in its charter—has no desire to moderate its language, especially when it is being supported financially and otherwise by Iran.

Dr. Deborah Lipstadt, commenting on her victory in the Irving trial, called Holocaust denial not a "clear and present danger," but a "clear and future danger." That future is much closer than it seemed when she won her case in the spring of 2000. The political use of Holocaust denial around the world has been ratcheted up considerably. And while it has always served as glue between various antisemitic forces, it now seems more like cement. It is no coincidence, for example, that Tony Martin, the African-American Wellesley professor who wrote the antisemitic book *The Jewish Onslaught* and used the Nation of Islam's book on alleged Jewish responsibility for slavery as a credible text in his classroom, was an honored speaker at David Irving's 2001 conference on "real history," held in Cincinnati before an audience largely populated by people from the world of white supremacy.

Holocaust Relativism

If Holocaust denial was not complicated enough, it is given a boost by Holocaust relativism. This term refers to not denial of the Holocaust outright, but its minimizing by unfair, and usually ignorant, comparisons. (Many antisemitic myths, by the way, have a "lite" version. The claim that neocons—read Jews—exercised inordinate influence over President George W. Bush leading up to the war in Iraq is a "lite" version of the claim that Jews are secretly in control of the U.S. government, for example.)

Sure, Hitler was a mass murderer ... but so was Stalin. Sure, the Nazis put Jews, Gypsies, Jehovah's Witnesses, and others in camps ... but America put Japanese-Americans in camps too. Sure the Nazis targeted innocent civilians ... but the Allies bombed Dresden. Sure the Nazis passed the Nuremberg laws ... but America had Jim Crow.

Like Holocaust denial, these immoral equivalencies rest on distortions. As horrid as the internment of Japanese-Americans was, they were not worked to death, shot, selected, or sent to gas chambers or crematoria. Whether or not it made sense for the Allies to bomb Dresden (some say it was justified by legitimate military goals, while others are not convinced), civilians had nothing to fear once the Allies gained territory; civilians had everything to fear once the Nazis gained territory. And so on.

A few years ago I attended a conference of the Northwest Coalition against Malicious Harassment. Two plenary speakers brought up the Holocaust in the most gratuitous and disturbing ways.

A Native American woman, speaking eloquently about the discrimination her people face daily, said in passing that the genocide of American Indians was "worse than" the Holocaust and that Hitler could not get his hand on any Indians, so he went after Jews.

Forgetting the absurdity of the notion that Hitler wanted to go after American Indians, the idea that the genocide of American Indians was "worse than" the Holocaust is bizarre. On what scale can one measure genocide? How can you rank these tragedies? It makes no sense to say that the Holocaust was "worse than" slavery, for example. How do you factor in the number killed, the percentage of the population destroyed, the time it took to commit the murder? Each genocide is unique. (What is unique about the Holocaust to me was the priority that killing Jews took over winning the war effort.) Each is another example of people's capacity to classify an "other," to dehumanize that "other," and when dehumanization becomes either central to one's ideology or commonplace and unremarkable, to kill that "other," including babies.

But the idea of "ranking" genocides seems to be necessary for some people's political goals, especially regarding slavery. There has been a push to call genocides "holocausts" and to call the Holocaust the "Nazi holocaust" or the "Jewish holocaust." This is calculated to rob the Holocaust of its uniqueness and is a disturbing trend that may succeed. In a generation, the Holocaust may be known by its Hebrew name, Shoah. But the attempt to rob the Holocaust of its name, or to enlist it in a contest of victimization, is counterproductive, and this American Indian speaker, who should have known better, unfortunately did not.

Then came a Hispanic poet who spoke passionately about the problems of getting quality public education for Hispanic children. He said that many teachers just assumed that a Hispanic child would not amount to much, so these children were neglected and not challenged to succeed. "This is a crime worse than Hitler," he said. "While Hitler attacked the body, these teachers attack the mind." Later he talked about the deportation of farm workers across the border back to Mexico in the first half of the twentieth century and said, "This was the same as the Holocaust."

Even allowing for poetic license, this was too much. As racist as those deportations were, farm workers were not lined up on the border and summarily shot nor taken to gas chambers, killed, had their gold fillings removed, and their bodies burned. There is a Holocaust-era picture of a girl hastily scribbling a note to someone, as she was about to be taken from her home and deported, presumably to one of the camps. Given the choice, she would have willingly suffered sitting in a classroom, being ignored by a racist teacher.

The people at this conference had worked in the trenches in the Northwest, combating groups such as the Aryan Nation and the racist militias. They should have been the last people who felt a need to minimize and distort the Holocaust to make the case that other racism should be taken seriously. They were speaking to a self-selected audience of sympathetic people. How much of this was latent anti-semitism, and how much of it was ignorance of the Holocaust? It is difficult to know, just as it is not easy to gauge how much was a tactic designed to win over an audience, and the related question of what that says about contemporary culture. Regardless, this type of relativism, and the distortion it promotes, makes the agenda of the hard-core Holocaust deniers that much easier.[29]

Comparing Israelis to Nazis, Israeli Leaders to Hitler

The use of the Nazi label to tar Jews in general and Israelis in particular is itself a form of Holocaust denial, because, while such comparisons unfairly defame Jews, they also belittle the crimes of the Nazis.

A leading French cleric was very insightful when, during an off-the-record discussion of current antisemitism in France, he traced part of the problem back to student protests there in 1968. "When I saw students calling police Nazis," he said, "that was the beginning."[30]

That watering down of what "Nazi" meant, chanted by students in France or casually bandied about at a Northwest Coalition meeting in a discussion of racism again Mexicans, made it easier for others to use that eviscerated and misunderstood adjective to target Jews and the Jewish state. The linkage is carefully calculated (especially in Europe) and has two purposes: to grant moral license to forget how Jews were victimized in the mid-twentieth century, and to produce in the speaker a feeling of moral smugness in targeting Israel.

But there is more to this than loose language. Could you imagine the outcry if people routinely used images associated with the horrors of slavery to describe other, clearly lesser, forms of discrimination? Could you imagine the response if such terms were used to complain about alleged black exploiters, and not about similar or worse acts by others? But that is how Holocaust references are used regarding Jews.

The Future of this Antisemitic Myth

In the decades to come, survivors will have died out, so there will no longer be people to say, "This is what happened to me."[31] Couple that with the fact that Holocaust denial is an ideological staple of the white supremacist, black supremacist, and Islamic supremacist movements. Add that the ignorance and jealousies that help promote Holocaust relativism and distortion make outright denial seem less outrageous. The result: Holocaust denial easily could become a mainstream "lie" that propels twenty-first-century antisemitism. Not only would that put individual Jews in harm's way, but it would also threaten the legitimacy of the State of Israel to those who do not know history. Perhaps most importantly, Holocaust denial will continue to help extremists who otherwise would not have anything to do with one another discover that they share basic ideological assumptions. Already, many white supremacist, black supremacist, and Muslim supremacist Web sites are two mouse clicks away from one another, with the connective tissue being antisemitism in general and Holocaust denial in particular. We should not forget that their common enemy is not only Jews, but also democracy and freedom.

Finally, Holocaust denial demonstrates the ease with which very different people, with markedly different politics, religions, identities, and agendas, can craft and/or absorb ideas presented with a patina of reasonableness and use them to promote Jew-hatred. It shows the power of antisemitic constructs to penetrate vastly different systems and cultures and become believed explanations of how the world works. While all antisemitic myths are objectively unreasonable, it is remarkable that this one—which necessarily posits a huge conspiracy of historians and others to hide the "real truth" of a war to which there were hundreds of thousands if not millions of witnesses—is so easily believed by so many, particularly in the Arab and Muslim worlds. That it is shows how easily people can embrace antisemitic hatred, especially when promoted by people in positions of authority and used in conjunction with political, religious, and/or racial zealotry.

*The constant singling out of one nation as the enemy
of humanity is in fact a campaign directed against the
Jewish people. We have seen that many anti-Jewish
outbursts in a number of countries have been rooted
in condemnations of Israel exploiting an antisemitic
terminology. Attacks on synagogues have been triggered by a
defaming language about the conflict in the Middle East.*

—Per Ahlmark, former deputy prime minister of Sweden[1]

Chapter Eight
Crafting a Working Definition of Contemporary Antisemitism for Today's Monitors

The last chapters have explored what antisemitism is and how it works as a system of thought. In order to develop strategies to counter it, governments and NGOs need more than anecdotes and impressions. They need data to document when antisemitism appears, how it manifests itself, whether it is becoming more or less prevalent, and other quantifiable facts. But until recently, there was no systematic attempt, in Europe or elsewhere, to define how to count, catalogue, and thus to compare antisemitism among various countries.[2]

One of the key organizations tasked with collecting data on antisemitism is the European Monitoring Centre on Racism and Xenophobia (EUMC). EUMC exists to provide "reliable and comparable information and data on racism, xenophobia, islamophobia and anti-Semitism at the European level in order to help the EU and its Member States to establish measures or formulate courses of actions against racism and xenophobia."[3] Yet it was roundly criticized in 2003, when it was accused of suppressing a report written for it by the Centre for Research on Antisemitism at Berlin's Technical University. The report (first leaked, and only later released by the EUMC) documented that a significant share of the hate crimes against European Jews since the collapse of the peace process in the fall of 2000[4] had been committed by young Muslims, something evidently uncomfortable for the EUMC to admit.

So it was no surprise that, when the EUMC released its own report entitled "Manifestations of Antisemitism in the EU 2002-2003" in March 2004, the controversy continued. This was so largely because its press release stated that while "it is not easy to generalise, the largest group of the perpetrators of antisemitic activities appears to be young, disaffected white Europeans."[5]

The irony was that, although the press release distorted reality, the March EUMC report was much more truthful than the press release suggested, and in some ways, superior to the earlier suppressed report as well. Recognizing that antisemitism came from a variety of sources, it did not downplay or diminish the role of young Muslims in the rash of arsons, vandalism, intimidation, and personal attacks. What was largely not noticed in the report, however, was a much more fundamental problem: the EUMC's troubling definition of anti-semitism.

While noting, correctly, that there was no universally agreed upon definition of antisemitism, the report—after many pages of intellectual throat-clearing—concluded that antisemitism was comprised of a series of stereotypes, including those of the Jew as "'deceit-ful,' 'crooked' [and] 'artful' [in] nature, [his] 'foreign' and 'different essence,' [his] 'irreconcilability,' 'hostility,' [and] 'agitation,' [his] 'commercial talent' and 'relation to money,' [and his] 'corrupt' nature." It also included notions relating to "Jewish 'power and influence,'" and a "Jewish 'world conspiracy.'"[6]

The "core of antisemitism," the EUMC therefore concluded, was:

> Any acts or attitudes that are based on the perception of a social subject (individual, group, institution or state) as "the ('deceitful,' 'corrupt,' 'conspiratorial,' etc.) Jew."

There were problems with this approach. First, it had cause and effect reversed. Stereotypes are derivative of what antisemitism is, not its defining characteristic.

Blinders Regarding Anti-Zionism as Antisemitism

But the real reason for this convoluted paradigm was apparent in the last part of the definitional section, under the heading "Antisemitism and Anti-Zionism," as follows:

> According to our definition, anti-Israel or anti-Zionist attitudes and expression are in those cases antisemitic, where Israel is seen as being representative of "the Jew," i.e., as a representative of the traits attributed to the antisemitic construction of "the Jew." ... But what if the opposite is the case and Jews are perceived as representatives of Israel? ... [W]e would have to qualify hostility towards Jews as "Israelis" only then as antisemitic, if it is based on the underlying perception of Israel as "the Jew." If this is not the case, then we would have to consider hostility toward Jews as "Israelis" as *not* [emphasis in original] genuinely antisemitic, because this hostility is not based on the antisemitic stereotyping of Jews.[7]

In other words, if a Jew were attacked on the streets of Paris because the perpetrator viewed Israelis as conspiratorial or money-grubbing or slimy, and then saw the Jew before him as a stand-in for that Israeli, that was antisemitism. But if the assailant was upset with Israeli policy and then attacked that same Jew in Paris as a surrogate for Israel or Israelis, this was not antisemitism. While the EUMC did not consider such attacks antisemitic, it nevertheless said that they should be monitored, although it did not say how this would be done.

Five days after the report was released, a Montreal Jewish elementary school was firebombed. A note left behind indicated that the attack was in retaliation for Israel's assassination of a Hamas leader—presumably not antisemitism according to the EUMC definition. The functional equivalent would be declaring the lynching of a young African-American man in the 1960s racist if the motivating factor were a belief that blacks were shiftless or lazy or destroying the white gene pool, but not if the same victim were swinging from the same

magnolia tree and the murderer was motivated by dislike of a speech
by the Reverend Dr. Martin Luther King, Jr., or the Voting Rights Act
of 1965.

The problems with the EUMC definition were threefold,
beyond its intellectual dishonesty: First, it bent logic like a pretzel in
order to disqualify almost any act motivated by dislike or even hatred
of Israel from the label "antisemitic." Second, it failed to consider the
denial to Jews of their right to self-determination in their homeland as
a manifestation of antisemitism. And third, it focused too much on
the mind and heart of the actor rather than on the character of the act.

Hearts, Minds, and Acts

The EUMC is not in the business of labeling any particular individual an antisemite. Nor for that matter are groups that monitor antisemitism, such as the Organization for Security and Cooperation in
Europe (OSCE), or Jewish defense organizations, which routinely
reserve the label only for the most clear-cut and outrageous perpetrators—a David Duke or a Louis Farrakhan—so as not to cheapen the
word.[8]

It is neither necessary nor helpful for groups that monitor or
combat antisemitism to get too far into the head of perpetrators: Do
they really hate Jews? Their method should instead be to look at the
act and see whether the Jew (or person or property mistakenly taken as
Jewish) was selected to be a victim simply because he was a Jew. If a
Jew on the streets of Paris is beaten up because he is a victim of a ran-
dom mugging, this is not antisemitism. But if he is beaten up because
he is a Jew, it need not matter whether the attacker thinks that his victim is one of the Elders of Zion, or picks on him because he is mad at
an Israeli prime minister. If the Jew is selected for attack because he is
a Jew, this is antisemitism, just as beating up a gay person because he
is gay is homophobia.

Definitions become harder, however, when looking beyond
criminal acts to matters of expression—hate speech, for example.

When is something antisemitic to be counted in a list of antisemitic events, and when is it not?

There are no ironclad rules, but some very good guideposts. What makes the matter complex, as we have seen, is that antisemitism has three overlapping strains. There is less difficulty classifying an act or expression as antisemitic when it comes from religious or race-based hatred. Matters get somewhat more problematic, or at least controversial, when dealing with anti-Zionism.

As has been noted, criticism of Israel is not antisemitism when it is engaged in a similar manner as one would criticize any other country, focusing on a program, a policy, a political leader or party. But when the alleged problems in Israel are used to attack its basic legitimacy, or to tarnish Jews collectively, that is antisemitism in effect, whether or not by design.

Some charge that when Israel is criticized for things that worse offenders are not, that is antisemitism too. It may or may not be, depending on whether the accuser's mandate is broad or narrow. If a group is supposed to look at human rights abuses globally, but spends the majority of its energies creating the impression that Israel is the world's worst human rights offender, that is a problem. But if its mandate is to look specifically at Israeli treatment of Palestinians, then other factors (such as the fairness of and the language it uses to describe its findings) have to be taken into account as well before reaching that conclusion.

Is Anti-Zionism Antisemitism?

Trickier still, is anti-Zionism antisemitism? Back in 1947, few would have claimed so. But it is today* when, for example, no one is clamoring for the undoing of Pakistan or Samoa or Bangladesh or Qatar or

---

* There are two rare exceptions to contemporary anti-Zionism being antisemitism, and they are so because they do not discriminate against the Jew and deny him a right of self-determination. Some ultra-Orthodox Jews believe that Israel should not exist until the Messiah comes. And there are some others who believe that there should be no nation-states, or that there should be no nation-states with links to

scores of other countries that became nations after the end of World War II—let alone for doing so while ignoring how many Pakistanis would be killed in an effort to deny them their self-determination, against which they would surely fight.

Or to put it in a different context, imagine a Palestinian state being created in 2010, and then in 2067 some voices assert that a mistake was made and, of all the peoples in the world, only the Palestinians should now give up their state. It would be hard to imagine such a claim not being labeled extreme, bigoted, racist, or insensitive to the bloodshed it would clearly produce. Correspondingly, there is antisemitism in play when it is said that of all the peoples on the globe (including the Palestinians), only the Jews are not permitted the right to self-determination in a land of their own (let alone in their historic homeland), and that the Jewish State of Israel should no longer exist. Or, to quote noted human rights lawyer David Matas:

> One form of antisemitism denies access of Jews to goods and services because they are Jewish. Another form of antisemitism denies the right of the Jewish people to exist as a people because they are Jewish. Anti-Zionists distinguish between the two, claiming the first is antisemitism, but the second is not. To the anti-Zionist, the Jew can exist as an individual as long as Jews do not exist as a people.[9]

Matas correctly terms this distinction "nonsense."[10]

A Working Definition for the EUMC and OSCE

To the credit of some key personnel at the EUMC and the OSCE, they listened to concerns about what was being counted as antisemitism and what was not. The EUMC staff carefully considered a draft working definition of anti-Semitism created by this author in consultation with many other experts around the globe during the sec-

---

any religion. These are not significant groups, and the latter groupings (anarchists and those who don't like religious-linked states) become problematic if they inordinately harp on Israel rather than, say, Spain or Russia. (There are also some Orthodox Jews who could be described as "non-Zionist," whose views are theologically driven and lead them not to care one way or another.)

ond half of 2004, and with some minor changes,[11] adopted it as a working definition. The final document stated:

A Working Definition of Antisemitism

(January 28, 2005)

The purpose of this document is to provide a practical guide for identifying incidents, collecting data, and supporting the implementation and enforcement of legislation dealing with antisemitism.

Antisemitism is a certain perception of Jews, which may be expressed as hatred toward Jews.

Rhetorical and physical manifestations of antisemitism are directed toward Jewish or non-Jewish individuals and/or their property, toward Jewish community institutions and religious facilities.

In addition, such manifestations could also target the State of Israel, conceived as a Jewish collectivity.

Antisemitism frequently charges Jews with conspiring to harm humanity, and it is often used to blame Jews for "why things go wrong." It is expressed in speech, writing, visual forms and action, and employs sinister stereotypes and negative character traits.

Contemporary examples of antisemitism in public life, the media, schools, the workplace, and in the religious sphere could, taking into account the overall context, include, but are not limited to:

— Calling for, aiding, or justifying the killing or harming of Jews in the name of a radical ideology or an extremist view of religion.

— Making mendacious, dehumanizing, demonizing, or stereotypical allegations about Jews as such or the power of Jews as a collective—such as, especially but not exclusively, the myth about a world Jewish conspiracy or of Jews controlling the media, economy, government or other societal institutions.

— Accusing Jews as a people of being responsible for real or imagined wrongdoing committed by a single Jewish person or group, or even for acts committed by non-Jews.

— Denying the fact, scope, mechanisms (e.g., gas chambers) or intentionality of the genocide of the Jewish people at the hands of National Socialist Germany and its supporters and accomplices during World War II (the Holocaust).

— Accusing the Jews as a people, or Israel as a state, of inventing or exaggerating the Holocaust.

— Accusing Jewish citizens of being more loyal to Israel, or to the alleged priorities of Jews worldwide, than to the interests of their own nations.

Examples of the ways in which antisemitism manifests itself with regard to the State of Israel taking into account the overall context could include:

— Denying the Jewish people their right to self-determination, e.g., by claiming that the existence of a State of Israel is a racist endeavor.

— Applying double standards by requiring of it a behavior not expected or demanded of any other democratic nation.

— Using the symbols and images associated with classic antisemitism (e.g., claims of Jews killing Jesus or blood libel) to characterize Israel or Israelis.

— Drawing comparisons of contemporary Israeli policy to that of the Nazis.

— Holding Jews collectively responsible for actions of the State of Israel.

However, criticism of Israel similar to that leveled against any other country cannot be regarded as antisemitic.

Antisemitic acts are criminal when they are so defined by law (for example, denial of the Holocaust or distribution of antisemitic materials in some countries). Criminal acts are antisemitic when the targets of attacks, whether they are people or property—such as buildings, schools, places of worship and cemeteries—are selected because they are, or are perceived to be, Jewish or linked to Jews. Antisemitic discrimination is the denial to Jews of opportunities or services available to others and is illegal in many countries. [Note: ECRI[12] in its *General Policy Recommendation No. 9*, 25 June 2004, has offered specific recommendations regarding the criminalization of antisemitic acts.]

How Anti-Zionism Should Be Defined by Other Monitors of Antisemitism

Whereas this definition provides a useful framework and concrete examples to help governmental organs and NGOs that monitor antisemitism decide what to include or exclude, Jewish defense and other independent organizations can be less reticent regarding anti-Zionism. (Again, we are not concerned with whether a person who spouts an anti-Zionist statement is motivated by hatred or ignorance or something else, but rather with monitoring, cataloguing, and hopefully educating about antisemitic expressions and acts.)

The immoral equation of Israel with apartheid-era South Africa, while perhaps a lighter version of the comparison between Israel and the Nazis, would not specifically or necessarily fall under the EUMC definition, but it should still be considered an expression of antisemitism. It is a twisting of history to paint Jews as demonic.[13]

And just as Holocaust denial is antisemitism, so is the similar antihistorical charge which denies any significant historic Jewish link to the land of Israel, whether it be claims that the Temple did not exist, or that this land was entirely an Arab land (let alone a Muslim or Palestinian one) from ancient times until European Jews started showing up a little over a century ago.

While it is not reasonable to expect a youngster born in Gaza to share the Zionist narrative, and, of course, everyone is entitled to his own point of view, people are not entitled to their own set of twisted facts. The distortion or wiping out of Jewish history in the Middle East (as opposed to giving different reasonable interpretations of that history) is no less antisemitic than the distortion or wiping out of Jewish history regarding the Second World War in Europe.

The Working Definition at Work

Ultimately, there probably is no perfect definition of antisemitism. Recall that U.S. Supreme Court Justice Potter Stewart, when faced with a similar quandary regarding the definition of obscenity, wrote, "I know it when I see it." To monitor antisemitism effectively—which has to be done before one can develop strategies and allocate resources to fight it intelligently—we need to rely on better guideposts than the subjective standard Stewart articulated. But it is also necessary to understand *why* we are looking at it, and conversely, the various reasons that some may have blinders when viewing antisemitism of certain types, or from particular perpetrators. Those who monitor or combat antisemitism need to make sure that, while they do nothing to cheapen the word, they also include all relevant acts and events, because the cataloguing of these incidents is the precondition to forming effective counterstrategies and smart allocation of resources.

The EUMC's working definition seems to be taking hold. The OSCE used it in its June 2005 report, "Education on the Holocaust and on Anti-Semitism: An Overview and Analysis of Educational Approaches,"[14] as well as in its Office for Democratic Institutions and Human Rights (ODIHR) Law Enforcement Officer Training Programme on Combating Hate Crimes.[15]

And on July 7, 2005, a Lithuanian court found that the editor-in-chief of the Vilnius daily *Respublika* had published material "propagating national, racial and religious enmity," when he alleged a "global plot" of Jews to rule "the world, money, mass media and politics." The court's decision specifically cited the EUMC's working definition and found that the newspaper's text "correspond[ed] to the ... hallmarks of anti-Semitism" enumerated by the EUMC.[16]

If the definition survives and becomes institutionalized in Europe, it will not only help clarify what antisemitism is, but will also help standardize research and analysis and monitoring of this problem across borders.

By failing to prepare, you are preparing to fail.

—Benjamin Franklin

Never interrupt your enemy when he's making a mistake.

—Napoleon Bonaparte

Chapter Nine
Combating Antisemitism:
The Importance of Strategic, Venue-Specific Thinking

Antisemitism in the twenty-first century is both a complex and a simple phenomenon. Simple because most variants take the form of seeing Jews—individually, collectively, or in their national expression (the State of Israel)—as conspiring to harm non-Jews. And most variants serve the purpose of explaining to people why "things go wrong."

The complexity is in categorizing the particular aspect of antisemitism with which one is dealing; identifying, researching, and understanding the venue and institutions which it is impacting; and then devising strategies with which to combat it. Too often, the response, even of some experienced Jewish institutions, is based on untested assumptions and other imperatives.

In some ways, the fight against antisemitism today is less sophisticated than it was in the immediate aftermath of the Second World War. Back then, the Jewish community employed a "quarantine" theory. The notion was that if antisemitism that had occurred was not reported in the papers or otherwise brought to light, its impact would not be amplified, and the purveyors of antisemitism would see that their activities did not get them the attention they craved.

There were problems with the quarantine theory, which today is generally rejected (clearly, one strategy does not fit all fact situations), but at least there was a theory to guide action. Today, while many initiatives are intelligent and thought-through, too often the approach seems to be to "shoot first and aim later."

The controversy around the 2004 Mel Gibson film, *The Passion of the Christ*, is instructive. The story of the death of Jesus is one that makes Jews nervous. The passion plays in Europe were occasions for arousing hatred, and Jewish history is replete with instances of pogroms at Easter time. While the telling of these passion stories has generally improved over the years as a result of interreligious dialogue, there was deep concern about the Gibson production for two reasons: Gibson belonged to an old-line Catholic group that rejected the teachings of Vatican II, and Gibson's father was a stone-cold antisemite and Holocaust denier.

Jewish antennae were legitimately raised because of the subject matter, the concerns about Gibson's views, and also the increase in global antisemitism at the time. Yet the Jewish communal response to the film was too ad hoc, and not nearly as effective as it might have been.

First, the movie potentially contained religious-based antisemitism. (As the movie had not yet been seen, it was impossible to tell.) It did not directly impact those for whom the crucifixion story had little or no meaning, and who were the main culprits behind the rise in global antisemitism—anti-Zionists and radical Islamists.

Second, since this potential antisemitism was, fortunately, isolable within one particular audience (Christians), there were logical things to do and not do.

For instance, while Jews were worried about increased antisemitism from the retelling of an old canard (i.e., Jews killed Jesus), this concern should never have been cast as a Jewish vs. Christian issue. The approach should have been instead, "This is an important story for Christians. How do Christians tell it faithfully and at the same time avoid promoting antisemitism?"

Rather than remaining largely an internal Christian issue about which Jews had some obvious interest, this became instead an interreligious conflict, with some in the Jewish community complaining about antisemitism before seeing what the film contained. Part of this, of course, was Gibson's fault for not accepting quiet overtures to review the film and take suggestions, as many of the promoters of traditional passion plays have done in recent years.

Because of the full-throttled manner in which the potential controversy about the film went public, the questions "What are we trying to accomplish?" and "How should we proceed?" were not sufficiently considered.

Clearly, Jewish agencies should not have remained silent, but perhaps it would have been better to explain clearly why this was not an "us versus them" issue, and (as a few Jewish groups tried to do[1]) to use the controversy as an opportunity for promoting religious dialogue and understanding. For once one Jewish organization jumps on such an issue in a very public manner, there is great institutional pressure for others to follow suit or be seen as ineffectual or timid.

Instead of understanding that the film could not be suppressed, that it had somewhat of a built-in audience, that this audience—especially in the United States and other countries where the teachings of Vatican II have been institutionalized—was not likely to become more antisemitic from seeing it, and that publicity was just what Gibson wanted, these Jewish groups walked right into the trap. In effect, though this certainly was not their goal, they helped promote the film, making it a huge success for Gibson. And while the film did not have any appreciable impact on antisemitism in the U.S., the publicity around it no doubt made it more likely that people in areas of the Christian world where Vatican II has not penetrated—such as parts of Latin America—would buy DVDs and expose their children to graphic images of the death of Jesus and the Jews' alleged role therein.

Undoing Some of the Damage of Durban

Conversely, a much more constructive approach emerged following the antisemitic events of the UN's World Conference Against Racism in Durban.

The antisemitism was understood to be largely from two sources: a combination of leftist and Arab-based anti-Zionism, on one hand, and Muslim religious-based antisemitism, on the other. There were clearly different institutions and strategies to employ for each.

Some Jewish NGOs, including the American Jewish Committee, began highlighting the antisemitism, anti-Christianity, and anti-Americanism ubiquitous in the Arab world—in its newspapers, in its textbooks, on its television stations. MEMRI.org began posting English-language translations of the Arab media material, much of it exceptionally vile. AJC commissioned examinations of Saudi and Egyptian textbooks, and exposed their intolerance. (For example, Saudi eighth-grade students learn that "the Muslims' power irritates the infidels and spreads envy in the hearts of the enemies of Islam-Christians, Jews and others ... a malicious Crusader-Jewish alliance [is] striving to eliminate Islam from all the continents." Ninth-grade students learn that "Jihad against the enemies is a religious duty." Tenth-grade students learn that "Western civilization [is] on its way to dissolution and extinction."[2])

Moreover, these NGOs attempted to reenergize the domestic debate about energy resources and conservation. What has this to do with antisemitism? Despite entreaties to do so, the U.S. government has not been willing to exact any meaningful "cost" for Muslim and Arab countries' incitement—even after September 11. Even with the recognition that countries such as Saudi Arabia are teaching about Jews in demonic terms and have never officially recognized the sovereign Jewish State of Israel, there has been great reluctance to use either a carrot or a stick, because of the American addiction to oil. The greater the U.S.'s energy independence, the less beholden it will be to these countries on a broad range of issues important to America. With less dependency may also come an increased willingness to use diplomatic and economic levers to combat these countries' incitement to hate Jews, Christians, and others.

A different, quicker-acting strategy was adopted regarding the leftist groups that either promoted the antisemitism in Durban or stood by in silence. The latter were groups with which many Jewish NGOs work on a variety of issues. Quietly, so as not to embarrass them publicly, they were talked to as friends about their roles in Durban. Overtures were made to board members of some of these organizations, many of whom were Jewish, to make them aware of the problem.

Jewish NGOs with credibility in the human rights field, such as the Jacob Blaustein Institute for the Advancement of Human Rights, began the slow work of turning the vocabulary of human rights back another 180 degrees. Whereas in Durban Zionism was painted by many as racism, JBI underscored the notion that freedom from antisemitism, like freedom from racism and sexism and homophobia, should be addressed as a basic human right. The clarity of this approach was that it understood the institution in which the antisemitism was expressing itself, understood what type of antisemitism was in play, and developed and implemented strategies to use the self-image of the human rights practitioners to engage them in a process of first understanding and then rejecting antisemitism promoted under the guise of anti-Zionism.

Is such a strategy guaranteed to prevent another Durban? No. But at least now the voices that were silent are better poised to speak out in an effective way at the right time. It was no coincidence that some of the people from human rights organizations who were silent (or worse) in Durban came to the OSCE's conference on antisemitism in Berlin.[3] Maybe it was some form of penance, but the first two questions—and they were challenging ones[4]—to Secretary of State Colin Powell at a closed meeting of Americans attending this conference came from non-Jewish human rights NGOs.

At the same time that groups such as the Blaustein Institute were raising antisemitism as a human rights issue, attention was being paid to the question of financial support for the antisemitic NGOs. While, of course, there is little that can be done about those groups subsidized by the Saudis and the Iranians, it turned out that many of the problematic groups were funded, in part, by the Ford Foundation. Embarrassed by this disclosure, the Ford Foundation announced that it would make sure that it did not fund such hatred in the future, and inserted clauses into its grant agreements to achieve this goal. It also began to fund European-based initiatives designed to combat antisemitism.[5]

Durban, clearly, had a larger role than the *Passion* in promoting contemporary Jew hatred, but rather than overreact, the Jewish community wisely analyzed the problem, saw places for action with people whose self-interest prompted them to help fix the problem they had, in part, created, and then quietly worked with them to put programs, initiatives, and themes in place designed to curtail at least one key ingredient—the anti-Zionism of left NGOs—that helped make Durban possible.

Anti-Zionism as the Anti-Globalism of Fools

Another such quiet initiative, focused on a particular type of antisemitism and the institutions through which it expresses itself, is the coming together of a group of leftists who share a long-time struggle against neo-Nazis and white supremacists in the U.S. and Europe. These are people who have much more in common politically with anti-globalists protesting the International Monetary Fund than with the mainstream Jewish community. Many are also severe critics of Israeli policy, but they understand antisemitism and they care about progressive politics.

One such activist was startled when his "progressive" roommate began ruminating about Jewish control of the media and of government, the exact canards he had heard from neo-Nazis. Others were distressed that their colleagues, in seeming support of Palestinian rights, were praising neo-fascist groups such as Hamas. How could it be that people who saw themselves as progressives were working to support movements that believe women should not be able to be educated or drive, and that homosexuals should be killed?

Some leftists who understand the danger of antisemitism among their cohorts are now speaking out more frequently and are organizing and building coalitions. But most Jewish organizations are not doing enough to help them. Why? Two reasons: First, because the general wisdom is that the left, particularly in recent decades, has been inhospitable to Jews and Israel. While this perception is partly true, it actually strengthens the case for aiding such initiatives. Unlike in the Muslim world, where there is little leverage and no embarrassment about promoting antisemitism, in the West there are values, theories, and contradictions to be explored among people on the left. They may never become supporters of Israeli policy, but they can be influenced about issues of bigotry.

The second problem is that most of the organized Jewish community, for understandable reasons and with good results, focuses its attention on key leaders and institutions. It values—correctly—statements of leading figures condemning antisemitism. At the same time, there has to be an understanding of the cultural norms among the left, which is more grassroots and activist. The goal of encouraging leading leftists to speak out should not preclude providing lesser-known people with the resources and training they need for countering antisemitism in the trenches. With the right support, they can be very effective monitors and exposers of antisemitism within their ranks.

Working with the Religious Right

The failure to understand the full importance of working with the left, despite the challenges and problems, is frequently coupled with a desire to work closely with the religious right, particularly Evangelical Christians, in support of Israel, without sufficiently appreciating the implications of this partnership. Clearly, Jewish organizations should work with people such as Pat Robertson and Jerry Falwell on issues such as the free exercise of religion in the former Soviet Union, or ending the slavery and genocide in Sudan. But it is problematic to assume that 1) because anti-Zionism is now a mainstream and troubling form of antisemitism; and 2) that there are few people speaking out in defense of Israel in its hour of need; and 3) the religious right supports Israel, therefore Jewish organizations should work uncritically with it in support of Israel.

Jewish organizations certainly should not be impolite or hostile toward members of the religious right (who, in the U.S., clearly outnumber those on the left). But they should be cautious and understand rather than overlook their theological agenda, the institutions they are trying to impact, and the implications all this has on antisemitism.

Evangelicals, who form an important constituency of the religious right, do not come to their support of Israel because they decided to study the Israeli-Arab conflict and concluded that equity is on the Jewish side. They are theologically driven to support Israel. They do so because they believe that the existence of the modern State of Israel is a precondition for the second coming of Jesus. Before that happens, the Jews have to be ingathered into Israel. Those who do not convert, however, will die. This view is an especially strong core belief for "dispensational" Evangelicals, who comprise about a third of the 40-50 million Christian Evangelicals in America.[6]

Because this belief is an imperative, it does not matter what Jewish groups do or do not do; Evangelicals will have the same attitude toward Israel regardless. But it is not always to be assumed—even if one is looking through the narrow lens of advocacy for Israel—that Evangelical support will always be a good thing. If a peace process involving territorial compromise with the Palestinians should ever actually appear likely to succeed (or if the Israelis decide to unilaterally withdraw from parts of the West Bank), many leading Evangelicals might oppose such a settlement because they see Jewish control over biblical Israel as a precondition for the Second Coming. Pat Robertson's comment that God punished Ariel Sharon with a stroke because Israel withdrew from Gaza[7] was not merely an offensive statement that required condemnation, but was also a window on this worldview which should be better understood.

Furthermore, some of the religious right in the U.S. too often promote an agenda that goes against the basic civil notion, so important in American democratic tradition, that while the majority rules, it must respect minority rights. Antisemitism is in no small measure a minor problem in the United States today because respect for religious beliefs requires government to stay far away from religion. The agenda of some elements within the religious right is to impose their own theological views on all Americans through law, on questions such as abortion or creationism or stem-cell research.

It should be remembered that Jews outside major Eastern cities and other urban settings such as Los Angeles are more likely to face what feels to them like religious-based antisemitism than any other kind. They may not be subjected to hatred, but rather to the notion that they somehow count less in the social compact. Their complaints frequently revolve around issues such as important school activities being scheduled on major Jewish holidays and the unwillingness of local authorities to treat this issue with the importance it deserves.[8] Sometimes, of course, these conflicts arise out of ignorance—not knowing when the Jewish holidays fall and their implications for students who choose to observe them—or insensitivity, as in not understanding why Christmas carols are not universal songs, but they must be dealt with in an increasingly diverse America.

The Christian right's agenda to create a "Christian America" carries with it—in the words of Rabbi Lori Forman—"the implications that non-Christians somehow do not belong,"[9] or if they do, have lesser claims of equality in the social order. In schools, the religious right wants increased entanglement of religion in public education, and supports school prayer and curricular changes to reflect a particular religious perspective (such as "scientific creationism"). It opposes a woman's right to have an abortion and tries to restrict people's rights because of their sexual orientation. While one can easily understand

why a believer's faith brings him or her to these conclusions (if one
believes that life starts at the moment of conception, then there is little distinction between abortion and taking a five-year-old off a swing
set and killing him), it is still a danger when one group wants to
impose its religious views on everyone else, as a matter of law.

Jewish organizations understood, and still understand, this challenge. Before the collapse of the Middle East peace process, Jewish
groups were much more vocal about the theological/political agenda
of the religious right. They spoke about how it posed a danger to religious freedom, and how it directly threatened Jews, whose religion was
seen as superceded and who were targeted for conversion. While still
opposing the religious right on issues such as abortion and a Constitutional amendment to prohibit gay marriage, Jewish organizations
have sometimes soft-pedaled their criticism of the organized religious
right because of its stance on Israel.[10] Israel is clearly an important issue
for many Jews, but it is shortsighted to let support for Israel be a
trump card that outweighs all other concerns, even antisemitism.

It is refreshing that there has been some attention paid at the
end of 2005 by both the American Jewish Committee and the Anti-
Defamation League to the question of religion in the public square
and to the dangers inherent in the wish of some leaders of the religious right to "Christianize America." There needs to be a continued
and clear focus on how to cooperate with the religious right on some
matters and to oppose them in the strongest terms on others.

Undoubtedly, the challenge of fighting antisemitism in the years
ahead will become more complex. Sometimes difficult choices and
trade-offs will have to be made. But the analytical process to balance
these considerations must be guided by a clear vision of how things
are, not how one wishes they were. Hard decisions must be made with
open eyes and with moral and intellectual consistency, as well as with
the understanding that shouting immediately or loudly is not necessarily the wisest thing to do. Just because someone is a supporter of
Israel does not mean that he should be given a free pass from criti-

cism.[11] Just as it is dangerous for people to pick and choose which type of antisemitism (religious, racial or political) they will condemn or disregard, people and organizations concerned with antisemitism also have to be consistent. Every type of antisemitism matters.

*To speak of Israel [on campus] is to speak of a "colonialist,"
"fascist," "ethnic cleansing machine" [and] to speak of Israel
at peace is the moral equivalent of defending apartheid in
South Africa.*

—Professor Laurie Zoloth, describing the climate at San Francisco State
University in 2002[1]

Chapter Ten
United States Campuses

Just as we have to be smarter about understanding and not minimizing the antisemitism from the religious right, it is equally or even more important to understand how to approach antisemitism from the political left, which usually manifests itself in its anti-Zionist form. While the left has a larger impact on the mainstream in Europe than in the United States, it has a singular influence in one very important American institution—the college campus. Our colleges and universities collect our brightest leaders of tomorrow. If they learn that antisemitism in any form is either unremarkable, a matter of "debate," or worse—truth—the potential danger is obvious.

On one hand, the campus is a remarkable reflection of how far Jews have come in America in the last decades. Not too long ago, there were quotas keeping Jews out of the elite universities. Now many of the leading colleges have presidents who are Jewish, and the door to campus life is open.

Yet, especially since 2000, there have been some troubling signs. Recall that Durban was meant to be the launching pad for a program to paint Israel as the "new South Africa" on campuses across the globe, but particularly in the United States. The strategy was simple: to replicate what had worked in the 1980s to force isolation of South Africa from all aspects of national "normalcy." That campaign was anchored on campuses, first through pushing for divestment of college investments and pensions from all companies having dealings with South Africa.

But September 11 was three days after Durban ended. The plan was postponed, and then launched again in February 2002. Soon divestment petitions were circulated at Columbia, Cornell, Duke, Harvard, MIT, Princeton, Rutgers, St. Lawrence University, University of California, Tufts, University of Massachusetts, University of Illinois, University of Maryland, University of Michigan, University of North Carolina, University of Pennsylvania, Wayne State, and Yale, among others.[2]

At MIT and Harvard, for example, a joint petition was signed with thirty-some-odd professors asking the university to divest from Israel. But a counterpetition with thousands of alumni signatures was immediately organized.

It quickly became clear that the divestment strategy was not going to win. Harvard President Lawrence Summers spoke out against divestment (and other forms of antisemitism) in the summer of 2002, describing those who were promoting the movement as "advocating and taking actions that are antisemitic in their effect if not their intent." Then Columbia President Lee Bollinger not only said Columbia would not divest, but termed the comparison between Israel and South Africa "grotesque" and "offensive."[3]

However, while no American university has, or will likely, divest, the campaign did not need to succeed in order to work. Just as Holocaust deniers do not think they are going to persuade people today that the Holocaust did not happen, but want to create the illusion that there is a reasonable "debate" about the historical facts, anti-Israel activists want to construct a linkage in peoples' minds between Israel and apartheid-era South Africa.

Shortly after the campus divestment movement was launched at a conference in Berkeley in February 2002, a series of antisemitic incidents occurred. A cinder block was thrown through a Hillel building

window there, and graffiti touting "F--k the Jews" appeared.[4] And
while there had been incidents of antisemitism on American campuses
before the divestment push (including even assaults[5]), the problem
accelerated thereafter.

At San Francisco State University—which historically has been
the "worst-case scenario"[6] of anti-Israel activity—a near antisemitic
riot broke out. Jewish students, some of whom were praying, others
departing after staging a peace rally, were harassed and threatened. As
Prof. Laurie Zoloth described it in an email, they were:

> ... surrounded by a large, angry crowd of Palestinians and their
> supporters.... They screamed at us to "go back to Russia" and they
> screamed that they would kill us all, and other terrible things.
> They surrounded the praying students, and the elderly women
> who are our elder college participants, who survived the Shoah,
> who helped shape the Bay Area peace movement, only to watch as
> a threatening crowd shoved the Hillel students against the wall of
> the plaza....
>
> As [they screamed] at the Jews to "Get out or we will kill you"
> and "Hitler did not finish the job," I turned to the police and to
> every administrator I could find and asked them to remove the
> counter demonstrators from the Plaza, to maintain the separation
> of 100 feet that we had been promised. The police told me that
> they had been told not to arrest anyone, and that if they did, "it
> would start a riot." I told them that it already was a riot....
>
> Was I afraid? No, really more sad that I could not protect my
> students. Not one administrator came to stand with us. I knew
> that if a crowd of Palestinian or black students had been there, sur-
> rounded by a crowd of white racists screaming racist threats,
> shielded by police, the faculty and staff would have no trouble
> deciding which side to stand on....
>
> There was no safe way out of the Plaza. We had to be marched
> back to the Hillel House under armed SF police guard, and we
> had to have a police guard remain outside Hillel. I was very proud
> of the students, who did not flinch and who did not, even one
> time, resort to violence or anger in retaliation. Several community
> members who were swept up in the situation simply could not

believe what they saw. One young student told me, "I have read about antisemitism in books, but this is the first time I have seen real antisemites, people who just hate me without knowing me, just because I am a Jew." She lives in the dorms. Her mother calls and urges her to transfer to a safer campus.

Today is advising day. For me, the question is an open one: What do I advise the Jewish students to do?[7]

University Presidents' Statement

Shortly thereafter, following many conversations with Prof. Zoloth, Richard Sideman, chair of AJC's Antisemitism Task Force, and I convened a conference call of five current or former presidents of major colleges and universities. We wanted them to hear directly from Prof. Zoloth and were eager to gain their perspectives about what was transpiring on their campuses. It turned out that a number of the problems at San Francisco State had followed shortly after the attacks of September 11, which some on campus had said was the fault of the Jews/Israelis, without contradiction by others.

Later there was a series of speakers brought onto campus who, according to Prof. Zoloth, made statements that had "nothing to do with Jews' stand on Israel, but to do with where Jews should live." These speeches played on themes, as she described them, of:

> Jews as the source of sinfulness in the world, Jews as the killers of innocent children, Jews as perhaps having an odd divided loyalty [suggesting that] "they seem like they're here but they really are agents of foreign Zionism," and then finally the notion that the campus itself was not a location that was safe for Jews. And this was said publicly at large rallies and privately to me by senior colleagues ... who felt it would be inappropriate for us to put up anything ranging from a succah ... to having a peace demonstration ... [T]here was a widespread concern that even expressing any solidarity, or any speech that had to do expressly with Israel, was, in fact, provocation.

Prof. Zoloth reported that some faculty at SFSU said that "to speak of Israel is to speak of a 'colonialist,' 'fascist,' 'ethnic cleansing machine' [and that] to speak of Israel at peace is the moral equivalent of defending apartheid in South Africa."

The SFSU campus even sported a poster with a picture of a dead Palestinian baby with the caption "canned Palestinian children meat, slaughtered according to Jewish rites under American license."[8]

Not every campus, of course, was like San Francisco State. Some had problems; others did not. But what raised concern beyond the incidents that gave rise to the conference call of presidents[9] were reports of Jewish students who were increasingly uncomfortable simply being able to be who they are. Some observant students would think twice before they decided to wear a *kippa* in public, or had to weigh taking a course in which they might want to speak out defending Israel, because to do so might mean sacrificing a good grade.

The presidents felt that the level of harassment on some campuses was not only harmful to Jewish students, but violated a basic tenet of free speech: that ideas could only reasonably be debated in a hate-free environment. They also agreed that it was the responsibility of university presidents to make sure that environment was cultivated and maintained.

They decided to circulate a statement among their peers affirming their duty to maintain an intimidation-free campus, and to give that statement a large distribution. While this was a project of college presidents, spearheaded by former Dartmouth President James O. Freedman and Brandeis President Jehuda Reinharz, AJC took on the administrative tasks.

The process of putting the statement together and gaining support for it was an education in itself.

First, there was debate about whether the term "Zionist" should be included in the text, since it had not only been Jewish students who had been harassed, but also Zionists, meaning supporters of Israel's right to exist.

Some objected to the idea, feeling it was a bit "in your face." But when a small group of Chicago-area Jewish students were told of the debate, their answer was clear: the statement had to include the word "Zionist." Otherwise, as one young woman put it, the whole effort would be "useless" since "people would condemn antisemitism in one breath and commit it in the next, under the guise of anti-Zionism."

In the end only one college president (a Jewish one) refused to sign because the text included the word "Zionist." A few others refused to sign because they had a policy not to sign statements, and a few more because they believed that alumni and others would interpret their participation as a confession that there were problems on their campus.

The statement read:

> In the current period of worldwide political turmoil that threatens to damage one of our country's greatest treasures—colleges and universities—we commit ourselves to academic integrity in two ways. We will maintain academic standards in the classroom and we will sustain an intimidation-free campus. These two concepts are at the core of our profession.
>
> Our classrooms will be open to all students, and classroom discussions must be based on sound ideas. Our campus debates will be conducted without threats, taunts, or intimidation. We will take appropriate steps to insure these standards. In doing so, we uphold the best of American democratic principles.
>
> We are concerned that recent examples of classroom and on-campus debate have crossed the line into intimidation and hatred, neither of which have any place on university campuses.
>
> In the past few months, students who are Jewish or supporters of Israel's right to exist—Zionists—have received death threats and threats of violence. Property connected to Jewish organizations has been defaced or destroyed. Posters and websites displaying libelous information or images have been widely circulated, creating an atmosphere of intimidation.
>
> These practices and others, directed against any person, group or cause, will not be tolerated on campuses. All instances will be investigated and acted upon so that the campus will remain

devoted to ideas based on rational consideration.

We call on the American public and all members of the academic community to join us.

After most of the presidents had already signed on, about a dozen presidents refused to sign (and one of the original signers— President Bill Chace of Emory—withdrew) because the text did not mention attacks on Arab and Muslim students too. Administratively, there was no way to change the statement at this point, but even if it could have been reworked, there was no reason to do so.

Arab and Muslim students were clearly covered by the statement as written—it was a declaration of a president's duty to all students. And while Jewish students and supporters of Israel were certainly active on campus, violence and intimidation were coming from only one direction.

The same week that Chace pulled out, a riot by pro-Palestinian students prevented former Israeli Prime Minister Benjamin Netanyahu from speaking at Concordia University in Montreal. Shortly thereafter, Jewish-linked property was defaced with swastikas at the University of Colorado at Boulder.

To have made the statement "symmetrical" in this environment, as this small group of presidents wished, would not only have created an immoral equivalency between chair throwers and placard holders, but also would have revised the narrative of the troubling facts that had given rise to the statement in the first place.

Recall that after the attacks of September 11, many college presidents and most human rights and Jewish defense organizations spoke out clearly about the wrong of scapegoating Arabs and Muslims. No one demanded that those statements not be issued unless they went from the particular to the general or specifically included Jewish students, despite the fact that antisemitic material blaming Jews and Israel for the terrorist attacks was already circulating on campus. Yet these few presidents complained when a statement that clearly went from the particular to the universal did not specifically mention Arabs.

There is little doubt that each of these presidents would have ably handled an antisemitic incident on their campus. Yet it is difficult not to be disturbed by their implicit statement that antisemitism does not really matter as much as other forms of bigotry. Imagine if the incidents giving rise to the statement had been antiblack (or antigay or antiwomen or anti-Arab). These presidents would not have been hesitant to speak out without feeling a need to couple their condemnation with mention of antiwhite (or antistraight or antimale or antisemitic) bigotry.

Why then the reluctance to mention antisemitic death threats, uncoupled with any other form of bigotry, as a sufficient reason to articulate a commitment to maintain a campus open to ideas, yet closed to bigotry?

None of those who refused to sign were antisemitic. But their action suggests other problems.

Does antisemitism matter to them as much as do other forms of bigotry? On many campuses (and elsewhere on the left) does antisemitism not rate because Jews are defined as a special class of "white," and whites, regardless of their subgroup, are not seen as victims, but victimizers?

Or could it be that the presidents, like many in the news media, have gotten into the habit of not being able to discuss attacks on Jews without discussing attacks on Palestinians? Some of this is lazy thinking and sloppy symmetry—the inability to report on a suicide bomber without mentioning a "cycle of violence," with no distinction between a terrorist who targets civilians and Israeli countermeasures that go after the attackers, but may hurt civilians by accident. But it also may be more. Some reporters who write about the deaths of Israelis due to terrorism cannot do so without mentioning the number of Palestinians killed, but can easily write about Israeli actions in the West Bank and Gaza without noting the terrorist attacks that are their predicate. Nor do they need a symmetrical couplet when writing about attacks on Jews by neo-Nazis.

The small group of presidents who refused to sign on this basis made an important statement by their stance: that when antisemitism comes from Arabs and Muslims, it has to be treated differently than if it comes from other sources. It can be noted and bemoaned, even criticized, but it has to be contextualized—the Arabs and Muslims are victims, too. Is there a bit of racism here?

The Palestine Solidarity Movement

While the circulation of the presidents' statement was a success (people debated about whether it should have included reference to Muslims and Arabs, but no one questioned the essential message—that antisemitism was a problem on some campuses which impacted the institutions' core values), other approaches to the problem have been uneven.

As mentioned, following Durban, the divestment movement on campus began. The focus of this effort, however, has subtly been altered, when it became clear that no campus was likely to divest. Instead, the center of gravity for this movement became the annual Palestine Solidarity Movement meeting.

The first conference was in Berkeley in 2002, followed by ones in Michigan, Rutgers,[10] Ohio State, Duke, and Georgetown. Each attracted many anti-Zionist and antisemitic speakers and produced many anti-Israel documents.[11]

The organized Jewish community developed an effective model to respond to these events. The understanding, by Jewish organizations both inside and outside the campus, was that antisemitism (as opposed to illegal activity[12]) was not a sufficient reason to bar these groups from meeting. Hateful ideas are not illegal. People may not like the implication of this fact, but it is a fact nonetheless. If Jewish organizations had pushed for the banning of this meeting, they would have 1) been demanding something they would not get, and thus been framing the battle as one they would lose, and 2) turned the PSM into a "First Amendment martyr," causing the question of its antisemitism and condoning of terror against Jews to be shunted aside.

Rather, Jewish groups argued, it is precisely because the PSM is allowed to hold its meeting, that campus leadership—from the president on down—have the obligation to use their own First Amendment rights to denounce bigotry. In other words, the game plan focused on the institutional self-perceptions and realities, and used these as tools.

Part of the problem with antisemitism in the guise of anti-Zionism is that it plays upon popular ignorance of Israel. Thus one counterstrategy was to have Israel-related programming—music, art, films—throughout the year. While the PSM was attempting to demonize Israelis, the Jewish organizations were helping students see Israelis instead as real human beings who cherish the same values as do Americans.

At Duke (the site of the 2004 PSM meeting), for example, the students circulated a statement asking people to declare their condemnation of the murder of innocent civilians, their support of a two-state solution, and their commitment to engage each other in respectful discourse. Most student groups were willing to endorse this statement—the PSM supporters were not. This was noticed.

The result on each of these campuses was that the PSM meetings were marginalized, while other groups came out of the woodwork asking the Jewish student organizations on campus about joint programs and initiatives. And attendance among Jewish students at Jewish-related campus events rose as well.

These efforts, however, were not without downsides. The energy and resources the Jewish organizations—on and off campus—allocated to counteracting the PSM were significant, and one has to ask the triage-related question: Were there not better uses for the efforts? (In fact, the PSM failed to get any university to consider divestment seriously, meaning that the Jewish community needed to put relatively little energy into the divestment fight on campuses around the country: Instead, their attention was drawn to the annual meeting of the pro-divestment organizers. This was a sign of success, not danger.) Second, Internet-circulated petitions—many of which contained factual errors (such as the assertion that the Rutgers president had kicked PSM off his campus because of its views [he did not], and other presidents should do the same)—created a drumbeat for cancellation that was counterproductive, and made the campus leadership feel itself under siege. There certainly is a place for creative activism, but it is unwise to ask for something that you know you will not get. Sometimes what feels good may be self-righteous indulgence and, what is worse, harmful.

Israel Studies: An Academic Response to an Academic Deficiency

The most important aspect of campus antisemitism is infrequently addressed—the influx of funding from Arab countries over the last decades to help establish Middle East Studies programs. As Martin Kramer chronicled in his book *Ivory Towers on Sand: The Failure of Middle Eastern Studies in America*, many of these departments are virtual propaganda machines that ignore the human rights abuses in every Arab country, but rail against Israel, and assert that its mere existence is an example of racism.

Couple this with the fact that the Jewish community's focus in terms of academic growth areas, over relatively the same period of time, has been the creation of programs teaching about the Holocaust. While it is clearly important to study the Holocaust, there is a dearth of programs that teach about contemporary Israel. Many Middle East Studies programs vilify the Jews in Israel, and instead of academic programs teaching about Israel from a less vitriolic narrative, there are programs teaching about Nazi Germany.

To remedy this problem, Brandeis University—in cooperation with the American Jewish Committee—has started a summer institute, enrolling twenty professors a year to teach about Israel. Some of the professors who participate in the institute are critics of Israeli policy, and that is fine. Whatever they think about Israeli actions, they must be committed to teaching—as opposed to indoctrinating—about contemporary Israel society, warts and all.

While such an initiative is intelligent because it understands both the type of antisemitism it is hoping to address and the institution within which it is aspires to have an impact, there are many problems with this model. There are over 3,000 colleges and universities in the United States. If no professor ever died, it would take 150 years to prepare at least one professor in Israel Studies for each campus.

Then there is the question of where should someone who teaches about Israel sit in the university? If they are included in the current Middle East Studies programs on many campuses, this will be suicide. If they are outside, they will be less relevant. There is no easy answer to this question, and, the options vary from campus to campus.

Other attempts to remedy this problem have been more problematic. For example, David Horowitz of *Frontpage Magazine* has asserted that university courses should be balanced and that schools adopt an academic "Bill of Rights" which would demand intellectual "diversity." But the purpose of a university is to shake up students' thinking and make them uncomfortable, not treat them as if they were passive scales that would become unbalanced if more ideas on one side of an issue were presented than those on another. Certainly a university is at its best when it offers students challenging exposure to all relevant theories in any field, with the best scholarship available. But that does not mean that an individual professor must pretend to teach without personal bias, or that every time a political science professor or history professor instructs his or her students about the destructive nature of the Ku Klux Klan, he or she must "balance" that presentation with sources that find value in the KKK. Further, when Pennsylvania held a legislative hearing on allegations brought by Horowitz that students were being mistreated by anticonservative ideologues, Horowitz was forced to admit that allegations he put forth to the panel could not be substantiated.[13]

Columbia University

While programs that use the campus culture to its advantage, such as the training of professors to teach modern Israel, are wiser in the long run, they do not address another problem—the intimidation of Jewish students who feel they cannot express their views openly in class without sacrificing their grades.

In the fall of 2004 an activist group called the David Project filmed Jewish students at Columbia University who had problems with the Middle East Studies program there. (Columbia, it should be noted, has a vibrant Jewish life, and the problem is largely limited to this department, known as MEALAC, short for Middle East and Asian Languages and Cultures.) One student—an Israeli—complained that when he asked a question, a professor replied by asking him if he had served in the Israel Defense Forces (IDF), and if he had killed any Palestinians. The professor would not answer the question unless the student answered his first. Another student recalled how she was talking with a professor after a class and, looking at her green eyes, he argued that she had no claim on the land of Israel, but he—with brown eyes—did. And another alleged that when she asked if it were true that Israel sometimes gave warnings before destroying buildings so that people could get out, a professor yelled, "If you're going to deny the atrocities being committed against Palestinians, then you can get out of my classroom!"[14]

No one really knows how widespread such incidents are at Columbia or elsewhere, and whether such behavior translates into students being given lower grades. In fact, although it was not clear from the film, it turned out that the episode with the Israeli (who was not even taking a class with this professor) did not happen in a classroom, but at a lecture at a sorority—a key difference.[15] What was certain was that there was no procedure in place to allow students comfortably to report incidents of intimidation while also protecting the professor's due process rights. Columbia, commendably, understood the need for having such a system, and embarked on creating one.

Meanwhile, however, people and groups from outside the campus (including some politicians and Jewish groups) began blasting Columbia in general, and the most problematic professor—Prof. Joseph Massad—in particular. Some even called for his dismissal. The problem was, no one had proved that Massad had done anything that would warrant firing. Further, Massad was coming up for tenure. It had been hoped, quietly, that because Massad was viewed as an inadequate scholar, when his tenure decision came up, he would be rejected on that basis. But immediately after the attacks began, academics from across the country started a campaign to support Massad, because they saw him as defending *their* rights to academic freedom, and because there is always an institutional instinct to rally around any beleaguered professor who is attacked by outside interests.

Long-term, the Jewish students taking courses in the MEALAC program are less likely to be subjected to intimidation of this sort with Massad gone, but those whose instincts were to yell and demand his firing may have actually made it more likely that he will receive tenure. And if he does not, it will be despite, and not because, of the tactics of some organizations that failed adequately to consult with the Jewish leadership on campus and jumped in without understanding the workings of the institution.

It was especially counterproductive when groups blasted the Columbia administration for appointing a faculty review committee that included members who had signed a petition calling for divestment from Israel as well as someone who had been a thesis adviser to Massad. They claimed that the committee thus constituted was selected to whitewash the situation, and even went so far as to put pressure on an Israeli official not to speak on the campus in protest. (The official cancelled, thereby harming the administration's plan to increase the Zionist narrative on campus.)

This stance was also insulting to the integrity of academics in general and the members of the committee in particular. It implied that a faculty member's political biases would render him or her incapable of answering the narrow question of whether a professor mistreated students. Further, according to this "logic," a professor who signed an anti-divestment petition should not have been allowed to sit on the committee either.

The worst part of this myopia was the focus on the process rather than the result, and a corresponding failure to understand the difference between campus and Jewish organizational cultures. If the committee had been made up of five Alan Dershowitzes, and had concluded that an anti-Israel faculty member engaged in improper behavior, many, perhaps most, of the faculty would have disregarded that conclusion as political. But if the committee—comprised of anti-Israel professors and Massad's thesis adviser—found, as it did, that some of the incidents had taken place, no one would question the credibility of that verdict.

Furthermore, these off-campus Jewish groups were so predisposed to attack the university that they blasted the report, even though it found that there were problems and that Massad had behaved as alleged.

The university deserved, but received too little praise for both the committee decision and a courageous speech by Columbia President Lee Bollinger in which he asserted that academic freedom applies to students and faculty alike, that academic freedom can be abused, and that abuses have consequences. Despite some missteps, the administration has been trying to do what it should, including actively increasing the study of Israel on campus by creating a new chair and holding symposia on Israel and other issues raised by this controversy. Further, acting on a process started before the allegations, it had put MEALAC into receivership. Its actions were designed to be accepted by faculty because they were driven by a desire to improve the intellectual life on campus, rather than to respond to outside pressures or political agendas.

A grassroots Jewish leader complained that there was any praise for Columbia's actions. When challenged to point to something unfair in the commendation of "positive steps," he laughed, saying, "This is not about fairness. We're in a war. We have to keep on the attack."[16]

His approach will probably succeed in raising money and fears, but it will not help the Jewish students at Columbia. Nor will statements, as some have made, comparing students on college campuses to "refuseniks" in the old Soviet Union. Clearly the administration of Columbia is not the KGB. The hysteria created from distorting the real problems into something much larger resulted in many calls to Jewish organizations from parents, asking whether they should send their child to Columbia. They asked with the same trepidation as if they were inquiring about sending their child to study in Ramallah. The irony is that such hysteria may indeed lead some Jewish parents to send their children to other schools instead of Columbia, thereby reducing the vibrancy of the Jewish community there in a way that Joseph Massad never could.

Rather than distort the situation and attack from outside, interested groups would be better advised to work with the professionals on the ground to address real needs. For example, Simon Klarfeld, the Hillel director at Columbia, reports that progressive Jewish students sometimes tell him that they have attended a pro-Palestinian program in which someone claims that "Jews control the media," and two days later it hits the student that that was antisemitism. In coordination with AJC, Klarfeld then invited a leftist expert on antisemitism (one of the members of the group mentioned in the last chapter) to run a workshop with progressive Jewish students to better understand antisemitism.

Testing for Bigotry

The fact is that many American campuses, including elite ones, are generally more left-leaning than the rest of society. What is needed are programs and publications that address sympathetically the progressive politics of many young students, and demonstrate how those politics are being subverted when it comes to questions of anti-Zionism. For example, they should be challenged to apply a basic test for identifying bigotry in any situation: Take the same scenario, change the players (gender, sexual orientation, religion, race, etc.) and see if the same rules apply.[17] In most instances regarding Jews and Israel, it is easy to document that the same rules do not apply. (Or as Emory University Professor Deborah Lipstadt put it, the problem is with the assumption that Israel is always wrong, which then ordains the debate to be about the question, "How wrong?"[18])

Conversely, there are too many instances when progressive Jewish students, who care deeply about both the security of Jews in Israel and the suffering of Palestinians, consider themselves marginalized by the mainstream Jewish organizations on campus. They feel pressured to "choose" a side, when their values lead them to support aspects of each. It is neither wise nor fair to put them in this position, nor to ignore their quandary.

One additional problem on campus in recent years (following the intifada which began in 2000) has been that too few students have had Israel experiences, which provide them with both the credibility and the context to address some of the issues that come up, as well as the bigoted charges. (For example, the claim that Jews in Israel are white Europeans, when the majority of Israeli Jews are Jews from Arab countries and their descendants, or the claim that Muslims have a prior claim to Jerusalem, which is effectively refutable when one can describe the Western Wall.) Hopefully there will be increased opportunity for programs such as birthright Israel[19] and Project Interchange, to take Jews (birthright) and leaders, including those from campuses (Project Interchange), to Israel.

Finally, there is a tendency among some in the Jewish community to make a single demand and a particular threat when confronting anti-Israel and antisemitic events on a campus: The demand is that the administration silence the haters, and the threat is that Jewish alumni will curtail or stop their financial support. Rather than being influenced by these voices to attack the university, the organized Jewish community should rather seek ways to work in partnership with the campus leadership, with an understanding that, if the problems are to be fixed, the changes have to come from within the structure of the academy, and in resonance with its goals and self-image. Rather than silence distasteful and dogmatic anti-Israel voices, the university should make sure that the Zionist narrative is taught too, and that serious scholarship is improved (which will then expose the shallowness of the dogmatic approach). Columbia, as noted, is not only going to create a chair in Israel studies, but is also bringing in visiting scholars from Israel. A major Jewish donor, instead of pulling funds, is instead providing money to create a series of symposia on the issues involved in the controversy. This is a much more intelligent approach.

Neither the initiatives outlined here, nor better internal Jewish communal analysis of the college situation, will "solve" antisemitism on campus. But each would be an important part in an overall program to address significant aspects of the problem.

We can't solve problems by using the same kind of thinking we used when we created them.

—Albert Einstein

Look at the bright side, but don't look too long or you'll be blinded.

—Emily Stern

Chapter Eleven
The Danger of Relying on Old, Unproven Gauges and Answers

In the last chapters we have examined what antisemitism is, how it manifests itself, what purposes it serves, and how it impacts different regions and institutions. And we have begun the discussion of how to combat it in the twenty-first century.

How we understand any particular manifestation of antisemitism is critical to how we craft counterstrategies. But as we have seen in Chapter One, antisemitism can be motivated by religious teachings, by views on race, by political considerations, or a combination of these factors. People who practice one kind of antisemitism may not fall on the radar screen of the measurement of another kind.

Surveys

The attitudinal surveys we use to gauge antisemitism focus almost exclusively on individual attitudes toward "Jews" and concentrate on stereotypes. The benefit of these surveys, which have been used for decades, is that they offer comparative snapshots. They give a relative measurement, from one survey to the next. Traditionally, they ask the randomly surveyed respondents whether they agree or disagree with certain stereotypes about Jews. For example: "Jews stick together more than other Americans; Jews always like to be at the head of things;

Jews are more loyal to Israel than America; Jewish businesspeople are
so shrewd that others don't have a fair chance at competition; Jews
have too much power in the U.S. today," and six similar questions.
Those who agree with 0 or 1 are considered nonantisemitic. Those
who agree with 2-5 are considered in the "middle," and those who
agree with 6 or more of 11 items are deemed "most antisemitic."[1]

As important as these surveys are, they have some problems.
First, labeling a certain part of the population most antisemitic and
another part not (since most reporting neglects to mention the "middle" figures, which have hovered between 35 percent and 41 percent
in recent years), creates a black-and-white picture, when the reality
comes in shades of gray. Antisemitism is not like a light switch—either
it is on or off. Most people are probably somewhat antisemitic, just as
most people are probably somewhat racist or homophobic or sexist.

Second, as many of the examples in the preceding chapters illus-
trate, antisemitism is not merely a matter of individual attitudes. It
plays out in social and political settings. Social psychology teaches that
ordinary people who normally would not harm another person will do
so when put in the right environment. Recall Durban, which had the
flavor of an intellectual gang rape. It was partly enabled by those who
would likely not be labeled antisemitic by such a survey, yet in this
environment did not step forward to defend the victims.

Third, these surveys tend to look at Jews in isolation. It is one
thing to announce that a certain percent of the American population
think Jews have too much power—a classic stereotype. But does this
statistic resonate differently when one considers it in comparison to
other groups? For example, in 1982 a Roper survey showed respondents a list of groups and institutions, and asked which ones do "you
feel have too much power and influence over our country's policies?"
Eighteen percent said "Israel" and 14 percent said, "the Jews." While
8 percent said WASPS, 8 percent said Spanish-speaking Americans,
and 8 percent said the Catholic Church, 39 percent said labor unions,
and 46 percent said the Arab oil nations. Furthermore, 63 percent

listed the wealthy, 52 percent large business corporations, 36 percent organized crime, and 41 percent the press.

Fourth, individual attitudes, while important, are not the arbiter of the level of antisemitism. There is no true index, but in any country such an assessment must include the frequency of antisemitic acts, the general political tenor, the willingness of leaders to speak out denouncing antisemitism, the strength of antisemitic political groups, the capacity of law enforcement and the Jewish community to respond, the content and frequency of stories in the media that might impact antisemitism, and the climate on campuses and in other key institutions, among other factors.

Another problem with the polls became clear in 2002. An ADL poll found that 17 percent of the American population was antisemitic, but that only 3 percent of college students were. However, that year AJC, ADL, and most Jewish organizations were putting more energy and resources into combating campus antisemitism than they had in memory. Was this anomaly because the 3 percent were more active than the 17 percent? Perhaps. Or perhaps the attitudinal surveys were gauging one type of antisemitism when another was in play.

Whereas the classic religious-based or race-based antisemite might have a problem with the individual Jew, this is much less likely with the contemporary political (anti-Zionist) antisemite. He or she would not have a problem with living next door to a Jew or marrying a Jew. In the United States, he or she would see Jews as just as much a part of the social compact as anyone else. This person would not even necessarily have a problem with the collective "Jew," but would have a problem with the political expression of that collective, the State of Israel. In fact, some of the purveyors of anti-Zionism on campus are Jews.

The surveys, then, fail adequately to pick up this important type of antisemitism. We need new instruments which, while still being able to produce data to be compared with the historic figures, also give insights into the contemporary ways in which antisemitic attitudes are being formed and expressed.

Education

Another presumption that drives much of the antisemitism programming in the U.S. and abroad is the belief that anti-bias education in general, and Holocaust education in particular, are an antidote to antisemitism.[3] Touched on briefly in the introduction, this subject deserves fuller treatment here.

A few years before the collapse of the Middle East peace process, there was a series of attacks on immigrants and also on some Jews in Germany. AJC, which had produced a highly acclaimed anti-bias educational program called "Hands Across the Campus," was contemplating exporting this product to Germany. It was also considering the possibility of working with another U.S.-based educational organization, Facing History and Ourselves, to combat the problem of hateful youngsters engaging in violence against racial and religious minorities there.

One question was whether educational programs that used the Holocaust as part of their lesson plan would be transferable to Germany where the Holocaust was part of its national history. But an even more basic question was: How do we know these educational programs work?

Many well-received programs had been evaluated to gauge what the teachers thought of them, but none to see whether they worked on the students over time. The Carnegie Foundation had funded one short-term review of "Facing History." During one school year the study looked at 212 eighth-grade "Facing History" students, and compared them to 134 similar non-"Facing History" students.[4]

While the study focused mostly at the program's impact on violence, it also included a scale on racism. Leaving aside some problems with the scale—it included opposition to affirmative action as an indication of racism (which it could be, but need not be), its findings were intriguing. It found that girl students and those classified as "nonfighters" emerged from the program less racist, but it made no difference for boys, and (as with the control group) those classified as "fighters" actually became *more* racist while going through the program. There was also no follow-up to see if even the minimal positive effects on girls and nonfighters (clearly not the type who were causing Germans their problem, by the way) held over time.

Unfortunately, there are ample precedents for costly educational initiatives having no lasting impact. As Cookie Stephan, a professor of psychology at New Mexico State University at Las Cruces, noted in her paper, "The Evaluation of Multicultural Education Programs: Techniques and a Meta-Analysis,"[5] there have been highly praised school-based anti-smoking campaigns for over a quarter century, and one of the most extensive is that in Washington State. It uses puppet play about second-hand smoke in elementary school, role-play on saying "no" in middle school, and testimony from tobacco trials in high school. A fifteen-year study was conducted covering 8,400 students. The result? Those who went through the program were just as likely to smoke as those who did not.

Stephan also cited the DARE program, which stands for Drug Abuse Resistance Education, popularly known as "just say no." The program started in 1983. Three quarters of the elementary schools in the United States use it. Over $126 million has been spent on it. And it turns out, kids who went through this program were just as likely to use drugs as those who did not. As one commentator noted, what felt good did not do good.

Stephan conducted a meta-analysis of the small number of studies on anti-bias curricula. None of these were long-term studies, and her conclusion—that these curricula likely help reduce prejudice—is suspect because, as she herself points out, "It is almost certain that evaluations showing no or negative differences were conducted but did not see print."

She also stressed that there was little data on the differences between the programs. Some use texts; others, experiential models, for example. Some are used in one grade, some another. Even if these programs do work, there is too little data to direct an educator to choose which type of program, targeted to which gender, at which age level, would be the best investment.

Fighting hate in general, or antisemitism in particular, is a zero-sum game. Money spent on educational programs cannot be spent elsewhere. Is it possible that those concerned with changing bigoted attitudes and behavior are defaulting to a safe-sounding formula that may be doing no good at all?

Studying Hate

The presumption that underlies much of this educational activity is that people are somehow blank slates, and that they get polluted with hate along the way. It is presumed that if we could somehow stop them from being so poisoned, or after they are exposed, give them an antidote, there would be less hatred and antisemitism.

That presumption is wrong. Hate is normative. AJC has a poster of cuddly little babies of different skin color, all in diapers, over the caption "No One Is Born Hating." True. But no one is born speaking either. At a certain point, not speaking is considered odd. Hatred is normative, too. We may need help identifying whom to hate, but to hate comes naturally.

In 2004 Gonzaga University's Institute for Action against Hate held the first International Conference to Establish the Field of Hate Studies. The principle behind the conference was that hate is a normative part of the human experience. For as long as there have been people, regardless of when or where, or what the major religion, economic or political system was, people have always demonstrated the capacity to label someone an "other," and then hate him, sometimes with deadly results.

We have integrated, interdisciplinary fields of academic inquiry addressing other basic human conditions. People get sick, so we have a discipline of medicine that is more than its component parts, such as biology and chemistry. People need shelter, so we have an academic field of architecture that is more than its component parts of mathematics, physics, and art. People have also always found ways to hate each other. Antisemitism, of course, is one of the most persistent types of hate, but it is also a subset of this human capacity.

While there is much to be learned from the different disciplines, including psychology, social psychology, history, political science, sociology, and many others, each looks at hatred in frustrating isolation. Hatred is not only a matter of what is going on in a person's mind, or what happens when the person is in a social setting, or how groups or nations function. It operates on all these, as well as additional, planes at the same time, and there is a crying need for a discipline that looks at hatred comprehensively instead of piecemeal.

Such a discipline will be critically involved in analyzing educational programs that supposedly reduce prejudice and/or antisemitism. Before we throw more money into these educational programs, simply on unproven faith that somehow they work, we need to make sure they do, and that their impacts are not short-lived, but hold over time. And if some of them do indeed work over time, we need to then ask which models work best (text-driven, experiential, etc.), at what ages, and in what environments.[6] And if it is proven that antibias education works, then it must a part of basic education. (We would not have outside groups come into schools and teach the only reading or math to which students were exposed, a program here, a lesson there. If there are educational tools that are proven to work, they should be part of the basic curricula.)

The challenge is that the providers of these programs, honestly believing they work, would rather put money into programs than evaluation. They also know that these endeavors are good public relations vehicles and money-raisers. And they are aware that a negative review would be devastating. Since they are not likely to test their own product, outside reviews need to be conducted. As the field of hate studies is becoming established, one of its first concrete projects should be a long-term study of anti-bias and Holocaust-related education.

Current Challenges

But even if hate studies scholars, or some other institution, undertakes such a study in the years ahead, what should we be doing now? At the present there is no proof that these programs work, and some evidence that they may be painting pictures of Jews that make it more difficult to unpack and challenge the contemporary ways in which anti-semitism is expressed.

At a minimum, until it is shown that Holocaust education pro-grams actually work, it is imperative that Jewish agencies and other institutions, such as the U.S. State Department, stop recommending Holocaust education as an antidote for antisemitism (as opposed to recommending it as important history with important historical les-sons to be learned). If educational initiatives are to be undertaken in the U.S., France, and other countries, they must address antisemitism in all its varieties, not simply the Holocaust. The vilification of live Jews, not only dead ones, needs to be the focus.[7]

Furthermore, because it is "politically correct" to prescribe Holo-caust education as a cure for antisemitism, Jewish agencies and well-intentioned people in the U.S. government are allowing countries that have a real problem with antisemitism too easy an out.

In France, for example, the main problem facing the Jewish community is multilayered. Its outward expression is the vilification of Jews and Israel by imams and others within the Muslim community, but further inside is a tradition of antisemitism that now finds its vent hole mostly regarding the State of Israel. France is certainly not an antisemitic country, but in recent years the question of whether French Jews are fully accepted inside the social compact is once again being raised.

These are real problems, but are they being adequately addressed by the promotion of Holocaust education? The evidence, particularly among progressives in Western Europe, is that the imagery of the Holocaust has become the stock tool of those *promoting* antisemitism. As Yehoshua Amishav wrote in *Ha'aretz*:[8]

> The dramatic development of the past three years is that blaming Israel, and condemnation of Jews' support for Israel, are based with increasing frequency on the use of the memory of the Holocaust.... This phenomenon is so widespread that a spokesman for the Israeli Embassy in Belgium asked two years ago that Yad Vashem discontinue the ceremonies for honoring the "Righteous of the Nations" (non-Jews who saved Jews during the Holocaust), because at almost every ceremony there was an incident involving ... disgraceful comparisons by one of the participants [along the lines of] ... "You are doing to the Palestinians what they did to you in the Holocaust."

This trend is not the result of poor teaching about the Holocaust, but the failure to address contemporary antisemitism and to show how images associated with the Holocaust are used to promote bigotry. The real educational challenge is how to teach about today's antisemitism, and how to evaluate that teaching over time to make sure it is having an impact.

It is unfortunate that an otherwise exceptionally valuable State Department Report on Global Antisemitism suggested that countries that have real problems with resurgent antisemitism should be praised, not for their response to these challenges, but for educating about or memorializing the Holocaust. Perhaps the schizophrenia of this approach was nowhere more apparent than in the report's section on Sweden, which noted both a dramatic increase in antisemitic hate crimes and the perception of the Jewish community that these incidents were linked to immigrant populations, leftists, and events in the Middle East. Yet the State Department document observed approvingly that "the Government took steps to combat antisemitism by increasing awareness of Nazi crimes and the Holocaust."[9] Meanwhile, not mentioned in the report were Swedish rallies that demonized

Israel and a riot by anti-Israel protestors at an Israel festival.[10]

A third, related, problem is that some organizations tend to focus uncritically on "new" vent holes for antisemitism, and highlight them, both for programming and fund-raising purposes, without a sufficient analysis of how significant they really are.

The Internet is a prime example. The first "hate" Web site, created by David Duke's protégé, Don Black, appeared in 1995. According to various estimates, there are probably about 4,000 hate sites worldwide.[11] There is no doubt that the Internet has provided haters a new and easier, interactive means of communication. It has also provided them with a sense of community and power that is clearly disproportionate to their numbers. But how significant are these sites?

While there are some terrible things on them, most antisemitism monitoring groups point to the number of sites, rather than to the more important quantity: How frequently are they visited? If there were a library with a million books, but ten visitors a day, and another with 10,000 books, but 500 visitors each day, which would have the larger real world impact?

In reality, these sites get very little traction. What is more, the total number of Web sites available today on the Internet is over one hundred million. Four thousand hate sites is a very small number.

The undue harping about hate sites on the Internet means there are fewer resources for other initiatives to combat more urgent, real-world problems of antisemitism. Which is more important, temporarily blocking a Web site with a collection of lies about Jews that have to be searched out to access (and that, if blocked, will likely reappear under another URL), or encouraging European countries better to address the challenge of foreign-funded imams teaching a growing segment of European society to see Jews in demonic terms? When Jewish groups claim that the Internet is a front-burner problem, European countries reluctant to face more urgent challenges are given license to avoid addressing them. Following our direction, they often choose the wrong target.

For example, the major conference held in recent years on hate and the Internet was in Paris in 2004, sponsored by the French government through OSCE. In France, where a wave of antisemitic violence started in 2000, the government wanted to do something to counter hate. But there was also a subtext to the conference: Many of the hate sites were run through American servers, so here was a way to blame the U.S. for a problem. The French, of course, wanted to have hate sites—including those based in America—banned, in violation of the First Amendment to the U.S. Constitution. Americans, of course, would not go along.

Saner voices prevailed at the conference—those focusing on what the countries could do in common, such as asking providers to enforce codes of conduct, monitoring, developing Web sites that expose haters and counter hatred, etc. But what was startling—though not surprising—is that no one could give a single example of someone committing a real-world hate crime, antisemitic or otherwise, because of the Internet, despite the conference's title: "OSCE Meeting on the Relationship between Racist, Xenophobic and Anti-Semitic Propaganda on the Internet and Hate Crimes."

Of course, the Internet should be of concern because it is used for transmitting encrypted messages for terrorists and other illegal matters. It should certainly be monitored for hate and antisemitism. And while there are some indications that certain white supremacist online forums[12] and new online gaming programs are growing concerns, the suggestion that it is either *the* or *a* major problem in contemporary hatred is as misplaced as suggesting that books or movies are the "cause" of the problem. Since there is no practical way to hide hatred on the Internet, to the extent that it is a real problem, let us develop curricula that teach youngsters how to identify and reject hate in this new medium.[13]

New Challenges for Jewish Communal Organizations

Unlike other communities that struggle to have even one or two communal defense agencies, the American Jewish community is blessed with many, most of which do very valuable work. But none of these organizations are immune from organizational challenges, competing pulls, and contradictions. All sincerely believe that their programs work, but do not have sufficient resources devoted to long-term testing to evaluate whether they are effective. These agencies are not like drug companies, which will be held accountable if they cannot prove that there is a reason to believe their products produce results.

Fighting antisemitism wisely requires making sure that the strategies selected fit the circumstances in which they will operate, and that presumptions about what will be effective are based as much as possible on proof and not belief. It is critically important that resources not be squandered on attractive-sounding, but ultimately ineffective initiatives. Jewish agencies should consider setting aside a portion of their budgets for thorough, long-term evaluation of their projects, solicit grant money to do so, or consider other ways of achieving this goal.

Those who combat antisemitism and bigotry in the years to come can ill afford to make assumptions based on faith rather than solid research. Jewish communal agencies should model how to integrate research into programs, and should insist on long-term evaluation of effectiveness of any initiative designed to change attitudes or behavior.

In 2050, there will be three times as many people living here as in 1960—420 million. White Americans will be a minority, 49 percent, and falling. Hispanics in the United States, over 100 million, will be equal to the entire population of Mexico today. Our Asian population will be almost as large as our African-American population today.

—Patrick Buchanan[1]

The Jewish population in the U.S. will drop from 5.7 million in 2000 to 5.6 million in 2020, to 4.7 million in 2050 and 3.8 million in 2080.

—Data from the *2000 American Jewish Year Book*[2]

Chapter Twelve
Looking Ahead in the United States

What is the battle against antisemitism likely to be in the near future?

No one has a crystal ball. Few in 1999 would have anticipated the implications of the collapse of the Middle East peace process, the level of the antisemitism at Durban, or the attacks of September 11, 2001. These "trigger" events are never easy to foretell. Nor can anyone fully predict the timing of other events that might, at least, have some moderating effect, perhaps ratcheting down the volume of demonization of Jews and Israel (such as a reinvigorated peace process).[3]

However, other things are predictable. In the United States, there will be significant demographic changes. By the year 2050, the American Jewish community will probably be smaller than it is today, both in real numbers and, even more so, as a percentage of the overall population. It is likely that this smaller community will have fewer resources and greater challenges. If the projections for 2050 hold true, America will then be majority nonwhite. For most Americans this change will likely be irrelevant, or even positive. But just as we have seen the rise of anti-immigrant and racist parties and personalities in Europe, something similar could occur here.

Christian Identity and Christian Patriotism

There are ideologies and theologies afloat that might provide some attraction to those who fear a nonwhite majority.[4] At the extreme are the views that animated the movers and shakers of the militia movement in the 1990s, namely Christian Identity and Christian Patriotism.

Christian Identity is an offshoot of British Israelism, a nineteenth-century theology that claimed that the residents of the British Isles were descendants of the lost tribes of Israel. This theology was embraced and then distorted by some leading American antisemites in the early part of the twentieth century. In its most basic formulation, Christian Identity preaches that there were two creations—a failed creation, which resulted in people of color, and a successful creation, which produced Adam and Eve. Eve, impregnated by Adam, produced Abel, whose descendants were white Nordic, Aryan people. Eve, impregnated by Satan, produced Cain, whose descendants are those people known today as Jews. This theology preaches, therefore, that nonwhites are subhuman (called "mud people"), and that Jews are literally Satanic.

While Christian Identity is a fringe phenomenon, it has had an impact. Some of the most important militia leaders were Christian Identity adherents.

Christian Patriotism is akin to Christian Identity, except that it is a uniquely American phenomenon. (One can be a Christian Identity adherent in Australia, Great Britain, etc.) Christian Patriotism preaches that the United States is the biblical Promised Land—promised, of course, to whites. It views the Constitution and the Bill of Rights as scripture, and the post-Bill of Rights amendments as in derogation of God's design. Thus equal rights for all people and citizenship for anyone born in the United States (the Fourteenth Amendment), suffrage for women (the Nineteenth Amendment), and the other post-Bill of Rights amendments are sacrilege. Terry Nichols, one of the Oklahoma City bombers, was a Christian Patriot.

While neither of these theologies/ideologies are likely to become mainstream, it is possible that they will pick up more adherents in the decades to come, because they make people feel that they are fighting for the survival of their "race," in service of God, against Jews and people of color, and the government that dares give members of such groups equal protection of the law. As mentioned earlier, Ken Toole, head of the Montana Human Rights Network and a state senator, described the militia movement during its heyday as a "funnel moving through space." At the wide end of the funnel, he saw everyday people being attracted by issues such as gun control, the intrusiveness of the federal government, and environmental regulations. A bit further in the funnel, people were being animated by conspiracy theories, including antisemitic ones. At the tip of the funnel were those who were eager to act on their beliefs, such as a Timothy McVeigh. The importance of this model is that it predicts that the greater the number of people at the outer stages of the funnel, the more pressure there will be for people to come out the small end.

History also shows that racist and antisemitic paramilitary groups are a part of American history—they were present in the 1920s with the KKK, in the 1960s with the Minutemen, in the 1970-80s with the Posse Comitatus, and in the 1990s with the militia movement. The likelihood is that they will appear again (some associated with the new anti-immigrant Minutemen have this pedigree), but if there is a more generalized fear of America's changing demographics, they might get more traction.

Additionally, while such movements will still likely be on the fringes, they will also have two other impacts. First, in smaller rural communities, racist groups from time to time have had disproportionate influence, whether electing public officials or running radio stations. While what happens in small towns in Montana and Idaho will not be noticed on the national stage, it can make life very difficult for people in those small communities.

Secondly, history also teaches that "beyond the pale" ideas pushed by fringe groups frequently get picked up by mainstream politicians, both because they see these issues as ones likely to work for them, and because they want to steal the thunder of those who are challenging their leadership.

The basic premise of these far-right extremist groups, as well as other such white supremacists, is that people of color pose a mortal danger to the survival of whites, and that Jews are behind this nefarious plot to destroy whites by promoting affirmative action, equal rights, and immigration, among other initiatives.

Immigration

Given the attacks of September 11, and the extreme likelihood that we will face such attacks again, it is also likely that those pushing an anti-immigrant line will be able to draw some people into their movement from the starting point of fear of terrorism, just as some of the militia types used the issue of gun ownership rights. It would not be surprising, therefore, to see a growing anti-immigrant movement gain steam in the decades ahead, and such a movement would be a vehicle through which much antisemitism and racism would be promoted.

What can be done about this? First, advocates, NGOs, and the media must ensure that people understand the difference between adequate and reasonable security measures to control who comes into our country, on the one hand, and racist exclusionary policies on the other. Secondly, they must expose those who would try to abuse people's fears to promote their own antisemitic and racist agendas. And thirdly, they should pay special attention to, and when appropriate work closely with Hispanic groups, who will likely face the most serious challenges on this issue in the years ahead from hate crimes, ballot initiatives, responding to politicians' speeches, media, etc.

Jewish groups are already cooperating on a variety of issues with Hispanics, and have created a Latino-Jewish Coalition. Working with other ethnic groups is especially important when addressing race-based antisemitism, as in the far-right racist movement, because all minority groups are targets, and can most effectively address these dangers in coalition.

But there is another reason, too. Survey data have shown Hispanics to be one of the more antisemitic subgroups in America, with new immigrants more antisemitic than those who have been in the United States for a time.[5] Recall that the surveys only look at attitudes derived from a standard index of anti-Jewish stereotypes. And note also that Hispanics come predominately from the heavily Catholic societies in Latin America, where the teachings of Vatican II have not penetrated as well as in other countries.

By such forward-looking initiatives as the Latino-Jewish Coalition, programs will be put in place to help counteract religious-based antisemitism within the Latino community, and address any Jewish groups that come under the sway of racist anti-immigrant appeals. Such a collaborative enterprise can productively combat all forms of antisemitism and bigotry. (Some of the Latino members of Latino-Jewish dialogue groups have traveled to Israel and are effective within their own communities debunking anti-Zionism.)

Hate Speech

If racism and antisemitism become stronger in the U.S. in the decades to come, especially when people are scared by acts of terror, it is likely there will be voices advocating suppression of freedom of speech. This is a very dangerous and usually counterproductive tact.

While clear appeals to, and incitement of, *imminent* violence against anyone is illegal, most racist and antisemitic incitement—while bone-chilling—is nonetheless protected speech. Only in the clearest, most extreme cases, should suppression be allowed.[6]

It is not the purpose of this book to argue the merits of the First

Amendment, or to question the laws in other democratic countries that attempt to limit speech for, among other reasons, the spread of bigotry. The problems with suppressing speech in the United States[7] are threefold.[8] First, such attempts would change the public debate from the bigotry expressed to that of the rights of the haters. Second, the debate about the suppression of the bigot's speech will actually give the bigot free publicity. And third, while laws are one part of the battle of bigotry, they tend to be a black hole, sucking away the awareness of and willingness to pursue other vehicles that might have better effect.

This debate has been engaged in one form or another since 1977, when the ACLU defended the rights of neo-Nazis to march in Skokie, Illinois. Over the decades many lesser known marches by white supremacists were held, and the communities have generally tried two different approaches (besides the tactic of trying to deny the haters a permit, which frequently ends up in a losing court suit): 1) encouraging businesses and others to close down during the march, effectively "pulling up the sidewalks" and figuratively turning their backs on the haters; 2) counterevents—either counterprotests (which are risky since they always have the potential for violence) or the holding of a community event against hatred in some other location.

While each of these tactics has its benefits, a group in Pennsylvania came up with another approach in the late 1990s. Faced with a neo-Nazi rally, the community decided to solicit donations, pledges tied to how long the hate fest ran. The longer it went on, the more money would be raised for community programs against hatred, police hate crime training, and the like. This brilliant tactic, while respecting the free speech rights of the bigots, actually inflicted a cost. Ten people might show up at the rally, but they would in effect raise thousands of dollars for initiatives that would be the haters' worst nightmare.

The beauty of this approach is that it understood that, except in the exceptionally rare case, hateful speech cannot be suppressed. Instead of fighting a losing battle and giving the haters a victory (and publicity for their message), they instead organized the community against hatred, gave people something they could do, raised money for combating bigotry, and created not only a dilemma for the haters, but actually a deterrent from holding future rallies.

This model, called Project Lemonade, has been used by other communities with success in recent years. Its broader use, in other situations in which hateful movements use public forums, would be much more effective than attempts at suppression.[9]

Further, attempts at prohibiting speech not only backfire, they also give an excuse for people in authority to disengage from the more difficult things they should be doing. For example, in the late 1980s and early 1990s, there was an attempt to impose "hate speech" codes on college campuses. Aside from their constitutional impossibilities, and their practical problems,[10] they were a subterfuge. College administrators could point to a rule saying "thou shall not say hateful things," and assert they were effectively dealing with bigotry and intergroup tension on campus. The real problems, of course, lay in lack of training of students and staff, absence of infrastructure for reporting incidents of hate, no clear understanding of what was supposed to happen when an incident occurred, failure to review the curricula, lack of a survey of intergroup tensions, and the reality that many students came to campus without having experienced living with students who were different from themselves.

Middle East Triggers

Another concern is whether events in or related to the Middle East will be a "trigger" for antisemitism in the U.S. This has been an historic fear of the Jewish community, but one which—while real—should not be overstated. Recall that during the Arab oil crisis of the 1970s, there was a concern that Jews would be blamed for the long lines and high prices at gas stations. They were not. Americans understood that the Arab regimes were responsible.

Yet, in recent years, tensions in the Middle East in general, and specific incidents relating to Israel, have been the backdrop for increased articulation of two antisemitic canards, one which combines claims of Jewish "dual loyalty" with visions of inordinate Jewish power; the other, a left-wing/religious-based singling out of Israel.

It was one thing for Pat Buchanan and Ralph Nader to talk of Jewish "cabals" and Israeli "puppeteers," but in the controversial lead-up to the second Iraq war,[11] many looked for someone to blame, and the answer for some was the "neoconservatives."

"Neocons," a shorthand term meaning "neoconservatives," were indeed among the intellectual architects of the war, including such people as Richard Perle, Douglas Feith, and Paul Wolfowitz. While many neocons are not Jewish, many are, and they are very clear in their support of Israel and their belief that it is good for both America and Israel if there is an increase in democracy in the Middle East.

That this group has some intellectual capacity to influence events in the Bush administration is without question, as President George Bush is himself a neocon. But there is a clear distinction between recognizing that the president sees the world in much the same way as a group with a distinct ideology, on the one hand, and the claim that outside think tanks and midlevel government officials somehow have taken control of the government, and that non-Jews in leadership positions when the decision to go to war against Iraq was made—President Bush, Vice President Dick Cheney, Secretary of State Colin Powell, National Security Advisor Condoleezza Rice, Secretary of Defense Donald Rumsfeld—were not making their own decisions, and instead were controlled by a group of Jews.

As mentioned earlier, this is a "lite" version of the *Protocols'* claim of a Jewish cabal, and the white supremacist assertion that the U.S. is secretly ruled by a "Zionist Occupied Government." It is "lite" because it does not necessarily presuppose a long-running, continuing, all-encompassing secret Jewish control over government, but rather claims such powers over particular government officials or policies under more narrow parameters. Nonetheless, the similarities—both in the tropes and the dangerous promoting of vilification of Jews—are real.

Such assertions became more commonplace in early 2003, typified by a claim by Congressman James P. Moran (D-VA) that "[i]f it were not for the strong support of the Jewish community for this war with Iraq, we would not be doing this." Secretary of State Colin Powell actually had to tell a House Appropriations Subcommittee: "The strategy with respect to Iraq has derived from our interests in the region and our support of UN resolutions over time. It is not driven by any small cabal that is buried away somewhere, that is telling President Bush or me or Vice President Cheney or [National Security Adviser] Condoleezza Rice or other members of the administration what our policies should be."

While such claims died down right after Saddam Hussein was defeated, they show signs of building again as U.S. troops remain in Iraq and things continue to go poorly. Likewise, if there is another terror attack in the U.S. and the perpetrators claim it is in retaliation for U.S. Middle East policy, or if a real peace process should ever emerge and it seems that the Israelis are not being forthcoming, the rumblings against Jewish political power may again be heard.[12]

In March 2006, two professors, John J. Mearsheimer and Stephen M. Walt, wrote a paper entitled *The Israel Lobby and U.S. Foreign Policy*, which was part of a series of "working papers" coming out of Harvard University's John F. Kennedy School of Government. While it would be unfair to dismiss the entire paper as antisemitic, it did contain whiffs of antisemitism in places, especially when it accused "the Lobby" of "[c]ontrolling the debate ... because a candid discussion of U.S.-Israeli relations might lead Americans to favor a different policy," and when it chose subheadings such as "The Tail Wagging the Dog."[13]

The problem with the Mearsheimer-Walt paper was not that it

raised the question of whether support of Israel was a logical American policy or that it examined the lobbying tactics of Israel's supporters. Rather, it suffered from substandard scholarship throughout (for example, simply asserting that support for Israel is against the U.S.'s interest, without citation of facts or giving a detailed analysis), and from the inevitable progression of dogmatic thinking. Walt and Mearsheimer firmly believe that Israel is a strategic liability and a state of questionable legitimacy that commits regular acts of repression. They cannot fathom that they might be wrong in their opinions, and cannot understand why the vast majority of Americans do not share their point of view, particularly about the Israeli-Palestinian conflict.[14] Since they are in their own minds so right, and everyone else so wrong, the only explanation plausible in the closed intellectual model they have constructed is that some unfair play must be involved: Enter the "Israel Lobby."

The long-term problem posed by the paper is not its scholarly or political errors so much as its diminishing of two taboos: accusing Jews of "dual loyalty" and undermining the legitimacy of Israel as a Jewish state. It was not only people such as neo-Nazi David Duke who endorsed the paper, but also intellectual figures such as Tony Judt, known for advocating that Israel be dismantled as a Jewish state.

Divestment and Boycott

The other foreseeable problem in the domestic battles over the Middle East is the move for divestment. As detailed in the chapter on the campus, this attempt to "South Africanize" Israel has not been successful. However, in 2004 the Presbyterian Church U.S.A. passed a resolution at its General Assembly, endorsing a program of selected and targeted divestment from companies doing business in Israel (such as Caterpillar, which supplies bulldozers that Israel has used to demolish the houses of the families of suicide bombers). There was concern, of course, that this action would mainstream and legitimize broader divestment and boycott schemes. While there have been some troubling developments, the situation is not as bad as had been feared for two reasons.

First, the organized Jewish community for the most part thought strategically and acted wisely. It did not throw out labels like "antisemitic," but reached out to the Presbyterians—and to other churches that might be influenced by the divestment decision—for renewed dialogue and discussion. Many Presbyterians began to understand that they had made an error in not discussing this issue with their Jewish cohorts, to get their views, before the matter came to a vote. Leaders of other religious groups vowed not to make the same mistake. The Episcopalian Church rejected divestment solely against Israel, and promised to consider both Palestinian terrorism and Israeli actions in the West Bank and Gaza in any new investment policy.

Rather than walk away from or condemn the Presbyterians, Jewish leaders reengaged with them and helped them to understand not only why Jews have a problem with such one-sided resolutions, but also how both communities really have the same goal—peace and security for both the Jewish State of Israel and for the Palestinian people, in a two-state solution. And the Jewish interlocutors emphasized that divestment is likely to hurt that goal, rather than help it, by encouraging the extremists.

This type of response makes sense. It understands the type of antisemitism (in this case, a combination of religious-based views with left ideology, but mixed with clearly non-antisemitic values, such as theological notions about the meek inheriting the earth, landless gaining land, and so forth). And it comprehends the institutions in play as well as the tools to impact them.

But success on the divestment front has not been uniform. The United Church of Christ, for example, considered a divestment resolution in summer 2005. It invited Dr. David Elcott, then U.S. director for Interreligious Affairs of the American Jewish Committee, to address its meeting, and the committee proposal that emerged thereafter spoke about the positive uses of economic leverage to promote opportunities for peace. Yet the resolution that was finally adopted by the synod was somewhere in between the Presbyterian document and the milder one offered by the UCC committee. It spoke about rejecting violence, but then termed the "occupation" as a manifestation of violence. And it advocated "divesting" from those companies that "refuse to change their practice of gain from the perpetuation of violence."[15] The document, however, did acknowledge the right of Israel to exist, deplored violence against its people, and condemned suicide bombings.

The UCC also passed a second resolution, entitled "Tear Down the Wall,"[16] which called for the dismantling of Israel's separation barrier, and in so doing, rejected an earlier draft that had called instead for the relocation of the barrier to land inside the "Green Line," meaning on the Israeli side of the 1948 armistice boundaries. While reflecting concerns for the disruption of the lives of Palestinians by the barrier, the document ignored the utility of a barrier in stopping suicide bombers from killing Israelis. There is certainly a religious theme in breaking down barriers, but where was the religious value in protecting lives? Barriers, after all, can be moved, while dead is dead.

Part of the challenge with the UCC was that, while there was a growing understanding of Jewish concerns among the laity from the significant grassroots dialogues, the leadership was concerned with responding to the agenda of church members from the Middle East who were pushing the divestment strategy.

While the UCC resolutions were both not as bad as they could have been, they were nonetheless disturbing, partly for their naivete, but also because—as with the other divestment and boycott initiatives—they reflect a psychological discomfort with the notion of Jews with power, let alone guns, which seems to be a recurring theme among some religious and progressive groups.

It is clear that before, and even in the immediate aftermath of, the 1967 war, there was great sympathy for Israelis from many on the left and progressive religious leaders, because Jews were indeed vulnerable, and the Holocaust was recent history.[17] But soon after 1967 the image of Israel became one of a militarized, racist, colonialist enterprise that oppressed Palestinians. Part of this was a result of the Cold War, and the push by the Soviet Union to curry favor with its Arab allies by claiming that Israel, an ally of the United States, was inherently racist. Part was driven by Marxist ideology, which saw Zionism not only as a colonial and racist idea, but also a movement that steered Jews away from the "truths" of socialism and communism.[18] But others, including many religiously affiliated but less dogmatically driven people, were nonetheless clearly uncomfortable with the notion of the Jew as powerful. This was especially so in the early 1980s, when Israel went into Lebanon in response to attacks by Palestinian terrorists, who were using the country as a base of operations. Rather than challenging the wisdom of Israeli policy, many church groups and others on the left began with the assumption that Israel's goals were always to oppress Palestinians and steal land. There was both antisemitic language about "Zionist control" of media, banks, governments, and so forth, as well as immoral equivalencies (terrorists targeting civilians on one side and a government trying to protect it citizens from harm by military means on the other) that are still prevalent today.

How to counteract this psychological problem, as well as the "politically correct" view among much of the left that Israel is the new apartheid is a difficult challenge. (Google "Israeli apartheid" and see how many hits you get.) Some are perplexed that the boycott/divestment movement has gained a degree of momentum during the time there was progress in the peace process, between Arafat's death and the electoral victory of Hamas. Clearly, when issues are seen in good-and-evil terms, political progress does not matter much, if at all.

The tools that have some chance of working against this unfair demonizing of Israel include grassroots organizing among the church and other institutions likely to take up the divestment/boycott issue, and legal measures when appropriate. It is no coincidence that the

UK's Association of University Teachers, which passed resolutions boycotting two Israeli universities in 2005, reversed itself only weeks later after one of them (the University of Haifa) and some individual AUT members filed notice that they might sue, the former for defamation, the latter because the AUT's bylaws did not allow it to take such actions. (The latter claimed that the AUT action put individual members in an untenable position, perhaps having to break contracts to abide by their union's policies, and thus the group's leadership might be personally liable for damages.) Whereas beforehand there was no potential cost, political or otherwise, for bigoted and improper actions, the legal threat imposed one.[19]

While political events in the Middle East might push the issue of divestment and boycott either more into the background or the foreground, the lesson is clear that there has to be continued engagement with those who are hearing distorted and ideologically driven messages that paint Israel as always in the wrong. Additionally, while there is little utility in branding whole religious movements as antisemitic, the members and leaders of these movements should be helped better to understand the problematic bases on which many of their assumptions lie, and should be concerned that, if they engage in activities that have potential legal costs, those costs will be exacted.

Physical Security

One other concern is the level of physical security of American Jewish institutions. That Jewish institutions are, and will likely remain, targets is no surprise, given the ideologies and theologies of antisemitism afloat, and the fact that a lone hater or small group can inflict great damage. Buford Furrow shot up the Jewish Community Center in Los Angeles in August 1999. Al-Qaeda material found after the war in Afghanistan mentioned the names and addresses of some American Jewish organizations.

Whenever an attack takes place, or a plot is exposed, the Jewish community focuses on the safety of its people and structures for a week or two, debating the level of security versus freedom appropriate for institutions. Then it seemingly moves on to other things. The American Jewish community lags far behind Jews in many parts of the globe, especially those in Great Britain, in creating an infrastructure to analyze security needs, provide protection, create immediate means of communication (both to share information about threats and to debunk rumors), and to deter attacks. Rather, the U.S. Jewish community relies largely on handbooks, manuals, and optimism.

One hopeful sign of increased realism and preparedness is the creation of the Secure Community Alert Network (SCAN) by the Conference of Presidents of Major American Jewish Organizations, which gives Jewish leaders across the country the ability to communicate immediately in a time of crisis and to receive information about imminent threats. But much more needs to be done, and the concern is that American Jews will not fully address this need until after some horrendous attack.

Finally, when we tackle antisemitism in the United States in the decades ahead, it will be in an America which will likely again be victimized by terrorism and challenged by other new circumstances and unanticipated trigger events. It will also be an America that will be figuring out how to approach monumental demographic changes. One demographic change will likely be the shrinkage of the American Jewish population and the growth of other groups (including Muslims and Arabs). Thus Jews can no longer afford to react in knee-jerk fashion, but rather need to understand the type of antisemitism being expressed, the institutions impacted by its expression, and the limitations of what can and cannot be done, and to use fully the opportunities that each instance offers.

Antisemitism, following its most devastating manifestation during the Holocaust, has assumed new forms and expressions, which, along with other forms of intolerance, pose a threat to democracy, the values of civilization and, therefore, to overall security in the OSCE region and beyond.

—OSCE Berlin Declaration

Chapter Thirteen
Conclusion

Unfortunately, there are reasons to be less hopeful about combating antisemitism abroad, especially in Europe. The demographic changes sweeping the continent, the long history of antisemitism, and the animus toward Israel (based partly on left-wing politics and partly on a post-Second World War psychology, wherein European guilt will be lessened if Israelis are cast as oppressors) make this a difficult problem. Some demographers have noted that the number of Jews in Europe is decreasing, with people moving to what are already the two great population centers for Jews in the world, the U.S. and Israel. This is a sad but real prospect, after millennia of a Jewish presence in Europe.

While there are reasons for concern about antisemitism in many parts of Europe, there are some encouraging signs. Rather than cataloging and rating all the initiatives that organizations and governmental institutions have been using to combat antisemitism, it is useful to highlight one promising structure through which many hopes are now being aligned, largely due to the efforts of an unheralded American diplomat named Stephen Minikes.

OSCE

Minikes was the U.S. ambassador to the Organization for Security and Cooperation in Europe (OSCE) from 2001 to 2005. There are, as he explained it, three multilateral groups that focus on Europe. One is

NATO, which includes the U.S. but not Russia. Another is the European Union, which does not include the United States. And the third is OSCE, to which both belong.

Shortly after the rash of antisemitic crimes began after the collapse of the peace process in 2000, Minikes set about the task of putting antisemitism squarely on the OSCE agenda. To understand the difficulties that entailed, know that the OSCE is a consensus-run organization. It can only take steps if all fifty-six countries that belong agree. Yet, through incredible diplomatic skill, Minikes was able to get the OSCE to hold a conference on antisemitism in Vienna in 2003. It was followed by a major conference on this issue in 2004 in Berlin, which resulted in an historic "Berlin Declaration,"[1] which not only addressed the easier religious and racial types of antisemitism, but also noted that "international developments or political issues, including those in Israel or elsewhere in the Middle East, never justify anti-Semitism." Such a statement might seem self-evident, but its inclusion in a European document about antisemitism was an important milestone.

However, declarations, no matter how historic, are only words until they are implemented. And while it is too early to tell whether OSCE will succeed, there are some indications that it may.

First, its Office for Democratic Institutions and Human Rights (known as ODIHR) was tasked with the responsibility to monitor and report on antisemitic incidents in the region. Second, it searched out "best practices" around the region for combating antisemitism.[2] Third, it has launched a project by current and former police officers, experts in hate crimes, to train European police officials on the best means of investigating and prosecuting such offenses, and already has done so in Spain, Hungary, the Ukraine, and Croatia. And fourth, it has created a special representative of the chair in office to oversee issues relating to antisemitism. Very fortunately, the person selected for this position, German parliamentarian Gert Weisskirchen, has a fire in his belly for this issue, and is held in great respect by many European leaders.

Rather than merely bemoan the situation in Europe, or as some have done, propose boycotts of countries where antisemitic attacks have occurred,[3] Minikes took the approach of using the institutions on the ground in Europe and soliciting them for the fight against antisemitism. There are many challenges, including assuring adequate funding for these OSCE initiatives and the continued reluctance of some OSCE member states to target antisemitism. But for the first time in history, an official of a quasi-governmental organization in Europe has responsibility to make sure that antisemitism is monitored and combated, and there is a growing structure for this work that may need protection, but at least no longer has to be created.

Diplomacy

Diplomacy will be one of the key tools in combating antisemitism in the years ahead. For the last decade or more, the American Jewish Committee has held meetings with foreign and prime ministers of scores of countries, especially in conjunction with the opening of each annual United Nations session. Each discussion is an opportunity to express and hear concerns and to forge relationships.[4] While antisemitism is not always dealt with as well as one would hope in the multinational forum of the UN, it usually is approached better internally as a result of these contacts. (Many of these countries also have developed good bilateral relations with Israel.) One irony, of course, is that the willingness of some countries to meet with AJC is no doubt traceable to an antisemitic assumption—that the key to Washington is somehow through the American Jewish community.[5]

While, as we have seen, there has been some progress in combating antisemitism in Europe in recent years, much more needs to be done there and beyond. What happens in the Arab and Muslim worlds not only resonates in those societies, but also impacts Europe, since many Middle Eastern countries have both imported the story lines of European anti-Semitism and also exported them back.

Consider some of the reactions in the Arab press to the U.S. Global Antisemitism Awareness Act, comments that not only resonate in the Middle East, but also reach an audience among Europe's growing Muslim population.

Muhammad Al-Samak, writing in the Egyptian government publication *Al-Ahram*, declared:

> [This definition] establishes a new reality in international relations, which divides the world into two axes—one that is accused of antisemitism, which includes the Islamic world, the Catholic world (Latin America), the Orthodox world (Russia), the Buddhist world (China), and the secular world (the European Union); and another opposing antisemitism, which includes only the U.S. and Israel. Implementing this American law will answer the question of whether this policy will manage to fight or at least calm antisemitism, or in igniting it across the world—not out of hatred for Jews, but out of resentment of Israel and the U.S.[6]

Columnist Ghazi Al-Aridhi, writing for the Saudi daily *Al-Riyadh*, opined:

> The Israeli intelligence apparatuses have carried out operations against Jewish targets in France, with the aim of blaming the Muslims and frightening and unsettling French Jews [so as to] underline that they must leave France for their motherland, Israel.... The [Global Antisemitism Review] Act enables Israel, by means of its [security] apparatuses, to carry out any operation against Jewish institutions or individuals across the world, and to blame its "enemies" [for it].[7]

While, as explained before, the United States must do more to combat the antisemitism in the Arab and Muslim worlds—such as complain about and exact a cost for the vilification of Israelis and Jews, as well as work to reduce America's dependency on foreign oil—this long-term challenge is not one for America alone. Europe must also play a part by pressing through diplomatic channels its rejection of foreign-funded imams coming to European soil and preaching hatred. This is a tall order, considering the European connection with its many former colonies, the internal demographics, and the constant drumbeat of anti-Israel rhetoric in the media and elsewhere. But one hope for the OSCE initiative is that it will help Europeans better understand the dangers of antisemitism to their own societies, and to see this not as a matter of pronouncements from the U.S. or Jewish NGOs, but as emerging from their own internal institutions.

Europe also has to condemn acts of terror against Israelis with the same vigor that it treats the increasing incidence of terror against its own citizens. As long as Europeans give the impression that they do not see bigotry, but rather political conflict, when a culture lauds killing Jews, they will not be effective in countering antisemitism.

Beyond Europe: Target Israel

One of the ironies of the pull of Zionism (as well as the push of antisemitism) is the increased concentration of Jews in Israel. While Jews are now able to defend themselves in a sovereign land, this density of Jews in a small area also makes them a target.

The level of Jew-hatred from many Arab countries is the only fair parallel to that of Nazi Germany. Jews are despised, vilified, called "apes and pigs" by imams, and demonized by the press and political leaders. Some Arab and Islamic commentators have even suggested that atomic, biological, or chemical weapons be used against Israel. Sure, Israeli Arabs would be killed too. But, they point out, there are so many more Arabs in the world than Israelis, it would be worth the cost.

While there are certainly non-antisemitic political dimensions to the Arab-Israeli conflict, the use of language that paints Jews as demonic, or lauds the prospect of genocidal attacks against Israelis as worthwhile pursuits, are stark reminders of antisemitism's potential. It is sobering that even a country such as Egypt, which has recognized Israel's right to exist and which, like Israel, is also under threat from Islamic extremists, regularly popularizes antisemitic myths through its institutions.

I write these words as Israel is again under attack, following the kidnapping of three soldiers. Hezbollah is sending rockets into northern Israel, and Israel has responded by attacking Hezbollah strongholds. While this battle certainly has a nation-to-nation component (Hezbollah is supported by Iran and Syria), antisemitism is also in play. In 1992 a Hezbollah statement proclaimed, "It is an open war until the elimination of Israel and until the death of the last Jew on earth." Ten years later Hezbollah's leader, Sheikh Hassan Nasrallah, encouraged Jews to move to Israel. "If they all gather in Israel," he said, "it will save us the trouble of going after them worldwide."[8]

While the Israeli Defense Forces and diplomatic maneuvers are a strong source of defense for Israel's Jews, the real possibility exists that some day there may be genocidal attacks against the Jews there, particularly with weapons of mass destruction, delivered either by antisemitic regimes, militias, or even small groups. In this worst nightmare, it will not necessarily take the full-scale organization of an antisemitic regime to commit a new genocide against Jews. A small group, propelled by antisemitism and armed with a dirty bomb or biological weapons, could cause massive damage. There is, of course, no way to entirely eliminate such danger. But a key component in reducing the level of threat is increasing the consistency with which leaders around the world identify antisemitism as a real peril, and speak out against it.

Conclusion

In conclusion, combating antisemitism is a multifaceted endeavor requiring the use of a wide variety of tools, some more appropriate for one situation than another. There is no silver bullet in this fight, nor is there reason to believe that a battle that has not been fully won in the last two thousand years will be successfully concluded in the near future. The challenge is to do the best we can, rather than merely what we assume is good. We need, always, to understand first what is the type of antisemitism we are facing; second, what institutions are being impacted; third, what are the assets that can be used, especially those that play on the self-image of these institutions; fourth, what tools are available to do the job; and fifth—and perhaps most importantly—how failure and success are to be gauged.

In the years ahead, money needs to be spent to test the assumptions upon which contemporary antisemitism is combated—including the notion that antibias education in general and Holocaust education, in particular, work. Those who combat antisemitism must be careful to analyze all the factors relevant to any situation before jumping in (and possibly make matters worse). If we approach antisemitism in a systematic and research-based manner, I have no doubt that the antisemitism our children and grandchildren will face will not be much worse, and may even be less, than what we or our parents had to endure.

Acknowledgments

I worked on this book on and off for over five years, and it could not have been written without the help and encouragement of many people.

Margie, Daniel, and Emily were supportive throughout, even though I would sometimes disappear for days to write. Daniel—who at fourteen has the potential to become a great chef if he chooses—kept me well fed. Margie, as always, was a kind critic and helped sharpen many ideas. And it was an especial pleasure to include one of Emily's incisive comments as a head note. At age twelve, she has the potential to combine three careers into one: writer, philosopher, and comic.

My colleagues at the American Jewish Committee were consistently helpful. Shula Bahat approved a sabbatical that allowed me to conduct the bulk of the early research. Sondra Beaulieu and Steven Koplin assisted with some of the research and also the tracking down of citations and other information, as did librarians Cyma Horowitz and Michele Anish. (Sondra also read an early version.) My former colleagues Jeffrey Weill and Sybil Kessler also helped by reading the material regarding Durban and offering useful suggestions. Roselyn Bell, as always, was an astute editor. Jeffrey Sinensky and Dr. David Elcott read earlier drafts and provided valuable comments. Richard Sideman and Martin Kaplan, as chairs of AJC's Antisemitism Task Force, also had a hand in some of the more important initiatives chronicled here. Joseph Mendels, the task force's newest chair, also helped crystallize and improve my thinking.

Special thanks go to David Harris, AJC's executive director, for whom combating antisemitism has always been a priority, and who consistently encourages AJC staff to "think outside the box."

Of all my colleagues, I am most grateful to Dr. Steven Bayme. Steve not only read over the manuscript with incredible care, made numerous improvements, and kept me from various errors, his work (on Jewish communal affairs and on Israeli-American Jewish relations) also reflects the type of careful analysis and planning this book advocates. Steve and I may differ in our politics, but his intellectual clarity and honesty have been a delight and a model.

The design of this book reflects the creative eye of AJC's talented art director, Linda Krieg, and the meticulous implementation of our indefatigable production supervisor, Sharon Schwartz.

Bob Mecoy, my former editor at Simon and Schuster, read a very early version of the manuscript and gave good counsel. Also instrumental were my friends Dr. Deborah Lipstadt and Barbara Grossman, both of whom were exceptionally supportive. Dr. Gerald Steinberg of Bar-Ilan University and NGO-Monitor read a draft of the chapter on Durban and offered valuable suggestions for improving it.

Finally, great parts of this book were written (and rewritten) while hiding out at Bard College, my alma mater, during winter break. Susan Barich, Erin Cannan, Jessica Kemm, Theresa Desmond, and Jamie Schultz helped make my stays there incredibly productive. There are few joys to rival working three or four days straight, from early morning to late at night, on one writing project. Unlike our work, too often, in the day-to-day combating of antisemitism, writing produces immediate tangible results. To do so back at an institution that is so unique and special was a joy (and also a marvel, since every time I returned there was at least one new building being erected, a testament to the vision and skills of Bard president Leon Botstein).

Notes

Introduction

1. The full title is "Report on Global Anti-Semitism, July 1, 2003-December 15, 2004, Submitted by the Department of State to the Committee on Foreign Relations and the Committee on International Relations in Accordance with Section 4 of PL 108-332." Although the report bears the date December 30, 2004, it was released on January 5, 2005.

2. See the report at pp. 3, 6, 8, 9 and in many country-specific references. Although the report also mentions the need for law enforcement and legislation, the references to tolerance education in general and Holocaust education in particular are replete throughout.

3. The U.S. State Department Report on Global Anti-Semitism, in its section on Turkey, noted the suicide attacks against two Istanbul synagogues in November 2003, which killed twenty-three people and injured more than 300 others. It then reported:

> In an incident that arose out of the bombings, the 17-year-old son of one of the alleged perpetrators of the synagogue attacks and three journalists were convicted of anti-Semitism and could face up to 3 years in jail. The youth said in an interview with the daily *Milliyet*: "The attacks did not touch the hearts of the members of my family because the target was Jews. We couldn't be happy, but we were satisfied. If Muslims hadn't been killed we would have been happy. We don't like Jews." The journalist and the editors of the newspaper were convicted of providing a platform for incitement against members of another religion. This was the first time in history that citizens were convicted of anti-Semitic activities.

Chapter One

1. "Worldwide Antisemitic Hate Crimes and Major Hate Incidents: From Jewish New Year 5761 (29/9/00)-Present (3/11/00): An Interim Report," Simon Wiesenthal Center, October 19, 2000; http://www.wiesenthal.com/site/apps/nl/content2.asp?c=bhKRI6PDInE&b=296323&ct=350239.

2. A more detailed discussion, with a longer definition proposed for those who monitor antisemitism, appears in Chapter 8.

3. Some portions of this chapter appeared, in a different form, in the publication *Antisemitism Matters* (New York: American Jewish Committee, May 2004).

4. Under the Nazi racial laws of 1935, if a person had three Jewish grandparents, they were Jewish. If they had two or one, they were classified as "*Mischlinge*," meaning mongrels.

5. Interestingly, even though the *Protocols* is a tool of racial and Muslim antisemites, its tone and imagery reflect the clear influence of age-old Christian anti-

semitism.

6. Black supremacists and black nationalists also engage in antisemitism. As noted above, the Nation of Islam and its leaders (notably Louis Farrakhan, but many others as well) have denied or demeaned the Holocaust, praised Hitler, called Judaism a "gutter" religion, and vilified Israel. Many Afrocentrists, including noted City University of New York professor Leonard Jeffries, not only twist history and science to argue that blacks are biologically and morally superior to whites, but also use classic antisemitic imagery to argue that Jews are a threat to African-Americans.

There is certainly a case to be made that antisemitism from the African-American community is "worse" than that from the majority community. African-Americans score higher than most other groups on attitudinal surveys measuring antisemitism, for example. Whereas few would ignore a white supremacist's agenda in order to pick out those isolated parts with which one might agree (neo-Nazi David Duke's environmental advocacy, for example), many inside and outside the African-American community regularly interact with and promote Farrakhan and the Nation of Islam despite its racism, sexism, and homophobia, let alone its antisemitism. While no public school or university is teaching the antisemitism inherent in Holocaust denial, many are incorporating Afrocentrist teachings. And while hate crimes against Jews by white supremacists occur from time to time, they are isolated incidents, unlike the 1991 violent antisemitic riots in Crown Heights, New York, promoted and fueled in part by black antisemitism and antisemites.

Yet today, in part because the African-American community is no longer the ascending nonwhite community, and in part because its antisemitism has not been energized in recent years by the same factors that have lead to the reemergence of global antisemitism as a challenge, I have not devoted a chapter to it in this book, although my writings about this issue can be found at www.ajc.org/site/apps/nl/content3.asp?c=ijITI2PHKoG&b=846637&ct=1102643.

7. Whereas anti-Zionism is a form of antisemitism in the current context, it was not always so. Before the establishment of the State of Israel there were debates, inside and outside the Jewish community, about whether the reestablishment of Jewish sovereignty in their historic homeland was a good idea.

8. Abba Eban, "Zionism and the U.N.," *New York Times*, November 3, 1975, p. 35.

9. See discussion of rare circumstances in which anti-Zionism may not be antisemitic in Chapter 8 footnote, pp. 100-01.

Chapter Two

1. Nazila Fathi, "Iran's President Says Israel Must Be ''Wiped off the Map,''" *New York Times*, October 26, 2005; http://www.nytimes.com/2005/10/26/international/middleeast/26cnd-iran.html?ex=1287979200&en=ac28fd408a57f88f&ei=5090&partner=rssuserland&emc=rss.

2. "In the Nazis' Words," collected by Gord McFee, http://www.holocaust-history.org/nazis-words/index.shtml.

3. *Encyclopedia Britannica,* Eleventh Edition, Vol. 2, s.v. "anti-Semitism," p. 134.

4. Ibid., p. 135.

5. Leonard Zeskind was the first to notice that ideological fallout from the collapse of the Soviet Union (though only indirectly associated with antisemitism) was readily apparent in the ideological pronouncements of the American militia movement. Many of the conspiracy theories about the Soviet Union—that the "evil empire" had secret plans for taking over America, sending loyal Americans to concentration camps and such—were "cut and pasted," with the U.S. federal government inserted in place of the Soviets in the new militia-think.

6. One labor leader told me that the first time she saw this growing interaction between people associated with the extreme right and left wings was in the early 1990s, during the protests against the North American Free Trade Agreement (NAFTA), when protestors marched with anarchists one day and with Pat Buchanan far-right supporters the next.

7. This flirtation reached the point in 2004 where left-leaning presidential candidate Ralph Nader was featured on the cover of Pat Buchanan's *American Conservative* magazine. Buchanan—famous for his assertion that a pro-Israel "cabal" was actually running the government—cited Nader, who claimed that Israel's leader was a "puppeteer" of the Bush presidency and of Congress.

8. Further, there had been a technological change in the 1990s due to the popularization of satellite television and the Internet. While too much has been made of the supposed impact of these media (as will be discussed in more detail in Chapter 11), they—especially television—certainly have played a role in bringing select images to targeted audiences to demonize Israelis.

9. Ironically, Jews were in the forefront of efforts to combat these groups, working against their agenda of curtailing immigration and in support of the new Muslim and Arab arrivals.

Chapter Three

1. "Statement of the Jewish Caucus on the NGO Process and Concluding Document," Durban, South Africa, September 1, 2001, World Conference Against Racism.

2. Seymour Martin Lipset, "The Socialism of Fools: The Left, the Jews and Israel," *Encounter,* December 1969, p. 24.

3. Ruth R. Wisse, "Blaming Israel," *Commentary* 77:2, February 1984.

4. Paula Span, "The Undying Revolutionary: As Stokely Carmichael, He Fought for Black Power. Now Kwame Ture's Fighting for his Life,'" *Washington Post,* April 8, 1998, p. D1.

5. Prepared remarks of Senator Daniel Patrick Moynihan in Kenneth Stern, editor, "The Effort to Repeal Resolution 3379" (New York: American Jewish Committee, 1991).

6. Serge Schmemann, "Annan Is Stern But Friendly on Israel Visit," *New York*

Times, March 26, 1998, p. 7. See "UN World Conference Against Racism: Talking Points," U.S. WCAR Working Group, July 18, 2001.

7. See http://www.un.org/WCAR/e-kit/backgrounder1.htm.

8. COBASE (Cooperativa Tecnico Scientifica de Base), "Are the NGOs Forum and WCAR Racist?" (Rome: COBASE, 2001).

9. "Statement of the Jewish Caucus on the NGO Process and Concluding Document." See also Tom Lantos, "The Durban Debacle: An Insider's View of the UN World Conference Against Racism," *Fletcher Forum of World Affairs* 26:1, Winter/Spring 2001, p. 35. The Israeli delegation was banned by Iran (as were Baha'i and Kurdish NGOs), and non-Israeli Jewish NGOS were only given visas when it was too late for them to come. See Harris O. Schoenberg, "Demonization in Durban: The World Conference Against Racism," *2002 American Jewish Year Book* (New York: American Jewish Committee, 2002), p. 90.

10. Arch Puddington, "The Wages of Durban," *Commentary*, November 2001, p. 30.

11. Ibid.

12. "Minister Melchior Briefs Press on Durban Conference," August 9, 2001, www.mfa.gov.il/MFA/Government/Speeches+by+Israeli+leaders/2001/Briefing+to+the+Foreign+Press (accessed 6/10/06).

13. Ibid.

14. Jonathan Mark, "The Slander at Durban: Israel's Left Warned of Apartheid Long Ago," *New York Jewish Week*, September 7, 2001, p. 18.

15. Arab Lawyers Union, "That is the fact ... Racism of zionism & 'Israel'", World Conference Against Racism, Racial Discrimination, Xenophobia and Related Intolerance, Durban, South Africa, 2001.

16. Andrew Srulevitch, "An Open Letter to the International Steering Committee of the NGO Forum and High Commissioner for Human Rights Mary Robinson Regarding the Distribution of Hate Literature" (Geneva: United Nations Watch, August 28, 2001).

17. Jeremy Jones, "Durban Daze: When antisemitism is 'anti-racism,'" *Review*, October 2001, p. 32.

18. "Statement of the Jewish Caucus on the NGO Process."

19. "The Palestinian Return Centre Explains Why Zionism Equals Racism," (London: The Palestinian Return Center, n.d., circa 2000-01).

20. "Occupied Jerusalem, a New Soweto?" Jerusalem Center for Social and Economic Rights, August 2001.

21. Andrew Srulevitch, letter to board of UN Watch, September 13, 2001.

22. "Statement of the Jewish Caucus on the NGO Process."

23. Jones, "Durban Daze," p. 32.

24. Flier, "Apartheid lives on in the land of Zionism," distributed by Free Palestine Campaign Committee, Dormerton, South Africa.

25. Abnaq el Balad, "A Palestinian Voice for Freedom and Democracy—A Cry from Inside the 53-Year-Old Israeli Apartheid State," Durban, August 2001.

26. Herb Keinon, "Ganging Up in Durban: How an Anti-Racism Conference

Turned on Racism's Ultimate Victims," *International Jerusalem Post*, September 14, 2001, p. 10. Apparently 20,000 of these flyers had been circulated. They were produced by Yousef Deedat of the Islamic Propagation Center, who reportedly claimed to be associated with Osama bin Laden and receiving money from the Bin Laden family. See Schoenberg, "Demonization in Durban," p. 98.

27. Interview with author, January 18, 2002.

28. "Jewish Youth Denounce Summit Document as Incitement to Violence," press release, Durban, South Africa, August 29, 2001.

29. The Eastern and Central Europe NGO Caucus put out a joint statement bemoaning various parts of the official NGO statement, including "ideas included in the chapters 'Globalization,' 'Palestinians and Palestine,' 'Reparations,' ... [etc.]" and called the "deliberate distortions made to the chapter 'Anti-Semitism' ... extremely intolerant [and] disrespectful." But while this gesture was welcome, it was inadequate to the quantity and quality of antisemitism on display. "Joint Statement by Eastern and Central Europe NGO Caucus and other NGOs at the NGO Forum on the World Conference Against Racism," adopted September 2, 2001, Durban, South Africa.

30. Jones, "Durban Daze."

31. Leaflet, "Hate Speech at the World Conference against Racism: Antisemitic, Anti-Zionism, and Anti-Jewish Remarks Directed against Jewish Delegates to the UN Youth and Non-Governmental Organization Conferences." See (regarding the yarmulke incident) "This Conference Is Racist!—Zionist View," *The New African: The New Voice of an Old Continent*, Johannesburg, August 30, 2001, p. 1.

32. Max Coslov and H. Ron Davidson, "The Durban Experience," *AJC Journal*, November 2001, p. 11.

33. Jones, "Durban Daze."

34. Srulevitch, letter to board of UN Watch.

35. Shimon Samuels, "On the Road from Durban Racism and Terror Converge. What Starts with Jews Is Often an Early Warning for Society at Large," *Ha'aretz*, October 13, 2001; interview with Jeffrey Weill.

36. Jones, "Durban Daze."

37. "Statement of the Jewish Caucus on the NGO Process."

38. Michael J. Jordan, "Inside the Durban Debacle: By Focusing the World on Israeli 'Apartheid' at the U.N. Racism Conference, Well-Organized Arab Activists Are Trying to Turn Israel into the South African of the 21st Century," Salon.com, September 13, 2001.

39. Rachel Swarns, "Rancor and Powell's Absence Cloud Racism Parley," *New York Times*, August 31, 2001, p. A3.

40. "WCAR Position Statement, The Revolutionary Committees Movement (Libya)," Durban, South Africa, August 31, 2001.

41. "Statement of the Ecumenical Caucus at the UN World Conference Against Racism, Racial Discrimination, Xenophobia and Related Intolerance," Durban, South Africa, September 4, 2001.

42. Letter of November 16, 2001, to Her Excellency Mary Robinson from the

Jacob Blaustein Institute for the Advancement of Human Rights.

43. Keinon, "Ganging Up in Durban."

44. Michael J. Jordan, "As Debris of UN Forum Clears, Jews Ponder the Consequences," Jewish Telegraphic Agency, September 14, 2001, p. 4.

45. Ibid.

46. For more about the Law of Return, see "AJC on Israel-Diaspora Relations" at http://www.ajc.org/site/apps/nl/content3.asp?c=ijITI2PHKoG&b=841113&ct=10 52401.

47. Sergio Della Pergola, "World Jewish Population, 2005" 2005 American Jewish Year Book (New York: American Jewish Committee, 2005), p. 97.

48. United Nations Population Fund, http://www.unfpa.org/profile/overview_arab.htm, accessed October 29, 2003.

49. Alan Dershowitz, The Case for Israel (Hoboken, NJ: Wiley, 2003), p. 156. Also see Alexander Yakobson and Amnon Rubinstein, "Democratic Norms, Diasporas, and Israel's Law of Return," at http://www.ajc.org/site/apps/nl/content3.asp?c=ijITI2PHKoG&b=846725&ct=875523.

50. "An Open Response to the Palestinian NGOs," Jewish Caucus, Geneva, August 9, 2001.

51. Of course, the refugees on both sides did not all have the same experiences. Some of the Palestinians who left their homes did so because they wanted to be out of harm's way while the Arab armies tried to kill Jews. Some were scared into leaving by Israeli forces. Likewise, some Jews were forced out of Arab and North African countries, but others were for a time willing to stay, for a variety of reasons, among them not wanting to give up their material possessions or because they thought they could continue to practice their religion without undue interference as long as they stayed away from political matters. While it is no easy task to sort out all the moral issues that had a hand in the creation of the refugees, three facts remain clear: 1) If the Arab population had accepted the UN solution of two states rather than declare war, the problems would likely have been much less severe. 2) On the basis of raw numbers, the populations on both sides were roughly equivalent. 3) The Israelis quickly absorbed the Jewish refugees, whereas the Arab states purposefully maintained the Palestinians as refugees for generations.

52. See Loolwa Khazoom, "Jews of the Middle East," at http://www.jewishvirtuallibrary.org/jsource/Judaism/mejews.html; Yaakov Kornreich, "A Guide to the Israeli-Palestinian Dispute," at http://www.youngisrael.org/israel.htm.

53. Rachel L. Swarns, "U.S. and Israel Threaten Boycott of U.N. Conference on Race," New York Times, September 3, 2001, p. A6.

54. Anne Bayefsky, "Human Rights Watch Coverup," Jerusalem Post, April 13, 2004. Bayefsky also alleges that HRW has been less than candid about its role at Durban.

55. Srulevitch, letter to board of UN Watch.

56. "Statement of the Jewish Caucus on the NGO Process."

57. "The Cause and the Effect: Two Excerpts," New York Times, September 4, 2001, p. A1.

58. Keinon, "Ganging Up in Durban," pp. 9-10.
59. Rachel L. Swarns, "Palestinians Give U.N. Racism Talks a Mixed Message: Arafat Condemns Israel—But Earlier, an Aide Announced Opposition to Labeling the Jewish State as Racist," *New York Times*, September 1, 2001, p. 1; Clyde Haberman, "Israeli Outrage at Arafat's Speech Makes Talks with Him Even Less Certain," *New York Times*, September 4, 2001, p. A8.
60. Herb Keinon, "U.S. and Israel Quit Durban—Peres: Racism Conference 'A Farce,'" *Jerusalem Post*, September 4, 2001, p. 13.

Also missing was an honest acknowledgment of the basis of the refugee status of many Palestinians. As Tova Herzl, the Israeli ambassador to South Africa at the time of the conference, noted:

> Why, of the more than 100 million people displaced in the quarter century after Hitler's rise to power in 1933, does only one of the major refugee problems that began during that period continue to garner the world's attention? ... Could it be that the Arab countries were less economically able to absorb several hundred thousands of their brethren? Or less willing? Among the displaced during that period were a comparable number of Jews forced to flee from Arab countries, effectively creating an exchange of population. If the wealth of Arab nations was not enough to bear the expense of assisting their brethren, surely Jewish property left behind in those countries would have covered the costs? ... Tragically, innocent people suffer as a result of war. Decent people help them, give them sanctuary and citizenship. (Other than Jordan, no Arab country did.)
>
> Tova Herzl, "If Israel Is Denied the Right to Exist, Who Is Being Racist?" undated article, circa August-September 2001.

60. Keinon, "U.S. and Israel Quit Durban."
61. Ibid.
62. "The Cause and the Effect," p. A1.
63. Charles Krauthammer, "Disgrace in Durban: The UN Conference on Racism Was Worse than Just Hot Air," *Weekly Standard*, September 17, 2001, p. 15.
64. "The Imam and Zionism," *Al-Hujjat* ("Officail [sic] Mouthpiece of the Ahlul Bait (AS) Foundation of South Africa"), August/September 2001, p.1.
65. Jordan, "As Debris of UN Forum Clears"; Morgan Campbell, "Israeli Mayor 'Happy' After Racism Forum," *Toronto Star*, September 10, 2001, p. NE03.
66. David A. Harris, "The Usual Game Has Ironclad Rules for Ganging Up on Israel," op-ed in *International Herald Tribune*, August 29, 2001, reprinted in David A. Harris: *In the Trenches*, Vol. II (Hoboken, NJ: KTAV, 2002); pp. 311-12. It wasn't only the raw antisemitism that demonstrated the force of the Islamic countries, there was an additional irony: A second major item discussed was the question of reparations from the United States and Europe for the African slave trade. Conspicuously missing was recognition of the Arab role in that slavery, or that it was Western democracies which put an end to this deplorable practice. Most signifi-

cantly, there was no focus on the fact that slavery as it exists today, in Mauritania and Sudan, is predominantly found in Islamic countries. Puddington, "The Wages of Durban," p. 31.

67. See Edwin Black, "Funding Hate," four-part series at http://www.jta.org/ford.asp (accessed January 6, 2005). When Ford's role in funding some of the groups calling for Israel's demise was later exposed, Ford agreed to address the problem by, among other things, creating guidelines which would prohibit such use of its funds (see Chapter 9). But the role of NGOs in promoting antisemitism as well as the network of funders who support them is a critical issue since, as Gerald Steinberg of NGO-Monitor has noted, there is a "halo effect," meaning that many governments, media, and other institutions tend to assume that reports issued by NGOs are credible when, in fact, they may well be biased. See Gerald M. Steinberg, "The Centrality of NGOs in the Durban Strategy," revised April 5, 2006; at www.ngo-monitor.org.

68. Ali Baghadi, "Rev. Jackson Lobbies for Perpetrators of Racism," *Final Call*, September 18, 2001. The piece also asserted that "Jackson stands with the most hated and despised two governments on earth, his 'friends' and benefactors, Israel and the United States."

69. Svati P. Shah, "A Report Back from the World Conference Against Racism," *Public Eye*, Fall 2001, p. 21. I wrote to Political Research Associates, the publisher of *Public Eye*, complaining about this reportage, and they responded, saying they agreed that they had missed the boat.

70. Tom Lantos, congressman from California, a Holocaust survivor, and a U.S. delegate to Durban, lamented that "the leaders of the great Western human rights NGOs like Human Rights Watch, the Lawyers Committee for Human Rights participated in the NGO forum in Durban [and] did almost nothing to denounce the activities of the radicals in their midst." Lantos, "The Durban Debacle," p. 50.

71. Press News Limited, Broadcast News (BN), April 4, 2002.

72. Diane West, "Resolved to Barbarism; EU Countries Condone Palestinian Terrorism," *Washington Times*, April 19, 2002, p. A21.

Chapter Four

1. Middle East Media Research Institute (MEMRI), "A New Antisemitic Myth in the Middle East Media: The September 11 Attacks Were Perpetrated by the Jews," Chapter III, at http://www.memri.org/AntisemiticMythBook/chapterIII.html.

2. Hale was sentenced to forty years in jail in 2005 for his part in a plot to murder a federal judge. See Natasha Korecki and Frank Main, "Supremacist Gets 40 Years; Hale Given Maximum for Trying to Have Judge Murdered," *Chicago Sun-Times*, April 7, 2005, p. 1.

3. Press release, "Pro-Israel Foreign Policy Costs Thousands of Lives Today," September 11, 2001, received via email.

4. "An Open Letter to the President of the United States," by David Duke, Sep-

tember 21, 2001, visited at www.stormfront.org on September 24, 2001.
5. David Duke, "Will Anyone Dare to Ask Why?" posted at http://www.storm-front.org/0901/duke-dare.htm. In another missive Duke ranted about "Jews cutting apart the bellies of pregnant women." See David Duke, "The Real Evil Spirit," David Duke's Official Web Site http://www.david-duke.org/; Tanzeemi-e-Islami, http://www.tanzeem.org/resources/articles/articles/david%20duke-the%real%evil%spirit.htm), cited in Harold Brackman, "9/11 Digital Lies: A Survey of Online Apologists for Global Terrorism," Simon Wiesenthal Center, 2001, p. 16.
6. The Camp David Accords were dated September 17, 1978. See http://www.mfa.gov.il/MFA/Peace+Process/Guide+to+the+Peace+Process/Camp+David+Accords.htm.
7. Tom Metzger, White Aryan Resistance (WAR), *Aryan Update* (September 16, 2001), http://www.resist.com, cited in Harold Brackman, "9/11 Digital Lies," pp. 16, 17.
8. The *Turner Diaries* is a fictional account of a white supremacist race war in the United States. It served as both the blueprint and inspiration for the 1980s terrorist group "The Order," which robbed banks and killed Denver talk show host Alan Berg, as well as for the Oklahoma City bombing. See detailed discussion in Kenneth Stern, *A Force Upon the Plain: The American Militia Movement and the Politics of Hate* (New York: Simon & Schuster, 1996).
9. William Pierce, National Alliance, in "White Nationalists War of Inevitable Attack on Canada," press release, September 17, 2001, www.natall.ca, quoted in Harold Brackman, "9/11 Digital Lies," p.16.
10. Jim Nesbitt, "Assault on America: Many American Right-Wing Racial Extremists Applaud Sept. 11 Attacks," http://www.newhousenews.com/archive/storyla092601.html.
11. Some black antisemites, most noticeably the deceased Khalid Abdul Muhammad, also have called New York "Jew York."
12. Jim Nesbitt, "Assault on America;" Billy Roper, National Alliance, Internet Bulletin Board, September 11, 2001, *Aryan Update* (November 4, 2001) cited in Harold Brackman, "9/11 Digital Lies," p.16.
13. Jim Ridgeway, "Osama's New Recruits," *Village Voice*, week of October 31-November 6, 2001, http://www.villagevoice.com/issues/0144/ridgeway.php.
14. Henry Rosemont, Jr., "Terrorist Attacks Expose Insecurity: Progressive Activists Can Help Explain Why This Happened," *Resist*, 10:8, October 2001, p. 1.
15. There were some bizarre comments from the left as well. Political Research Associates, the publisher of the *Public Eye* (See Chapter 3, footnote 69), for some strange reason felt a need to state: "We concur with the observation of the Black Radical Congress that *this* [the September 11 attack] *is not a revolutionary act.*" Message from Political Research Associates, dated September 19, 2001.
16. *Crime in the United States-2000, Uniform Crime Reports*, Federal Bureau of Investigation (Washington, D.C.: Department of Justice, 2001), p. 60. It is possible that crimes against some who might have been mistaken for Muslims could be included under the total of 173 crimes against other religious groups or among the

44 crimes in the anti-multi-religious group. In the following year (2001) the number of hate crimes against Jews was reported as 1,043, and those against Muslims as 481. Also, the number of attacks on people based on their "national origin/ethnicity" jumped from 911 in 2000 to 2,098 in 2001. For more on the FBI Hate Crime Statistics Acts, see http://www.adl.org/Learn/hate_crimes_laws/HCSA_FBI.asp.

17. This was especially so in the aftermath of the first Gulf War, when the U.S. had a large military presence in Saudi Arabia.

18. Paul Berman, *Terror and Liberalism* (New York: W.W. Norton & Co, 2003), pp. 79-80.

19. Atta was likely inquiring about flight schools at least as early as March 2000 and enrolled in a Florida flight school in July 2000. Tim Golden, Michael Moss and Jim Yardley, "A National Challenged: The Plot: Unpolished Secret Agents Were Able to Hide in Plain Sight," *New York Times*, September 23, 2001, Section 1B, p. 1.

20. Various e-mails from Dan Levitas to author, September 2001.

21. MEMRI, "A New Antisemitic Myth in the Middle East Media: The September 11 Attacks Were Perpetrated by the Jews," Chapter II, at http://www.memri.org/AntisemiticMythBook/chapterII.html.

22. MEMRI, "A New Antisemitic Myth," Chapter III, at http://www.memri.org/AntisemiticMythBook/chapterIII.html.

23. The article on the Qatar-based Web site continued:

> According to reliable sources, the EoZ met at a secret spot in Europe after the Durban Conference to analyse the factors behind the anti-Israel and anti-Zionism sentiments of the world. The meeting decided to adopt strategic measures to change the world scene and divert the anti-Israel sentiments to some other direction like that of Muslims. The EoZ, which has controlled the world politics for long, planned devastating attacks against American cities.... Allah ... says about the Jews: "Every time they kindled the fire of war, Allah extinguished it; and they (ever) strive to make mischief on earth. And Allah does not like the mischief-makers." [*The Holy Qur'an* (5:65)]

"Zionists Could Be Behind Attack on WTC and Pentagon," Islam Web (posted 10/21/01, accessed November 15, 2001), http:www.islamweb.net/.

24. Columnist Ahmad Al-Musallah of *Al-Dustour*, cited in MEMRI, "A New Antisemitic Myth," Chapter II, at http://www.memri.org/AntisemiticMythBook/chapterII.html.

25. Columnist Rakan Al-Majali of *Al-Dustour*, cited in ibid.

26. *Al-Manar*, cited in ibid.

27. Jonathan Rosen, "The Uncomfortable Question of Anti-Semitism," *New York Times Magazine*, November 4, 2001.

28. Sheikh Gamei'a also reportedly said that "Jews disseminate corruption in the land." In an interview he stated:

> We know that they have always broken agreements, unjustly murdered the prophets; do you think they will stop spilling our blood? No. [Jews

are] everywhere, disseminating corruption, heresy, homosexuality, alcoholism, and drugs…. [Because of Jews] there are strip clubs, alcoholism, homosexuals, and lesbians everywhere. They do this to impose their hegemony and colonialism on the world.

Rachel Donadio, "Imam Abu-Namous: a Q and A," *Forward*, October 26, 2001.

29. Muslim Public Affairs Council: "Israel a Suspect in WTC/Pentagon Attacks," e-mail from Yehudit Barsky to author, 9/24/01. Rachel Zoll, "In the wake of Sept. 11, Muslim leaders criticized for statements on terrorism," Associated Press, October 24, 2001.

30. Scott MacLeod, "In the Arab World, Conspiracy Theories and Anti-Semitism Deflect Attention from Real Problems," June 10, 2002, http://www.time.com/time/europe/magazine/2002/0617/antisemitism/arab.html.

31. MEMRI Special Report No. 8, "A New Antisemitic Myth in the Middle East: The September 11 Attacks were Perpetrated by the Jews," MEMRI, September 2002, p. 14.

32. At http://www.physics911.net/olmsted.htm. See also *Saut Al-Haqq, Wa-Al-Hurriuua* (Israel), October 19, 2001, cited in MEMRI, Special Report No. 8.

33. Khalil Al-Sawahri, *Al-Ayyam* (Palestinian Authority), October 2, 2001, cited in MEMRI, Special Report No. 8.

34. Dr. Zahran of Suez Canal University, *Al-Ahram* (Egypt), October 7, 2001, cited in ibid.

35. Ahmad Abu Zayid, *Al-Wafd*, October 27, 2001; *Al-Ahram*, October 29, 2001, cited in ibid.

36. Sheikh Gamei'a, www.lailatalqadr.com/stories/p5041001.shtml, cited in ibid.

37. Hilmi Al-Asman, *Al-Dustour* (Jordan), September 29, 2001, cited in ibid.

38. Dr. Amira Al-Shinwani, *Al-Akhbar*, (Egypt, October 26, 2001) cited in ibid.

39. At http://www.whatreallyhappened.com/fiveisraelis.html. See also *Al-Usbu'* (Egypt), November 5, 2001, cited in ibid.

40. Abu Zayid, *Al-Wafd*, October 27, 2001; *Al-Ahram*, October 29, 2001, cited in ibid.

41. Ahmad Al-Musallah, *Al-Dustour*, (Jordan), September 13, 2001.

42. Syrian ambassador to Tehran Turky Muhammad Saqr, *IRNA*, Iran, October 24, 2001. See also Al-Manar TV (Lebanon) September 17, 2001, www.paknews.com, and Abu Zayid, supra, all cited in MEMRI, Special Report No. 8.

43. Zahran, op. cit. See also Saqr, ibid.; Kayhan (Iran), October 2, 2001, Raed Salan, *Saut Al-Haqq, Wa-Al-Hurriyya* (Israel), October 5, 2001, *Al-Hayat* (London), September 30, 2001, *Al-Ahram* (Egypt), October 7, 2001, and *Al-Hayat* (London), September 24, 2001, all cited in MEMRI, Special Report No. 8.

44. Most of these assertions are contained in "A New Antisemitic Myth in the Arab Press: The September 11 Attacks Were Perpetrated by the Jews," MEMRI, Special Report No. 8, September 10, 2002. See memri.org and also chretiens-et-juifs.org.

45. *Al-Hayat* (London), September 24, 2001.

46. See "The Fake Bin Laden Video Tape at http://www.whatreallyhappened. com/osamatape.html and http://www.911blimp.net/vid_fakeOsamaVideo.shtml.

Chapter Five

1. Jeffrey Goldberg, "Behind Mubarak: Egyptian clerics and intellectuals respond to terrorism," *New Yorker*, October 8, 2001, p. 51, citing MEMRI.

2. Robert S. Wistrich, *Muslim Anti-Semitism: A Clear and Present Danger* (New York: American Jewish Committee, 2002), p. 4.

3. Goran Larsson, *Fact or Fraud?: The Protocols of the Elders of Zion* (Jerusalem: AMI-Jerusalem Center for Biblical Studies and Research, 1994), p. 43.

4. Wistrich, *Muslim Anti-Semitism*, p. 6.

5. Y. Harkabi, *Arab Attitudes to Israel* (Jerusalem: Israel Universities Press, 1972), p. 293, cited in C.C. Aronsfeld, "Arab Antisemites' Nazi model," *Patterns of Prejudice*, May-June 1972, p. 14. See also Robert S. Wistrich, *Antisemitism: The Longest Hatred* (New York: Pantheon, 1991), p. 196.

6. Koran, Sura 2:61/58, Sura 5:60/65, 2:65 and 7:166.

7. See, for example, Aluma Solnick, "Based on Koranic Verses, Interpretations, and Traditions, Muslim Clerics State: The Jews Are the Descendants of Apes, Pigs, And Other Animals," Middle East Media Research Institute (MEMRI), Special Report-No. 11, November 1, 2002, available at Memri.org.

8. Norman Stillman, "The Nineteenth Century and the Impact of the West: Social Transformations," in *The Jews of Arab Lands in Modern Times* (Philadelphia Jewish Publication Society, 1991) at http://arabworld.nitle.org/texts.php?module_ id=6&reading_id=54.

9. Wistrich, *Muslim Anti-Semitism*, p. 14.

10. *Al-Mussawar*, August 4, 1972, cited in http://www.jewishvirtuallibrary.org/ jsource/myths2/TreatmentofJews.html#_edn10.

11. Lillian Ickowitz, "Wild Words: Blasphemy Charge at the UN," *Australia/Israel Review*, April 10-May 1, 1998 at http://www.aijac.org.au/review/ 1998/234/wildwords.html. See also Steven Stalinsky, "Passover Hate: A Lie Continues to Spread," at http://www.nationalreview.com/comment/stalinsky20040406 0909.asp (visited July 3, 2006).

12. Letter dated June 10, 1997, from the chargé d'affaires of the Permanent Mission of Israel to the United Nations addressed to the secretary-general, at http:// domino.un.org/UNISPAL.NSF/85255a0a0010ae82852555340060479d/1f77a7e 6b8c0b375802564c20032c3c5!OpenDocument. See also "American Jewish Committee Calls for Yasser Arafat to Repudiate AIDS Slander Against Israel Made by Palestinian Observer to U.N. Commission of Human Rights," AJC press release, May 2, 1997.

13. Palestine Liberation Army mufti Sheikh Colonel Nader Al-Tamimi, quoted on Al-Jazeera (Qatar) on October 24, 2000, and in a column by 'Adel Hamooda entitled, "A Jewish Matzah Made from Arab Blood," in *Al-Ahram* (Egypt), October

28, 2000, reported in MEMRI, Special Dispatch No. 105 (Egypt), November 6, 2000.

14. Hillel Halkin, "The Return of Anti-Semitism," *Commentary*, February 2002, p. 31.

15. Norman Cohn, "The Myth of the Jewish-World Conspiracy: A Case Study in Collective Psychopathology," *Commentary*, June 1966, p. 8. See, for example, "Jewish Control of the World Media," by Seif 'Ali Al-Jarwan, in the largest Palestinian Authority daily, *Al-Hayat Al-Jadida*, July 2, 1998 at http://memri.org/bin/articles.cgi?Page=archives&Area=sd&ID=SP0198 (accessed October 30, 2003) and Ramadan television special, "The Protocols of the Elders of Zion," MEMRI, Special Dispatch #309, December 6, 2001, at http://memri.org/bin/articles.cgi?Page=archives&Area=sd&ID=SP30901.

16. Wistrich, *Antisemitism: The Longest Hatred*, p. 245.

17. Comment by Michael Korcok on "the Grand Mufti of Jerusalem," at http://www.ndtceda.com/archives/200204/0664.html.

18. See Wistrich, *Muslim Anti-Semitism*, supra at p. 2, citing Moshe Pearlman, *Mufti of Jerusalem* (London, V. Gollancz, 1947) p. 49. Wistrich's footnote 7 says:

> Haj Amin al-Husseini's speech began with several anti-Jewish quotations from the Koran. On March 1, 1944, speaking again on Radio Berlin, the mufti of Jerusalem called on the Arabs to rise up and fight. "Kill the Jews wherever you find them. This pleases God, history and religion. This saves your honor. God is with you."

See also Robert S. Wistrich, *Hitler's Apocalypse* (New York: St. Martin's Press, 1986), pp. 164-71 for Haj Amin's belief in the strong ideological similarities between Islam and National Socialism, especially in their authoritarianism, anti-Communism, and hatred of the Jews.

19. Harkabi, *Arab Attitudes to Israel*, p. 230.

20. The Six-Day War began on June 5, 1967, following a series of aggressive actions by Arab armies in the months before, including the demand that the UN forces on the border between Egypt and Israel be removed (they were); an Egyptian blockade of the Strait of Tiran, thus closing off Israeli access to these international waters; and the movement of Arab forces from a coalition of Arab states encircling Israel, threatening it with 465,000 troops, over 2,880 tanks, and 810 aircraft. When political attempts to defuse the situation failed, and Egyptian troops deployed in the Sinai, the Israel Defense Forces were given the go-ahead to strike against this imminent threat to Israel's existence. The war was a resounding victory for Israel, with the Arab armies losing in just six days.

21. ADL press release on "A New Worldwide Anti-Semitism," March 5, 1974, p. 5.

22. "Anti-Semitic Propaganda Published in Arab States being Distributed World-wide, AJCommittee Reports," Jewish Telegraphic Agency, October 30, 1974 reporting on "Political and Religious Anti-Semitism: Weapon in the Arab-Israeli Conflict: A Background Memorandum," AJC, May 8, 1974.

23. Eliahu Salpeter, "Islam Coopts the Jewish Satan," http://www.cdn-friends-icej.ca/antiholo/jewish_satan.html.

24. The 1988 platform of Hamas, entitled "The Movement of Islamic Resistance," says:

> The Jews have taken over the world media and financial centers. By fomenting revolutions, wars and such movements as the Free Masons, Communism, Capitalism and Zionism, Rotary, Lions, B'nai B'rith, etc.— they are subverting human society as a whole in order to bring about its destruction, propagate their own viciousness and corruption, and take over the world via such of their pet institutions as the League of Nations, the U.N. and the Security Council. Their schemes are detailed in the *Protocols of the Elders of Zion.*

Quoted in Larsson, "Fact or Fraud?" p. 45.

25. Sam Skolnik, "Arabs continue to generate antisemitic propaganda," *Washington Jewish Week*, December 23, 1993.

26. See Kenneth S. Stern, *Hate and the Internet* (New York: American Jewish Committee, 1999).

27. Arnon Groiss, *The West, Christians, and Jews in Saudi Arabian Schoolbooks* (New York: Center for Monitoring the Impact of Peace and the American Jewish Committee, 2003), pp. 104-05. These schoolbooks also contain scandalous accusations against Christians and Americans.

28. Kenneth R. Timmerman, *Preachers of Hate: Islam and the War on America* (New York: Crown Forum, 2003), p. 53 (uncorrected proof).

29. Cohn, "The Myth of the Jewish-World Conspiracy," p. 5.

30. "American Jewish Committee, in Meeting with Turkish Minister, Decries Official and Press Expressions of Anti-Semitism," AJC press release, February 24, 1996.

31. "Islamic Anti-Semitism," *New York Times*, October 18, 2003, p. A12.

32. This agenda included the undoing of many of the lessons of the Holocaust, including the need for compassionate asylum policies for people fleeing persecution, regardless of their racial or ethnic background.

33. There was no end to the story lines about Jews conspiring to harm non-Jews promoted in the Arab world. A ninety-five-page publication entitled *Arab Theologians on Jews and Israel* was distributed at Durban. It presented papers from the Fourth Conference of the Academy of Islamic Research, convened in Cairo in 1968, with titles such as "The Jews are the enemies of human life as is evident from their Holy Book," "Good tidings about the decisive battle between Muslims and Israel, in the light of the Holy Quran, the prophetic traditions, and the fundamental laws of nature and history," "Jihad in the cause of Allah," and "The Jihad is the way to gain victory," among others. As D.F. Green, who found and exposed this book, noted, it calls Jews not only enemies of humanity, but also "enemies of God," and the "dogs of humanity"; it states that they are "riff-raff and do not constitute a true people or nation," that Jews are inherently "evil" and "deserve their fate," that

the State of Israel is a "culmination of ... depravity [which must] be destroyed [by] Jihad—a Holy War," and that the "superiority of Islam over all other religions is ... a guarantee that the Arabs will ultimately triumph." Green concludes: "The ideas expounded in this volume could lead to the urge to liquidate Israel (politicide) and the Jews (genocide). If the evil of the Jews is immutable and permanent, transcending time and circumstances, and impervious to all hopes of reform, there is only one way to cleanse the world of them—by their complete annihilation." D. F. Green, *Arab Theologians on Jews and Israel: The Fourth Conference of the Academy of Islamic Research*, third edition (Geneva, 1976).

34. Todd Robberson, "Iranian President Talks up a Storm: Anti-Israel Remarks Isolate Nation as He Tries to Win Power at Home," *Dallas Morning News*, December 17, 2005, p. 1A.

35. Wistrich, *Muslim Anti-Semitism*, p. 37.

36. Stuart Schoffman, "Deconstructing Durban," *Jerusalem Report*, October 8, 2001, p. 36.

37. Ahmad Ragab of Egypt, in Goldberg, "Behind Mubarak," p. 51.

38. "David Duke in Saudi Paper," *Arab News*, May 28, 2002.

39. See "The Jewish Population of the World" at http://www.jewishvirtuallibrary.org/jsource/Judaism/jewpop.html, accessed January 6, 2005.

40. In between these two assertions is the allegation that the American system of lobbying has led the American government to a more pro-Israel position than is otherwise justified. This allegation may or may not be an example of antisemitism, depending on how it is presented, but regardless, antisemites will use it to support their claim of Jewish control over non-Jews.

41. Harris O. Schoenberg, "The Scapegoat," *Jerusalem Post*, July 27, 2001, p. A11.

42. Note that the communiqué released by those claiming responsibility for the July 7, 2005, London subway bombings referred to the "British Zionist Crusader government." "Al-Qa'idah Europe claims responsibility for London blasts," BBC Monitoring Middle East, July 7, 2005.

43. Wistrich, *Muslim Anti-Semitism,* p. 17, citing *Response* (Fall 2001), Vol. 22, No. 3 (Simon Wiesenthal Center Report), p. 9.

44. Charles Krauthammer, "Disgrace in Durban: The UN Conference on Racism was Worse than Just Hot Air," *Weekly Standard*, September 17, 2001, p. 15.

45. 'Atallah Abu Al-Subh, "Terror in America," Hamas Weekly, *Al-Risala* (Gaza), from Special Dispatch: Jihad and Terrorism Studies, No. 297, November 7, 2001 at http://www.dynet.com/bbs/mideast/100010-0.html), quoted in Harold Brackman, "9/11 Digital Lies: A Survey of Online Apologists for Global Terrorism," Simon Wiesenthal Center, 2001, p. 10.

46. David Pryce-Jones, "Priests of Killing: The Palestinians and the Cult of Death," *National Review*, April 22, 2002, LIV: 7. See also, Wistrich, *Muslim Anti-Semitism,* p. 35.

47. While Palestinians voted for Hamas for a number of reasons, including opposition to the corruption associated with the then-ruling Fatah Party and

Hamas's track record of providing health and other communal services, clearly neither its Islamo-fascist ideology nor its embrace of terror and suicide bombings made the party beyond the pale.

48. Grey Myre and Steven Erlanger, "Israel Seals West Bank and Gaza to Suppress Violence," *New York Times*, July 14, 2005, p. 3.

49. Wistrich, *Muslim Anti-Semitism,* p. 31.

Chapter Six

1. Community Service Trust briefing, May 27, 2002.

2. The best book on this topic is Gabriel Schoenfeld, *The Return of Anti-Semitism* (San Francisco: Encounter Books, 2004). See also various publications of the American Jewish Committee, Community Security Trust (UK), and the Stephen Roth Institute for the Study of Contemporary Antisemitism and Racism (Israel).

3. Michael Melchior, speech to American Jewish Committee, May 9, 2002. See http://www.ajc.org/site/apps/nl/content3.asp?c=ijITI2PHKoG&b=851489&ct=11 18833.

4. For example, the State Department report cited the inclusion of a "Saudi Arabian book 'Terror and Zionist Thinking' (featuring a cover illustration of a person standing in a pool of blood with a skull and a Star of David)" at the Frankfurt (Germany) book fair.

5. Remarks of Robert S. Rifkind, chairman of the Administrative Council of the Jacob Blaustein Institute for the Advancement of Human Rights, delivered at the NGO Preparatory Meeting for the OSCE Conference on Anti-Semitism, Berlin, April 27, 2004. See http://www.ajc.org/InTheMedia/RelatedArticles.asp?did =1231.

6. While many try to paint the Jews as the successors to colonialist white cowboys of the American West and the Palestinians as present-day Indians, the historical parallel is quite the other way. Jews—like today's Indians—are striving to reclaim a part of their ancestral homeland surrounded by hostile others.

7. Under international pressure, Syria diminished its control of Lebanon in 2005.

8. The ironies this produces are too delicious if they weren't so harmful. For example, which state—Israel or the future Palestinian state—exhibits more of the bone-chilling bigotry of apartheid? While there is no question that there are indeed instances of discrimination against Arabs in Israeli society, Arabs are citizens of the country and can vote and be elected to the Knesset (Israel's parliament). Conversely, where is the criticism from Europe or the left of the Palestinians' failure to extend similar political rights and protections to Jews who live in settlements that will one day be part of a Palestinian state in the West Bank? (In areas such as Hebron Jews have lived throughout history until they were forced out—many in 1948—only to return after 1967.)

9. Rifkind, Remarks to NGO Preparatory Meeting.

10. See "Knowledge and Remembrance of the Holocaust in Sweden" at http://

www.ajc.org/site/apps/nl/content3.asp?c=ijITI2PHKoG&b=846741&ct=1042063.

11. See, for example, primary sources noted at http://www.honestreporting.com/articles/45884734/critiques/Sad_Situation_in_Sweden.asp.

12. Melchior, speech to American Jewish Committee.

13. Report of Valerie Hoffenberg, AJC representative in France, to the AJC Antisemitism Task Force, May 2, 2006.

Chapter Seven

1. Harold Evans, "Anti-Semitic Lies and Hate Threaten Us All," *Times* (London), June 28, 2002, pp. 2;8.

2. Wistrich, *Muslim Anti-Semitism*, p. 41.

3. Ibid.

4. American Jewish Committee, *The Effort to Repeal Resolution 3379: An American Jewish Committee Conference November 8, 1990 at the United States Mission to the United Nations, New York, New York* (New York: American Jewish Committee, 1991), p.41.

5. Of course, the deniers fail to point out that reparations work the other way—benefiting the survivors, not the victims—so if there were a motive to play with the numbers, it would be to reduce the number who died. Nor do the deniers point out that the Jewish yearning for a return to their homeland is ancient, not a post-1945 invention, and the modern Zionist movement can be traced from the First Zionist Congress held in 1897.

6. One of the earliest Holocaust deniers, Paul Rassiner, actually came from the left, but that some earlier deniers were not from the right does not change the character of the movement.

7. See Kenneth S. Stern, *Holocaust Denial* (New York: American Jewish Committee, 1993), pp. 80-81.

8. Ibid, p. 65.

9. "Holocaust Denier Zundel Deported and Arrested," http://history1900s.about.com/b/a/151685.htm.

10. "Execution 'Engineer' Settles Criminal Case," *New York Times*, June 13, 1991, p. 11.

11. All statements from the Irving-Lipstadt trial can be found at www.Holocaustdenialontrial.org, or its shortcut www.hdot.org.

12. See, for example, "Transcript from Day 22: Final Solution: In East: Mass Shootings: Hitler: Role in: Himmler's Phone Log, November 30, 1941: Interpretation of Language" at hdot.org.

13. See http://www.holocaustdenialontrial.com/evidence/evans004.asp.

14. On July 25, 1998, Rebecca Gutman, then a local assistant director of the American Jewish Committee in Sarasota, Florida, attended an Irving lecture in Tampa, Florida. The meeting was organized by the National Alliance, the American neo-Nazi group then headed by William Pierce. Ms. Gutman supplied the court with a sampling of National Alliance literature available at the Irving event, which

was not only blatantly antisemitic, but also spoke in the overt language of Nazism, including calls for white "living space." Irving denied any contact with the National Alliance, but Irving's extensive diaries demonstrated that not only had he corresponded with National Alliance members (at least one of whom had written to Irving on National Alliance stationery), but also that the NA had regularly organized events for Irving in the United States, including two in 1995, three in 1996, and two in 1997.

15. Including Ernst Zündel, Ewald Bela Althans; (far-right party) Deutsche Volksunion (DVU) and its leader, Gerhand Frey; Ostrat Günter Deckert; Karl Philipp; Ernst-Otto Remer; Christian Worch; Ingrid Weckert; Michael Swierczek; and Udo Walendy, among others.

16. The diary also showed Irving's racism and misogyny. An example of the former is a "ditty" he wrote for his young daughter, Jessica:

I am a Baby Aryan
Not Jewish or Sectarian
I have no plans to marry—an
Ape or Rastafarian.

He has also written in his diary that "God works in mysterious ways, but here, we agree, he appears to be working [unreadable word] towards a Final Solution, which may cruelly wipe out not only Blacks and homosexuals but a large part of the drug addicts and sexually promiscuous and indiscriminate heterosexual population as well."

17. Even before the collapse of the peace process, Syria was actively promoting Holocaust denial. For example, its official newspaper, *Tishreen*, ran an editorial on January 31, 2000, by its editor-in-chief, which asserted that "Zionists created the Holocaust myth to blackmail and terrorize the world's intellectuals and politicians." See "American Jewish Committee Denounces Syrian Support for Holocaust Denial," AJC press release, February 1, 2000.

18. See Stern, *Holocaust Denial*, pp. 49-52, for examples. For examples in the Palestinian Authority see http://www.pmw.org.il/holocaust.htm (visited July 3, 2006).

19. While Jewish history denial has been given an intellectual framework in the wake of the Holocaust deniers, it did not start there. In fact, Saudi Arabia's King Faisal, as part of his call to the world's Muslims to "recover our sacred places [from] Zionist and Communist menaces," has said that Jews not only were "accursed" by God, but also have "no right to Jerusalem [as they] have no connection with Jerusalem and no sacraments there.... When the Romans occupied Jerusalem they took the Temple with them and therefore the Jews have no connection nor right to have any presence in Jerusalem or any authority there." "Faisal Attacks the Jews: Urges Islam to 'Rescue' Jerusalem," *Washington Post*, December 31, 1973, p. A1.

20. See http://www.expatica.com/source/site_article.asp?subchannel_id=26& story_id=27150&name=Germany+prevents+rightist+from+travelling+to+Iran.

21. See Stern, *Holocaust Denial*, pp.53-54.

22. As of this writing, Zundel's trial in Germany for Holocaust denial is still not completed. (Richard Bernstein, "Civility vs. Free Speech: A Democratic Quandry," *International Herald Tribune*, May 5, 2006, p. 2), and Irving has been convicted of Holocaust denial in Austria and sentenced to three years in jail. "British Author Jailed in Austria for Holocaust-denial Banned from News Media," Associated Press, March 7, 2006.

23. See December 20, 1989, issue of *Al-Istiqlal (Independence)*, cited in Stern, *Holocaust Denial*, p. 50.

24. For example, Seif Ali Al-Jarwan, writing in a Palestinian newspaper in 1998, said that Jews "concocted horrible stories of gas chambers which Hitler, they claimed, used to burn them alive. The press overflowed with pictures of Jews being gunned down ... or being pushed into gas chambers.... The truth is that such persecution was a malicious fabrication by the Jews." *Al Hayat Al-Jadeeda*, July 2, 1998, "Jewish Control of the World Media" (translated by MEMRI and cited in Wistrich, *Muslim Anti-Semitism*, p. 39).

25. For example, a Palestinian newspaper during this period sported a crossword puzzle with the correct answer being "Yad Vashem," Israel's Holocaust museum. The question: "The Jewish center for eternalizing the Holocaust and its lies." See Wistrich, p. 55, n.136.

26. "Arab Revisionists Meet in Jordan," Stephen Roth Institute for the Study of Anti-Semitism and Racism, Tel Aviv University, citing "Revisionist Historian Forum a Great Success," Middle East News Online, 16 May 2001; "JWA Pulls off Revisionist Historians' Conference," Jordan Times Online, 15 May 2001; "Exclusive Interview with Dr. Ibrahim Alloush," Middle East News Online, 7 May 2001; "The Jordanian Writers Association Sets a New Date for Its Forum," Free Arab Voice Online, 15 April 2001; AZAR, 18 May 2001 (MSANEWS).

27. Eliahu Salpeter, "Islam Coopts the Jewish Satan," *Ha'aretz*, September 6, 2001. See http://www.haaretz.com/hasen/pages/ShArt.jhtml?itemNo=71584 (visited July 3, 2006).

28. Khaled Abu Toameh, "The Haji: Arafat's New Prime Minister," *Jerusalem Post*, March 10, 2003, p. 2.

29. Such demeaning of the Holocaust is not, as some have suggested, an inevitable outcome of victim-group "competition." In 1998 there was an uproar when the Ellis Island Museum used the term "concentration camp" in the title of an exhibit (belonging to the Japanese National Museum) about the Japanese-American experience during World War II. The American Jewish Committee invited Jewish and Japanese-American leaders to meet, and reaffirming their close and constructive relationship, the issue was resolved. The joint text released noted:

> A concentration camp is a place where people are imprisoned not because of any crimes they have committed, but simply because of who they are. Although many groups have been singled out for such persecution throughout history, the term "concentration camp" was first used at the turn of the century in the Spanish-American and Boer Wars.

During World War II, America's concentration camps were clearly distinguishable from Nazi Germany's. Nazi camps were places of torture, barbarous medical experiments and summary executions; some were extermination centers with gas chambers. Six million Jews were slaughtered in the Holocaust. Many others, including Gypsies, Poles, homosexuals, and political dissidents were also victims of the Nazi concentration camps.

In recent years, concentration camps have existed in the former Soviet Union, Cambodia and Bosnia. Despite differences, all had one thing in common: the people in power removed a minority group from the general population and the rest of society let it happen.

"AJCommittee and the Japanese American National Museum Reach Agreement over the term 'Concentration Camp' Used in Ellis Island Exhibit," AJC press release, March 17, 1998.

30. Off-the-record meeting of clerics with AJC's Antisemitism Task Force, May 2003.

31. Regarding Holocaust reparations, it should be noted that some critics made it seem as though it were only Jews who were seeking restitution and were doing so because they were "greedy," as opposed to acknowledging that many seeking compensation were non-Jews and the litigation was to help those who had suffered as they were entering their last years, and also to bring some measure of justice. Some commentators, most noticeably Norman Finkelstein, took the reparations issue to a new level. Whereas Holocaust deniers start with the assumption that the Jews made up the Holocaust, and then used their conspiratorial ways to attack non-Jews, Finkelstein starts with belief that the Holocaust did happen, but then employs conspiracy theories and antisemitic stereotypes to explain the reparations lawsuits.

Chapter Eight

1. Remarks of Per Ahlmark at an international conference on "The Legacy of Holocaust Survivors," Yad Vashem, April 11, 2002, at www1.yadvashem.org/about _yad/what_new/data_whats_new/whats_new_international_conference_ahlmark. html.

2. A slightly different version of this chapter was first published as "Proprosal for a Redefinition of Antisemitism" in *Antisemitism Worldwide: 2003/2004*, Stephen Roth, ed., Institute for the Study of Contemporary Antisemitism and Racism, Tel Aviv University (Tel Aviv: 2005), p. 18.

3. European Monitoring Centre on Racism and Xenophobia, at http://eumc. eu.int/eumc/index.php?fuseaction=content.dsp_cat_content&catid=2 (visited July 5, 2006).

4. The report covered incidents that occurred during the first half of 2002. See "Manifestations of Anti-Semitism in the European Union: First Semester 2002, Synthesis Report," Draft 20, February 2003, p.5, at http://UK-ORG-BOD.SUP-PLEHOST.ORG/EUMC/EUMC.PDF.

5. "EU Anti-Racism Body Publishes Antisemitism Reports," EUMC Media Release, March 31, 2004.

6. European Union Monitoring Centre, "Manifestations of Antisemitism in the EU 2002-2003" (Vienna: 2004), p. 237.

7. Ibid., p. 240.

8. Note that even after making vocal criticisms of Mel Gibson's film *Passion of the Christ*, Abe Foxman of the Anti-Defamation League of B'nai B'rith said that the movie was not antisemitic. (See ABC's *Primetime Live*, "Mel Gibson's Passion," February 16, 2004.) Yet some (generally smaller or fringe) Jewish groups and individuals do use the word antisemitism too loosely from time to time, thus giving credence to those who claim that if they criticize Israel or aspects of the Jewish community, they will be labeled antisemites. Of course, some antisemites use the a priori claim that their views will be labeled antisemitic to suggest that they are being unfairly smeared (perhaps by an all-powerful Jewish conspiracy), or that their hateful expressions are brave. One would hope that if someone were honestly concerned that their expressions or actions might be considered antisemitic that 1) they would look at the credibility of the Jewish groups making that claim, and 2) their first reaction to an assertion of antisemitism by a credible organization would be to look inward (as they would likely do if their expressions were called racist by the NAACP or sexist by NOW), rather than reflexively to deny and counterattack.

9. David Matas, "Combatting Antisemitism," a paper based on discussions at the Jacob Blaustein Institute Seminar on Human Rights Methodology and Antisemitism, Vienna, Austria, June 17-18, 2003, p. 15.

10. The problem here is a matter of practical concerns versus intellectual honesty. If some people are reluctant to define acts of antisemitism as including Jews being stabbed because the attacker does not like Israel's actions, they are hardly likely to include any but the most outrageous expressions of anti-Zionism in a definition of antisemitism. The few groups on the political left that are concerned about antisemitism in their own community are likely to be similarly reluctant. As one leftist organizer concerned about antisemitism noted, it is not good strategy to go to a person who views himself as an anti-Zionist and tell him he is an antisemite before the discussion begins. (Statement made to author in an off-the-record meeting about antisemitism on the left, New York, February 2003.)

11. The original definition suggested to the EUMC read:

> Antisemitism is hatred toward Jews because they are Jews and is directed toward the Jewish religion and Jews individually or collectively. More recently antisemitism has been manifest by the demonization of the State of Israel.

> Antisemitism frequently charges Jews with conspiring to harm humanity, and it is often used to blame Jews for "why things go wrong." It is expressed in speech, writing, visual forms and action, and employs sinister stereotypes and negative character traits. (It may also be manifested on people mistaken as Jews, or on non-Jews seen as sympathetic to Jews.)

Contemporary examples of antisemitism in public life, the media, schools, the workplace and in the religious sphere include, but are not limited to:

— Calling for, aiding, or justifying the killing or harming of Jews in the name of a radical ideology or an extremist view of religion.

— Making mendacious, dehumanizing, demonizing, or stereotypical allegations about Jews—such as, especially but not exclusively, the myth about a world Jewish conspiracy or of Jews controlling the media, economy, government or other societal institutions.

— Accusing Jews as a people of being responsible for real or imagined wrongdoing committed by a single Jewish person or group, or even for acts committed by non-Jews.

— Denying the fact, scope, mechanisms (e.g., gas chambers) or intentionality of the genocide of the Jewish people at the hands of National Socialist Germany and its supporters and accomplices during World War II (the Holocaust).

— Accusing the Jews as a people, or Israel as a state, of inventing or exaggerating the Holocaust.

— Accusing Jewish citizens of being more loyal to Israel, or to the alleged priorities of Jews worldwide, than to the interests of their own nations.

Examples of the ways in which antisemitism manifests itself with regard to the State of Israel include:

— Denying the Jewish people their right to self-determination, e.g., by claiming that the existence of the State of Israel is a racist endeavor.

— Applying double standards by requiring of it a behavior not expected or demanded of any other democratic nation.

— Using the symbols and images associated with classic antisemitism (e.g., claims of Jews killing Jesus or the blood libel) to characterize Israel or Israelis.

— Drawing comparisons of contemporary Israeli policy to that of the Nazis.

— Holding Jews collectively responsible for actions of the State of Israel.

However, criticism of the policies of any Israeli government similar to that leveled against any other democratically elected government should not be regarded as antisemitic.

Antisemitic acts are criminal when they are so defined by law (for example, denial of the Holocaust or distribution of antisemitic materials in
some countries). Criminal acts are antisemitic when the targets of attacks,
whether they are people or property—such as buildings, schools, places of
worship and cemeteries—are selected because they are, or are perceived to
be, Jewish or linked to Jews. Antisemitic discrimination is the denial to
Jews of opportunities or services available to others and is illegal in many
countries.

12. The European Commission Against Racism and Intolerance.

13. But at the same time monitors need to be careful to look at the context of the
statement, to see if, in fact, it is an immoral equivalency. References to "Israeli
Apartheid" (see, for example, http://electronicintifada.net/bytopic/149.shtml) are
antisemitic. Scholarly statements, such as concerns during the Oslo process that the
division of the West Bank into "A," "B," and "C" areas might create problems similar to those seen under apartheid, may not be.

14. OSCE/ODIHR *Education on the Holocaust and Anti-Semitism,* at http://194.
8.63.155/documents/odihr/2005/06/14897_en.pdf.

15. OSCE/ODIHR *Combating Hate Crimes in the OSCE Region,* June 2005,
http://194.8.63.155/documents/odihr/2005/06/14915_en.pdf.

16. "Decision," Vilnius City District 2 Court Judge A. Cininas, #A11-01087-
497/2005, dated July 7, 2005.

Chapter Nine

1. David Elcott, former director of U.S. Interreligious Affairs for the American
Jewish Committee, was one of the few who articulated this vision. See David Elcott,
"*The Passion of the Christ* Could Cause Unwarranted Polarization," *Boston Globe,*
February 2004, at http://www.ajc.org/site/apps/nl/content2.asp?c=ijITI2PHKoG&
b=1531915&ct=1152501.

2. Arnon Groiss, *The West, Christians, and Jews in Saudi Arabian Schoolbooks,*
(New York: American Jewish Committee and the Center for Monitoring the
Impact of Peace, 2003), pp. 3, 4, 7.

3. Their presence was largely due to the tireless work of Stacey Burdett of the
Anti-Defamation League, who, perhaps better than anyone else, understood how
important it was for them to be there.

4. The NGOs wanted the United States to push for the appointment of a special representative on antisemitism inside OSCE in order to institutionalize the
OSCE's commitment to fighting antisemitism. The U.S. had not fully developed its
position on this issue, but the questioners kept hammering on the need and the
urgency. Eventually this became the U.S. position, and the appointment of a special
representative was made.

5. Joe Berkofsy, "Ford guidelines on funding colleges spark both challenges and
applause," *Jewish Telegraphic Agency,* May 12, 2004; http://www.fordfound.org/
news/view_news_detail.cfm?news_index=151.

6. As Timothy P. Weber notes in his article "On the Road to Armageddon," which appears on the Web site beliefnet.com, dispensationalism is "a particular way of understanding the Bible's prophetic passages, especially those in Daniel and Ezekiel in the Old Testament and the Book of Revelation in the New Testament. [Dispensationalists] ... believe that the nation of Israel will play a central role in the unfolding of end-times events." At http://www.beliefnet.com/story/151/story_15165_1.html.

7. "Robertson Suggests Stroke Is Divine Rebuke," *New York Times*, January 6, 2006, p. 14.

8. In some sense, these objectively small slights that bear long-lasting scars (a teenager having to decide whether to play football on Yom Kippur; a librarian being told she cannot take off Thanksgiving because she gets "her" holidays off) are almost inevitable in towns where the "culture" is presumptively Christian, and a Muslim or Buddhist would face the same challenges as a Jew.

9. Lori Forman, *The Political Activity of the Religious Right in the 1990s: A Critical Analysis*, (New York: American Jewish Committee, 1994), p. 24.

10. In 2003, when the then-prime minister of Malaysia, Mahathir Mohamad, gave a speech in which he claimed Jews ruled the world by proxy, all major Jewish organizations—correctly—issued strong statements decrying this overt anti-semitism. It is ironic that, years earlier, in his book *The New World Order*, Pat Robertson wrote something very similar. The difference? Mahathir was against Israel, and Robertson a supporter.

Robertson traced much world upheaval to the workings of a secret group called the Illuminati, aligned with the Freemasons. He wrote that in 1782:

> [T]he headquarters of Illuminated Freemasonry moved to Frankfurt, a center controlled by the Rothschild family. It is reported that in Frankfurt, Jews for the first time were admitted to the order of Freemasons. If indeed members of the Rothschild family or their close associates were polluted by the occultism of Wishaupt's Illuminated Freemasonry, we may have discovered the link between the occult and the world of high finance. Remember, the Rothschilds financed Cecil Rhodes in Africa; Lord Rothschild was a member of the inner circle of Rhodes' English Round Table; and Paul Warburg, architect of the Federal Reserve System, was a Rothschild agent.
>
> New money suddenly poured into the Frankfurt lodge, and from there a well-funded plan for world revolution was carried forth.

Pat Robertson, *The New World Order* (Dallas: Word Publishing, 1991), p. 181.

11. Because detractors and supporters of Israel might represent different types of institutions or have different histories and connections with Jewish and other institutions, the tactics used to respond to them might well be different.

Chapter Ten

1. Richard Sideman and Kenneth Stern, "Minutes of June 6, 2002 Conference Call on Anti-Semitism on the College Campus," American Jewish Committee, internal document, June 18, 2002.

2. Steven Koplin, "Grid of Campus Divestment Activity," American Jewish Committee, internal document, 2002.

3. Megan Greenwell, "Divestment Issue Not Supported Nationwide," *Columbia Spectator*, November 12, 2002, at http://media.www.columbiaspectator.com/media/storage/paper865/news/2002/11/12/News/Divestment.Issue.Not.Supported .Nationwide-2038132.shtml?sourcedomain=www.columbiaspectator.com&MIIH ost=media.collegepublisher.com.

4. Tanya Schevitz, "UC Berkeley's conflicts mirror Mideast's pain, Tension growing between Jewish, Palestinian students," *San Francisco Chronicle*, April 5, 2002, at http://www.sfgate.com/cgi-bin/article.cgi?file=/c/a/2002/04/05/MN1742 07.DTL.

5. See, for example, Joe Eskenazi, "Alleged assault near Berkeley campus troubles Jews," *Jewish News Weekly of Northern California*, October 19, 2001, at http://www.jewishsf.com/content/2-0-/module/displaystory/story_id/17071/edition_id/336/format/html/displaystory.html.

6. There are reports that the situation at San Francisco State has improved somewhat recently.

7. Laurie Zoloth, "Fear and Loathing at San Francisco State," at http://www.aish.com/jewishissues/jewishsociety/Fear_and_Loathing_at_San_Francisco_ State.asp.

8. Sideman and Stern, "Minutes of June 6, 2002 Conference Call."

9. There were other episodes as well, including a graduate student offering a class on the poetry of Palestinian resistance at Berkeley, about which he noted that "[c]onservative thinkers are encouraged to seek other sections." Joe Eskenazi, "Crisis on Campus, E. Bay federation head wants 'dangerous' class canceled at Berkeley," *Jewish News Weekly of Northern California*, at http://www.jewishsf.com/content/2-0-/module/displaystory/story_id/18239/edition_id/365/format/html/displa ystory.html (visited July 7, 2006).

10. The organizer of the Rutgers meeting was an extreme ideologue who offended her cohorts so much that that year's meeting was moved to Ohio State instead. However, the local organizers in New Jersey went ahead with their anti-Israel event, even though they also lost the right to hold it on campus, since they did not fill out the paperwork that the university required for such events.

11. Following are excerpts from a statement adopted at the Third National Student Conference of the Palestine Solidarity Movement, November 7-9, 2003:

> 2. The Third Conference believes that the Palestinian people must ultimately be able to decide their future in Palestine. Certain key principles ... grounded in, but not limited to, international law, human rights, and basic standards of justice, will be funda-

mental to a just resolution to the plight of the Palestinians. These include:

> — ... the recognition and implementation of the right of return and repatriation for all Palestinian refugees to their original homes and properties; and

> — an end to the Israeli system of Apartheid....

3. Just as the Third Conference condemns the racism and discrimination inherent in Zionism underlying the policies and laws of the state of Israel, the Third Conference rejects any form of hatred or discrimination against any group based on race, ethnicity, religion, gender, or sexual orientation....

4. As a solidarity movement, it is not our place to dictate the strategies or tactics adopted by the Palestinian people in their struggle for liberation.

5. The 3rd Conference seeks to promote the following campaigns:

> — divestment from Israel

> — ending U.S. aid to Israel;

> — Right of Return

At http://www.palestineconference.com/principles.html accessed January, 2005.

12. After the 2006 PSM meeting at Georgetown, Columbia student Bari Weiss wrote about it in the journal she founded, the *Columbia Current*. She quoted a PSM speaker named Joe Carr as stating, "We work with Hamas and Islamic Jihad." It is unclear what this admission means. But if it were proved that PSM did indeed work closely with terrorist organizations, there might be a legal basis to refuse its request to hold meetings meetings based on its actions and not its views. Bari Weiss, "Lessons from the Palestinian Solidarity Movement," *Columbia Current*, Spring 2006, at http://www.columbia.edu/cu/current/articles/spring2006/weiss.html.

13. Jennifer Jacobson, "Conservative Activist Admits Lack of Evidence for Some Allegations of Faculty Bias," *Chronicle of Higher Education*, January 20, 2006, at http://chronicle.com/weekly/v52/i20/20a03301.htm. *Campus Watch*, created by Daniel Pipes in recognition of the poor scholarship, frequent intolerance of differing points of view, reported instances of intimidation of students, and tremendously anti-Western and anti-Israel bent in Middle Eastern Studies generally, keeps an eye on professors it deems to be violating these goals and standards, posting quotations from them. While, on one hand, this is a service that shines light on a real problem, it plays into the perception (real or not) that outside groups are trying to challenge the rights of professors to speak. Thus, some professors who were not on the *Campus Watch* list asked to be included, as a sign of solidarity. The debate, then, has shifted away from the troubling dogma and intolerance of the programs, which rightly concern Pipes, into one of free speech.

Likewise, the assertion that Title VI grants be better structured so not to be used for one-sided bashing of the U.S., Western civilization, and Israel is also complex. On one hand, campuses have no inherent right to these funds, and if Congress wants to provide them with strings attached, that is its prerogative. On the other hand, this approach feeds into an "us versus them" mentality, which again recasts the issue as one of academic freedom and free speech.

14. *Columbia News*, "Ad Hoc Grievance Committee Report," at http://www.columbia.edu/cu/news/05/03/ad_hoc_grievance_committee_report.html.

15. While such a reply is unseemly and inappropriate, it does not directly engage the prospect of a student feeling unable to express his or her opinions, for fear of receiving a lower grade.

16. Off-the-record phone conversation between author and leader of one off-campus Jewish group, March 31, 2005.

17. See Kenneth S. Stern, *Why Campus Anti-Israel Activity Flunks Bigotry 101*, http://www.ajc.org/site/c.ijITI2PHKoG/b.848707/apps/nl/content3.asp?content_id=%7BB2CCEEE5-B039-42D0-8762-FB2EAACAA7CA%7D&notoc=1.

18. Comment by Dr. Deborah Lipstadt, at a consultation on the campus, American Jewish Committee, New York, May 24, 2005.

19. At the PSM conference at Duke in 2004, Jewish anti-Israel activists spoke about going on birthright trips and then using the opportunity for anti-Israel activity.

Chapter Eleven

1. *Anti-Semitism in America 2002* (Anti-Defamation League, 2002) at http://www.adl.org/anti_semitism/2002/as_survey.pdf, accessed January 7, 2005.

2. Tom W. Smith, *What Do Americans Think About Jews* (New York: American Jewish Committee, 1991), p. 39.

3. Some portions of this chapter first appeared in a different form in Kenneth S. Stern, "The Need for an Interdisciplinary Field of Hate Studies," *Journal of Hate Studies* 3:1 (Spokane: Gonzaga University, 2004), p. 17 ff.

4. L.H. Schultz, D.J. Barr, and R.L. Selman, "The Value of a Developmental Approach to Evaluating Character Development Programmes: An outcome study of Facing History and Ourselves," *Journal of Moral Education* 30:1, 2001, pp. 18-19.

5. In Walter G. Stephan and W. Paul Vogt, *Education Programs for Improving Intergroup Relations: Theory, Research and Practice* (New York: Teachers College Press, 2004).

6. A hate studies program might also give birth to some new social initiatives. For example, social psychology research suggests that when people work together on a "superordinate goal," stereotypes break down. It might be worthwhile to create and test pilot projects bringing students from different backgrounds together (perhaps during the end of the senior year in high school), and send teams (a Jew from New York, an African American from Chicago, an American Indian from South Dakota, etc.) to another part of the United States (the rural South, for example) to work together to help a local community for a few weeks. If such an initiative

demonstrates a reduction in bigoted attitudes that holds over time, or other positive outcomes, the program might be expanded.

7. The OSCE's Office of Democratic Institutions and Human Rights report, *Education on the Holocaust and on Anti-Semitism: An Overview and Analysis of Educational Approaches*, noted: "Holocaust education cannot be deployed, either preventively or as a corrective, against all contemporary forms of anti-Semitism." June 1, 2005, p. 2, http://194.8.63.155/documents/odihr/2005/06/14897_en.pdf.

8. Yehoshua Amishav, "Anti-Semites Are Using the Holocaust," *Ha'aretz*, December 28, 2003.

9. U.S. State Department's "Report on Global Antisemitism, July 1, 2003-December 15, 2004, Submitted by the Department of State to the Committee of Foreign Affairs and the Committee on International Relations in accordance with Section 4 of PL 108-332," 2005, p. 46.

10. "About 5,000 protest against Israel; no violence reported," Associated Press, April 7, 2002; "Anti-Israel demonstrators detained in Sweden," *Nordic Business Report*, March 22, 2004.

11. BBC News, April 20, 2004, at http://news.bbc.co.uk/2/hi/technology/3641895.stm.

12. T.K. Kim, "Electronic Storm," *Southern Poverty Law Center Intelligence Report*, at http://www.splcenter.org/intel/intelreport/article.jsp?aid=551.

13. Kenneth S. Stern, *Hate and the Internet* (New York: American Jewish Committee, 1999). I am not suggesting that Europeans scrap their laws against the publication of hate speech. They have a different tradition and are entitled to it, just as Americans are entitled to theirs. However, the reality is that hate on the Internet cannot be buried in ostrich-like fashion, both for technological and other reasons. The Europeans should see hate on the Internet as an educational opportunity to teach students about the existence of hatred in the real world and how to recognize and reject it.

Chapter Twelve

1. Patrick J. Buchanan, "America in 2050: Another Country," WorldNetDaily, at http://www.wnd.com/news/article.asp?ARTICLE_ID=37720.

2. Sergio DellaPergola, Uzi Rebhun and Mark Tolts, "Prospecting the Jewish Future: Population Projections, 2000-2008," *2000 American Jewish Year Book* (New York: American Jewish Committee, 2000), p. 123.

3. Michael Whine, of the Community Security Trust in the UK, has noted that if one holds up a chart of incidents of antisemitic hate crimes and another of the frequency with which tensions in the Middle East are mentioned in the press, the two are nearly identical.

4. There is, of course, the abstract possibility that such xenophobia will have some benefit to Jews, who, in an increasingly charged atmosphere defining whites on one side (aligned with those presumably with more power) and non-whites on the other, would be seen as members of the white grouping. But the historical evi-

dence is strong that antisemitism is a likely product in any circumstance that gives license to bigotry and intergroup conflict.

5. *American Attitudes Towards Jews in America* (Anti-Defamation League, 2005) at http://www.adl.org/anti_semitism/Anti_Semitic_Attitudes_files/frame.htm.

6. Of course, illegal acts can be prosecuted or prohibited, even if they are related to speech. For example, a person has no right to sexually harass a coworker, or to repeatedly call someone on the phone in the middle of the night, even though the means through which he or she acts is through speech.

7. There is an argument to be made that some speech that is otherwise permitted should be curtailed during wartime. One problem with this approach is that, while it has some merit, the current war is not one against a particular nation state and thus has no clearly definable end. The war against Islamists is likely to go on for years, if not decades, and will go through periods of greater and lesser intensity, so unless we are willing to give up free speech on a quasi-permanent basis, this argument should not apply.

Some also argue that calls for genocide should be made illegal, because they have no redeeming social value. While this is true abstractly, the sanctioning of such theoretical assertions, rather than calls for imminent action, would raise too many legal, factual, and functional problems.

8. There may also be a fourth problem when attempting to suppress a particular text. Some people advocate civil and criminal lawsuits in Europe and elsewhere against promoters of *The Protocols of the Elders of Zion*. Leaving aside the questions of whether laws against the *Protocols* are a good idea and whether they can be enforced, there is the more basic problem of identifying the danger that the *Protocols* presents. Is it dangerous because it is a text or because it is an idea? Is there danger that attempts to suppress the text might also promote the idea?

9. From time to time, a hate group "adopts" a stretch of highway to keep clean, and state officials cannot refuse such groups as the Ku Klux Klan or the American Nazi Party based on their odious views. A good solution is to rename that part of the roadway for someone such as Rosa Parks or Martin Luther King, Jr. Having white supremacists pick up trash on the Rosa Parks Highway is somehow fitting.

10. See Kenneth S. Stern, *Bigotry on Campus* (New York: American Jewish Committee, 1990).

11. The time in question was before it became clear there were no weapons of mass destruction, that other "justifications" for the war were dubious, that the occupation would continue to cost Americans and Iraqis their lives, and that the stability in the region would be jeopardized.

12. Another trigger might be a high-profile criminal case involving claims that a Jew or Jewish group compromised American security to help the Israelis. One of the major antisemitic incidents in the late nineteenth century involved the trial of Alfred Dreyfus in France, and the claim that while a captain in the French military, he secretly aided the Germans. The antisemitism was so thick during this affair that chants of "Death to the Jews" were heard in the streets of Paris, although in the end Dreyfus was exonerated.

There were concerns that something similar could happen when Jonathan Pollard, a United States Navy intelligence analyst, was caught spying for the Israelis in the mid-1980s. He claimed he was turning over material that was important for the security of an ally—Israel—relating to Soviet arms shipments in the region, the chemical weapons programs of Syria and Iraq, the Pakistani atomic bomb, and Libyan air defenses. But, of course, turning over such material to an "ally" is no excuse—once the information is compromised, there is no way to tell who else knows it. The Israelis were clearly embarrassed and promised never to make this mistake again. It was certainly possible that there might have been anti-Israel and antisemitic backlash if the case had gone to trial, but Pollard pleaded guilty and received a lengthy jail sentence. In all likelihood, the Israelis—concerned about the backlash—told Pollard to make the best plea deal possible, and then they would use political and diplomatic tools to attempt to gain his freedom. That a few individual Jews—like individual Germans or Iraqis or Nicaraguans or others—could be confused about their allegiance first to the United States and then to the country of their national origin or heritage affiliation is inevitable. And when someone acts on this internal conflict to the detriment of the United States, they—like Pollard—should be punished.

There have also been, in recent times, allegations that AIPAC (American Israel Public Affairs Committee) may have forwarded to Israel some information given to it outside normal channels in a way that violated the law. While, at this writing, it is unknown whether the rumors are credible, one must assume that if AIPAC made a mistake, it, like any other credible organization, would admit its error, suffer the appropriate consequences, and institute procedures to make sure it would not happen again. There may, of course, be nothing to these charges. But a case like this could well be a trigger of claims of "dual loyalty." If so, it is incumbent on, not only Jewish agencies, but also others to debunk the canard and put any wrongdoing in proper perspective.

13. John J. Mearsheimer and Stephen M. Walt, *The Israel Lobby and U.S. Foreign Policy*, Harvard University John F. Kennedy School of Government Faculty Research Working Papers # RWP06-011, March 2006, pp. 15-16, 25. (Harvard removed its logo from the paper, further distancing itself from the scholars, shortly after a shortened version was released by the *London Review of Books*.)

14. The Mearsheimer-Walt paper never noted, for example, that while many Palestinians cheered when America was attacked on September 11, 2001, Israeli society shared America's grief.

15. United Church of Christ, Twenty-fifth Synod, Resolution 8: "Concerning Use of Economic Leverage in Promoting Peace in the Middle East," at http://www.ucc.org/synod/resolutions/gsrev25-15.pdf.

16. Ibid.

17. Some assert that this shift reflects the difference between the "old left" and the "new left." There may be some truth in that observation, as members of the "old left" had memories of Jews as refugees, which members of the "new left" do not.

18. See, for example, *Prairie Fire: The Politics of Revolutionary Anti-Imperialism*—

A Political Statement of the Weather Underground (Communications Co., 1974), pp. 103-08.

19. In early 2006 the American Association of University Professors, long committed to academic freedom, scheduled (but later cancelled) a conference about the wording of its policy against academic boycotts. AJC submitted an analysis of the policy, which analyzed why academic boycotts are inappropriate in general, and why the case for a boycott against Israel fails any reasonable test. The full text of the AJC submission to AAUP is available at the AJC Web site at http://www.ajc.org/site/lookup.asp?c=ijITI2PHKoG&b=2213809.

Chapter Thirteen

1. For the full text of the Berlin Declaration, see http://www.osce.org/documents/cio/2004/04/2828_en.pdf.

2. Kathrin Meyer, who works on antisemitism issues at the OSCE, has been an unsung heroine in this project. She has reached out to NGOs (including the Berlin office of the American Jewish Committee) and has been working to include material about combating contemporary antisemitism into programs already in existence to teach about the Holocaust.

3. Not only would boycotts be counterproductive, but the Jewish communities in countries such as France are against this approach, instead arguing that *more* people should come and raise the issue of antisemitism while there.

4. The background of these diplomatic meetings is chronicled in David Harris's four-volume series, *In the Trenches* (Hoboken/Jersey City: NJ: KTAV, 2000, 2002, 2004, 2006).

5. This model—of reaching out to different countries and meeting at the highest level about our respective concerns—has also been adopted domestically. The aforementioned Latino-Jewish Coalition is the result of such an initiative. The principle is that no group fighting bigotry can be effective going it alone, and the more each ethnic and religious group knows about and understands each other, the more likely they can count on each other in times of need.

6. MEMRI, "Arab Reactions to the U.S.'s Global Antisemitism Review Act of 2004," December 8, 2004, Inquiry and Analysis Series #198 at http://memri.org/bin/articles.cgi?Page=archives&Area=ia&ID=IA19804 (accessed January 17, 2005).

7. Ibid.

8. "Nasrallah's Nonsense," *New York Sun*, March 11, 2005, p. 10.

Index

Abbas, Mahmoud, 68, 90
Abortion, 115-16
Abu Dabi, 58
Academic "Bill of Rights," 129
Academic freedom, 131-32. *See also*
AAUP
Affirmative action, 11, 139-40, 151
Afghanistan, 18, 35, 62, 75, 161
African Americans, 98-99, 120, 148
Ahlmark, Per, 96
Ahmadinejad, Mahmoud, 15, 61-62, 89
Al Shara, Farouk, 36
Al-Ahram, 58, 166
Al-Aqsa Mosque, 63, 66
Al-Aridhi, Ghazi, 166
Al-Asmar, Hilmi, 52
Al-Azhar University (Cairo), 60
Al-Aziz, Mamdouh bin Abd, 53
Al-Ghazi, Issam, 66
Al-Hujjat, 38
Al-Husseini, Haj Amin, 59
Ali, Orkhan Muhammad, 51
Al-Jazeera, 58
Al-Khatib, Mu'taz, 53
Allies (World War II), 91-92
Al-Marayati, Salam, 51
Al-Maydan, 66
Al-Muhajiroun, 70
Al-Musallah, Ahmad, 53
Al-Qaeda, 47, 161
Al-Riyadh, 166
Al-Samak, Muhammad, 166
Al-Sawahri, Khalil, 51
American Association of University Professors (AAUP), 202
American Civil Liberties Union (ACLU), 153
American Free Press, 17
American Indians, 92
American Jewish Committee, vi, 39, 59, 70, 78, 110, 116, 121-22, 128, 138-39, 141, 158-59, 165; history of, v

American Jewish Committee Antisemitism Task Force, 121
American Jewish Year Book, 148
American Nazi Party, 45
Amin, Idi, 66
Amishav, Yehoshua, 144
Amman, Jordan, 60
Amnesty International, 34
Anarchists, 101
Annan, Kofi, 25
Anthrax, 67
Anti-Americanism, 64-69
Anti-Arab bigotry, 45-46, 124. *See also*
September 11, attacks of
Anti-bias education, 139-43, 169
Anti-Defamation League of B'nai B'rith (ADL), 8, 116, 138
Anti-globalists, 17, 112-13
Anti-Israelism related to antisemitism, 1, 95,144, 155
Antisemitism
  Anti-Zionism as antisemitism, 98-99, 127
  Arab antisemitism, 58
  as a perception of Jews, 102
  as a system of ideas, 78-79
  as explanation for why things go wrong, 8, 9, 14, 102, 107
  as having "lite" version, 91, 155-56
  as reflecting discomfort with notion of Jews with power, 159-60
  as self-defense, 72
  as suppressed truth, 79
  bright people, engaging in, 79
  charge not to be used loosely, 158, 161
  claim would disappear if Middle East conflict settled, 72
  comparison with 1930s, 8
  comparison of Israelis and Nazis, 1, 103. *See also* Israel
  connection between Europe and Mus-

lims, imported and exported, 73, 165
conspiracy theories regarding Jews as,
vi, 5, 7, 8, 9, 11-14
definition of, 8, 96-106
dehumanizing of Jews as, 102. *See also*
Jews
denial of Jewish historic link with land
of Israel as, 3, 13, 99, 104-05
denial of Jewish right to self-determination as manifestation of, 101, 103.
See also anti-Zionism
denial of application of the word to
Arabs, 26-27
denial of meaning of word, 40
dismissed as less significant than other
forms of hatred, 125, 126
dual loyalty accusations as, 103, 155
Europe, in, 70-77. *See also* specific
countries
freedom from, as human right, 111
holding Jews responsible for Israel's
acts as, 103
Holocaust denial as, 103
in the Arab world, 55-69, 73
in the Muslim world, 55-69, 73
Israeli-Palestinian peace process related
to, vii, 8, 19-21, 23
Jesus, associated with death of, 9. *See
also* Jews
left-wing politics associated with, vi,
13-14, 19, 21, 74-75, 125; flirtation
with right-wing politics over, 17-18,
89, 110, 155, 158
legal tools against, 161
Middle East events as triggers for dis-
plays of, vii, 154-57
myths associated with, 43, 51, 57, 78,
79, 94-95, 102, 167. *See also* individual myths, e.g. blood libel, Holocaust
denial, September 11, etc.
"New" antisemitism, vii, 6, 8, 23
on campus, vii. *See also* U.S. campuses
political antisemitism, vii, 12-14, 117,
136, 138, 164. *See also* anti-Zionism
quarantine theory of, 107
race-based antisemitism, 10-12, 117,

136, 138, 164
racist concept, termed, 32
related to charge of Jewish power,
vi,102, 155
religious antisemitism, 8-10, 108,
110, 115, 117, 136, 138, 143, 145,
152, 158, 164, 166
spelling of, 1
stereotypes, as a series of, 97-98
subset of human capacity to hate, 142
Temple Mount, claim does not exist,
as, 104
triggers for, 154-57
twisted in Durban, 36
Working Definition of, 102-06. *See
also* European Monitoring Centre on
Racism and Xenophobia
Anti-Zionism, 12-14, 37, 41-42, 98, 105,
108, 110-13, 118-19, 121-23, 126, 134,
138, 152, 160; as antisemitism, 98-99,
100-06, 111, 114, 127
Antwerp, Belgium, 71
Apartheid (comparison with Israel), 25,
27-29, 32-33, 35, 38-39, 42, 104, 118,
122, 157-161
Arab cartoons, 55
Arab extremists, 60
Arab land, 74, 104
Arab Lawyers Union, 28
Arab leaders, 64
Arab League, 39
Arab media, 19, 58, 62-63, 65-69, 90,
110, 165-66. *See also* specific publications
Arab oil crisis, 154-55
Arab refugees, 34
Arab states, 6, 11, 13, 19, 60-61, 64, 110,
128, 134, 137, 154-55, 160, 165, 167-68
Arab voters, 22
Arabs, 25, 26, 39, 44-45, 49-54, 56, 62,
66, 59, 72-73, 77, 88-91, 95, 110, 124,
126, 162, 166-68; as allies of Nazi Ger-
many, 59
Arafat, Yasir, 36-37, 40, 160
Argentina, 7
Aryan Nation, 72
Asian-Americans, 148

Assad, Bashar, 62-63
Association of University Teachers (UK), 161. *See also* American Association of University Professors
Atta, Muhammad, 47, 51
Attitudinal surveys, 136-39, 152
Auschwitz, 3, 25, 81, 82-84
Australia, 7, 28, 69, 71, 149
Austria, 7, 22

Baby killing, 92
Baghdad, 55
Bangladesh, 100
Barak, Ehud, 53
Bay Area peace movement, 120
Beirut, 89-90
Belgium, 7, 71, 144
Ben Itto, Hadassa, 78
Berlin Declaration, 163-64, 176-178
Berlin, 2, 3, 59, 71, 85-86, 96, 111, 164
Berman, Paul, 47
Bible, 59
Bigotry finder test, 133-34
Bill of Rights, 149-50
Bin Laden, Osama, 46-47, 52, 53, 63-64
Birthright Israel, 134
Black Death, 9
Black supremacists, 94-95
Black, Don, 145
Blood libel, 9, 19, 20, 31, 55, 57-58, 62, 75, 78, 103, 122
Bollinger, Lee 119, 132
Bosnia, 7
Boycott (by pro-Israel forces), 165
Boycott (of Israel or Israelis). *See* Divestment
Brandeis University, 122, 128
Brazil, 7
British, 73, 82, 88
British Broadcasting Company (BBC), 53
British Israelism, 149
British Jewry, 31
British National Party, 22, 87
Brussels, Belgium, 71
Buchanan, Patrick, vii, 7, 17, 148, 155
Buddhism, 166

Bush, George W., 1, 43, 47, 91, 155-56
Butz, Arthur, 82, 87
Byrd, James, 48

Camp David Accords, 47
Campus. *See* U.S. Campuses
Canada, 7, 69, 71, 82, 84, 98, 124
Carnegie Foundation, 139-40
Carto, Willis, 80
Caterpillar Corporation, 157
Catholic Church, 137
Catholic societies, 152, 166
Central Intelligence Agency, 66
Centre for Research on Antisemitism, 96
Chace, Bill, 124
Chechnya, 18
Children, exploitation of, 41, 68-69
Chile, 45
China, 74, 166
Chirac, Jacques, 21, 72
Chomsky, Noam, 89
Choudary, Anjem, 70
Christian Identity, 11, 68, 149-51
Christian Patriotism, 149-51
Christianity, 9, 10, 15, 18, 48, 55, 57, 60, 63, 108, 110, 113, 116
Church of the Holy Sepulcher, 63
Church of the Nativity, 63
Cincinnati, 91
Civil liberties, 46
Civil rights, 39
Clarendon Club, 87
Cockburn, Alexander, 17
Cohen, Norman, 60
Cold War, 17, 19, 160
Colonialism, 20, 32, 35, 36-37, 65, 66, 73, 118, 121, 160, 166
Columbia University, 119, 130-33
Communism, 65, 160
Concordia University, 124
Conspiracy Theories. *See* specific topics (e.g., September 11, antisemitism)
Cornell University, 119
Cotler, Irwin, 8
Crusaders, 110
Crusades, 9

Cycle of Violence, 125

Damascus, 57, 62
Dartmouth College, 122
Darwin, Charles, 10
David Project, 130
Deicide charge. *See* Jesus
Democratic Party, 7
Demography, 12, 21, 23, 77, 148-50, 162, 163, 166
Denying the Holocaust: The Growing Assault on Truth and Memory, 84
Dershowitz, Alan, 132
Destruction of Dresden, The, 82
Dhimmis, 10, 56
Diary of Anne Frank, 2, 80
Divestment (from Israel), 118-20, 126, 131-32, 157-161. *See also* Apartheid, Israel
Dresden, 91
Dreyfus, Alfred, 15
Drug Abuse Resistance Education (DARE), 140
Duke University, 126, 127-28
Duke, David, vii, 43-44, 48, 63-64, 87, 99, 145
Durban, South Africa, 3,4,7,14,23,27, 28, 30, 33-34, 36, 38-42, 45, 48, 52, 62, 109-12, 118-19, 126, 137, 148. *See also* United Nations World Conference Against Racism Racial Discrimination, Xenophobia and Related Intolerance
Dutch, 73

Easter, 108
Eastern Europe, 76, 81. *See also* specific countries
Eastpointe, Michigan, 45
Eban, Abba, 12
Ecumenical Caucus, 32
Education on the Holocaust and Antisemitism: An Overview and Analysis of Educational Approaches, 105
Education, 139-144, 146
Egypt, 11, 13, 38, 51, 52, 56, 58, 59, 61, 63, 66, 69, 74, 166-67; textbooks in, 110

Einsatzgruppen, 3, 85
Einstein, Albert, 136
El Salvador, 45
Elcott, David 158-59
Elders of Zion, 50, 60, 99. *See also Protocols of the Elders of Zion*
Emory University, 124, 134
Encryption, 146
Encyclopedia Britannica, 15-16, 22
Energy, 110
England, 7, 22, 24, 56, 66, 69, 70, 84-85, 149, 161-62
Episcopal Church, 158
Erbakan, Necmettin, 61
Ernstein, France, 70
European Commission Against Racism and Intolerance (ECRI), 104
European Monitoring Centre on Racism and Xenophobia (EUMC), 7, 96-106; working definition on antisemitism, 7, 101-06
European Union, 96, 164, 166
Evaluation of Multicultural Education Program: Techniques and a Meta-Analysis, The, 140-41
Evangelical Christians, 113-17; dispensational, 114

Facing History and Ourselves, 139-40
Faisal, King, 58
Falwell, Jerry, 113-14
Farm workers, 93
Farrakhan, Louis, vii, 88, 99
Fascism, 14, 62, 81, 89, 118, 121
Faurrison, Robert, 82
Federal Bureau of Investigation (FBI), 46
Feith, Douglas, 155
Fez, Morocco, 55
Final Call, The, 40
Ford Foundation, 40, 112
Ford, Henry, 11
Forman, Lori, 115
Forster, Arnold, 8
France, 7, 13, 15, 20, 21-22, 69, 70-71 72, 73, 77, 82, 94, 143, 166; riots in, 20
Frank, Otto, 80

Franklin, Benjamin, v, 107
Free Exercise of Religion, *See* United
States Constitution, First Amendment
Freedman, James O., 122
Freedom of Speech. *See* United States
Constitution, First Amendment
Freemen, 67
French, 73, 82; Jews, 143, 166. *See also*
France
Frontpage Magazine, 129
Furrow, Buford, 72, 161

Gamei'a, Muhammad, 50-51, 52
Gaming programs, 146
Gas chambers, 81, 82, 84, 90, 93
Gay marriage, 116
Gaza, 104, 115. *See also* Palestine
Geneva, Switzerland, 41
Genocide, 34, 64, 76, 92, 114, 168. *See
also* Sudan
Georgetown University, 126
German Jews, 85-86
Germany, 7, 8, 15, 33, 59, 71, 72, 73,
82, 84, 85-88, 139, 140
Ghettos, 9
Gibson, Mel, 108-09
Gobineau, Joseph, 10
Golan Heights, 63
Goldstein, Baruch, 57
Gonzaga University, Institute for Action
Against Hate, 141
Graf, Jürgen, 89
Gray, Charles, 84, 87-88
Greece, 7
Gulf War, 45, 47
Gun control, 150-51
Gypsies, 91

Ha'aretz, 144
Hadith, 56
Haider, Jörg, 22
Hale, Matt, 43
Halimi, Ilan, 77
Halle, Germany, 87
Hamas, 60, 67-68. 90, 98, 112, 160;
referring to *Protocols* in charter, 60, 90

Hands Across the Campus, 139
Harkabi, Y., 59
Harris, David A., 39
Harvard University, 119, 156
Hate crimes, 26, 31, 45, 46, 69, 70-72,
73, 77, 96-97, 99-100, 103, 105, 119,
144, 151, 164
Hate speech, 99-100, 126-27, 135, 152-
54; codes, 154
Hate studies, 141-43
Heydrich, Reinhard, 85-86
Hezbollah, 60, 168
High Court of Justice (in London), 84-85
Hillel, 119-20, 133
Himmler, Heinrich, 84, 85-86
Hispanics, 93, 148, 151-52
History, 142-43
Hitler, Adolf, vi, 2, 3, 4, 15, 20, 28, 29,
31, 32, 51, 55, 58, 59, 63, 72, 78-79, 83-
85, 87-88, 90, 91, 92, 93, 120
Hitler We Loved and Why, The, 82
Hitler's War, 82
Hoax of the Twentieth Century, The, 82
Holocaust, 2, 3, 20, 25-26, 28, 29, 38,
40, 42, 50, 62, 73, 75, 76, 79-95, 103,
119, 120, 139-41, 143-44, 160, 163
Holocaust denial
  as glue between various antisemitic
  movements, 91, 94-94
  in Arab countries, 88-91
  claim that Anne Frank diary is a fraud,
  80
  claim that Hitler protected the Jews,
  85-86
  claim that Jews made up to justify creation of modern State of Israel, 79,
  89-91
  claim that Jews made up to obtain
  reparations, 79
  claim that fewer than six million Jews
  were killed, 78, 83-84
  claim that Nazi crematoria could not
  handle so many bodies, 80, 103
  claim that there were no gas chambers,
  81, 83-84
Holocaust deniers, vii, 21, 78-95, 108

Holocaust education, 2, 4, 76, 128, 139-144, 169
Holocaust relativism, 91-94
Holocaust survivors, 2, 84, 94
Homophobia, 99, 111, 113, 116, 125, 137
Horowitz, David, 129
Human rights, 24, 27, 29, 30, 35, 37, 39, 40-41, 74, 100, 111
Human Rights Watch, 34, 46
Hungary, 164
Hussein, Saddam, 41, 156

Iberian Peninsula, 9
Idaho, 151
Immigration, 11, 20-22, 72, 88, 144, 149-52
Imperialism, 40, 61, 65, 74
Inquisition, 9
Institute for Historical Review (IHR), 80, 87, 89
Interministerial Committee on Human Rights, 25
International Association of Jewish Lawyers and Jurists, 78
International Conference to Establish Field of Hate Studies, 141
International Monetary Fund, 112
Internet, 7, 44, 60, 88, 95, 127-28, 145-46
Interreligious dialogue, 108-09
Intifada (First), 58
Intifada (Second), 2, 7, 134
Iran, 18, 25, 31, 32, 38, 39, 51, 61, 69, 78, 89, 112, 168
Iraq, 18, 45
Iraq War, 91, 155-57;
  charge Jews (or neocons) responsible for, 155-57
Irving, David, 82-89, 90-91;
  antisemitic politics and connection with far-right figures, 87-88
Irving v. Penguin and Lipstadt, 84-88
Islam, 18, 32, 55, 59
Islamic Cultural Center, 50
Islamic Jihad, 60

Islamic States, 73
Islamism, 3, 10, 18, 22, 23, 38, 46-48, 50, 57, 64, 66, 70, 94-95, 108, 167
Islamo-fascism, 57
Islamophobia, 21, 36
Israel Defense Forces (IDF), 130, 168
Israel studies, 128-30, 132, 135
Israel, 13, 14, 17, 18, 19, 36, 39, 42, 102, 113-17, 121-35, 143, 164, 166;
  attacks on legitimacy of, 74, 99, 103, 156-57
  birth of, 56
  as collectivity of Jews, 13, 34, 35, 138
  criticism of as not antisemitic, 100, 103, 112
  call for genocide against, 70
  compared with Nazi Germany, 4, 20, 28, 72, 90, 94-95, 103, 104
  demonization of, 4, 19, 20, 27, 31, 61-69, 70, 76-77, 110, 118-19, 121-22, 128, 143-45
  denial of Jewish people's historical connection with, 27, 74, 89, 99, 104
  denial of equal treatment with other states, 23, 30, 34-35, 38, 41, 76, 100, 103, 157-61
  depleted uranium, claim shoots Palestinians with, 37
  drugs, accused of spreading, 62, 69
  historical homeland for Jews, 74
  HIV, claim inject Palestinians with, 58
  Holocaust, linking need for with, 62
  Holocaust denial, used to deny legitimacy of, 88-91, 94
  ignorance of, 127-29
  lost tribes of, 149
  population figures, 33
  prostitution, accused of spreading, 62,
  Protocols, allegations policies reflect, 58
  regarding September 11 attacks, 43-54, 63, 121
  seen as enemy of humanity, 96
  seen as too powerful, 137
  support for seen as provocation, 121
  target of antisemitism, 102
Turkey, relations with, 61

use of classical antisemitic images to demonize, 103
War of Independence of 1948, 59
water and food, accused of poisoning, 62, 69
See also Six-Day War and Yom Kippur War.
Israel, calls for destruction of, 15, 29, 34, 39, 61, 78, 101, 148, 166, 167-68; by chemical weapons, 167; by biological weapons, 66, 167, by atomic weapons, 78, 167
Israel-Lebanon War (1982), vi
Israel-Lebanon War (2006), 168
Israeli puppeteers, charge of, 155
Israeli-Arab conflict, 3, 10, 167
Israeli-Palestinian conflict, 64, 157
Israeli-Palestinian peace process, vii, 2, 7, 8, 19-21, 23, 27, 90, 116, 139, 148, 156, 160, 164
Italy, 7
Ivory Towers in the Sand, 128

Jackson, Jesse, 36-37, 40
Jacob Blaustein Institute for the Advancement of Human Rights (JBI), 30, 73, 111
Jehovah's Witnesses, 91
Jenin, 75, 76
Jerusalem, 24, 59, 63, 66, 134
Jesus, Second Coming of, 114; charge that Jews responsible for death of, 9, 31, 35, 63, 75, 78, 103, 107-09
Jewish "cabals," charge of, 155
Jewish Caucus (at the United Nations World Conference Against Racism), 23, 35
Jewish Centre, the (at United Nations World Conference Against Racism), 31
Jewish defense organizations, 99, 104, 109, 113-14, 116, 124, 126-27, 131-35, 143, 145, 147, 152, 158, 161-62
Jewish extremism, 57
Jewish holidays, 115
Jewish Onslaught, The, 91
Jewish population (United States), 46, 148

Jewish Question, 76
Jews, 17, 18, 19, 25, 26, 34, 40, 59, 91, 134, 138, 150. *See also* specific countries (e.g., French Jews)
    as a collective, 131
    as a people of the book, 55
    as a people, 10, 41
    as antisemites, 138
    as apes and pigs, 56, 167
    as denied human rights, 23
    as harming or being part of a conspiracy to harm non-Jews, 43, 44, 53, 55, 58, 60, 61-64, 75, 81, 88, 102, 107
    as hating non-Jews, vi
    as having progressed in United States, 118
    as infidels, 56, 58
    as poisoners of wells, 9, 53, 61, 70, 75, 80
    as refugees from Arab lands, 34
    as Satan's offspring, 44, 61-62, 72, 149
    as slayers of prophets, 56, 63
    as synonymous with neocons, 91
    as viewed in Arab and Muslim worlds, 55, 69
    attacks on, 7, 70-72. *See also* hate crimes
    blamed for Islamist acts of terror, 18
    calls for murder of, 29, 32, 167-68; with biological weapons, 168
    charge that control American foreign policy, 44
    charge that control government, 13, 14, 65, 91, 102, 112, 155-56. *See also* Zionist Occupied Government
    charge that control industry, 14, 79
    charge that control media, 11, 14, 44, 50, 60, 79, 102, 105, 112, 133
    charge that control politics, 53
    charge that control things generally, 60-62, 67, 102, 105, 150
    charge that control world economy, 53, 102, 105
    charge that responsible for death of

Jesus, 9, 31, 35, 63, 75, 78, 103, 107-09
charged with having advocated sex with children, 60
charged with being colonialists, 73
charged with being victimizers of Germany, 81
charged with using alcohol to harm non-Jews, 58
charged with using prostitution to harm non-Jews, 58
claim that Jews in Israel are "white," 134
compared with Nazis, 93-95
danger to from Islamic extremists, 70
death threats against, 120
demonization of, 27-30, 31, 55, 60, 64-69, 77, 102, 104, 110, 128, 143, 145, 148, 156, 166-67
denial of equal treatment for, 41, 94
discomfort of some non-Jews seeing Jews defending selves, 75
discomfort of some with Jews in positions of power, 159
dual loyalty, accusations of, 103, 121, 155, 157
European guilt for Holocaust related to, 163
expulsions of, 9
forced conversions of, 9
intimidation of on campus, 130. See also University presidents' statement
lies about on Internet, 145
limited employment for, 9
population in Israel, 33, 64
population in United States, 162
returning to historic homeland, 57
seen as a special class of whites, 125
seen as agents of Zionism, 121
seen as enemies of God, 90
seen as enemies of Islam, 90
seen as killers of innocent children, 121, 122
seen as powerful in antisemitic imagery, vi, 102, 155
seen as representatives of Israel, 98-99,

103, 107
seen as responsible for wrongs committed by non-Jews, 103
seen as responsible for wrongs committed by single Jew, 103
seen as source of sin in the world, 121
September 11 attacks, related to or responsible for, 7, 14, 43-54, 121
special clothes for, 9, 55
stereotypes of, 152. See also stereotypes of Jews
surveys measuring stereotypes about, 136-39
taxes on, 9
threats against safety of on campus, 121
viewed favorably by some non-Jews only when in role of victim, 75
yellow star, forced to wear, 55
Jihad, 43; calls for, 39, 110
Jim Crow, 91
Jones, Jeremy, 28
Jordan, 31, 60, 69, 74
Jordan Times, 28
Jordanian Writers Association, 90
Judaism, 40-41, 55, 57
Judt, Tony, 157

Kahane, Meir, 57
KGB, 133
Khatib, Ghassan, 68
King, Martin Luther, Jr., 24, 99
Klarfeld, Simon, 133
Koran, 10, 56
Kramer, Martin, 128
Krauthammer, Charles, 38
Kries, August, 44
Ku Klux Klan, vi, 43, 79, 129
Kuwait, 47

Labor unions, 137
Lane, Edward William, 56
Latin America, 109, 152, 166
Latino-Jewish Coalition, 152
Latinos, 152
Lausanne, Switzerland, 71

Law enforcement, 138
Law of Return (Israel), 33
Le Pen, Jean-Marie 22
Lebanon, 63, 74, 89, 160, 168
Left-wing politics, 70, 73, 111-13, 133-34, 144; inhospitable to Jews, seen as, 133; inhospitable to Israel, seen as, 113. *See also* Antisemitism
Leuchter, Fred, 83-84
Levitas, Dan, 48
Liberty Lobby, 80
Libya, 31-32, 61
Lieberman, Joseph, 7
Lipstadt, Deborah, 84, 87-88, 91, 134
Lithuania, 105
London, 2, 67, 84-85
Los Angeles, California, 71, 72, 115, 161
Lutheran World Federation, 32
Lutsk, Ukraine, 71
Lyon, France, 70, 71

Mahdi, Ibrahim, 68
Maher, Ahmed, 61
Mahler, Horst, 89
Mahoud, Abdel Halim, 60
Manchester, England, 71
Manifestations of Antisemitism in the EU 2002-2003, 97
Marcellus, Tom, 87
Marr, Wilhelm, 8, 26
Marseilles, France, 70, 71
Martin, Tony, 91
Marxism, 160
Massachusetts Institute of Technology (MIT), 119
Massachusetts, 83
Massad, Joseph, 131
Matas, David, 101
Matzah, 57-58
Matzah of Zion, 58
McCarthy era, 65
McVeigh, Timothy, 67, 150
Mearsheimer, John J., 156
Mein Kampf, 14, 59
Melchior, Michael, 8, 27, 37, 41, 64, 70-71, 76

MEMRI.org, 110
Metzger, Tom, 44
Mexicans, 93-94
Mexico, 7, 93, 148
Middle East and Asian Languages and Cultures (MEALAC), 130-33
Middle East studies programs, 128-33
Militia of Montana, 67
Militias (Middle East), 168
Militias (United States), 39, 67-68, 149-51
Milli Gazete (Turkey), 61
Minikes, Steve, 163-65
Minority rights, 115
Minutemen (1960s), 150
Minutemen (2000s), 150
Mohamad, Mahathir, 61
Montana Human Rights Network, 67-68, 150
Montpelier, France, 71
Montreal, 98, 124
Moran, James P., 156
Morocco, 7, 71
Mossad, 49, 51, 63
Moynihan, Daniel Patrick, 24
Mud people, 149
Mufti of Jerusalem, 59, 66, 73
Multnomah County Courthouse, v
Muslim Extremists, 60
Muslim Public Affairs Council, 51
Muslims, 1, 3, 10, 13, 18, 21, 22, 25, 39, 45-46, 49-54, 55-56, 61, 63, 72-73, 77, 95, 97, 104, 110, 113, 124, 126, 134, 143, 162, 165-66; antisemitism from seen as less serious, 126

Nader, Ralph, 155
Namibia, 36
Nasrallah, Hassan, 168
Nation of Islam, 11, 32, 40, 64, 91
Nation, The, 17
National Alliance, 44
Nazi cartoons (as resembling anti-Israel propaganda), 28
Nazi Germany, 4, 11, 16, 32, 81, 128, 167

Nazis, 1, 3, 20, 59, 62, 64, 69, 76, 78, 80-81, 84, 85, 87, 90, 91-95, 103, 104, 144

Nazism, 58, 88

Neo-Conservatives (neocons), 91, 155-56

Neo-Fascists, 112

Neo-Nazis, 4, 11, 13, 14, 22, 29, 31, 43-44, 58, 60, 62, 63, 80, 81, 878, 89, 112, 125, 153, 157

Netanya, Israel, 68

Netanyahu, Benjamin, 124

Netherlands, The, 7

New Mexico State University at Las Cruces, 140

New York City, v, 2, 50, 67, 68; as "Jew York," 44

NGO Conference before OSCE meeting on Antisemitism, 73

NGO Declaration (at Durban), 23

Nice, France, 71

Nichols, Terry, 150

Non-Aligned Movement, 39

Nongovernmental organizations (NGOs) 24, 25, 28-35, 73, 96, 104, 110-12, 151, 167

Non-Zionist Jews, 101

North Africa, 20

North Atlantic Treaty Organisation (NATO), 164

Northwest Coalition Against Malicious Harassment, 92-94

Northwestern University, 82

Norway, 38

Nuremberg Laws, 91

Nuremberg Trials, 81

"Occupied Jerusalem: A New Soweto?," 29

Office for Democratic Institutions and Human Rights (ODIHR)'s Law Enforcement Officer Training Programme on Combating Hate Crimes, 105, 164

Ohio State University, 126

Oil, 110, 166

Oklahoma City bombing, 49, 67, 150

Organization for Security and Coopera-

tion in Europe (OSCE), 2, 73, 99, 102-06, 111, 146, 163-65, 167. *See also* Berlin Declaration

Organization of the Islamic Conference (OIC), 39, 61

OSCE Conference on Antisemitism (2004), 111

OSCE Meeting on the Relationship between Racist, Xenophobic and Anti-Semitic Propaganda on the Internet and Hate Crimes, 146

Oslo Accords, 19, 47, 90

Ottoman Empire, 57

Pakistan, 100-01

Palestine (including West Bank and Gaza), 29, 32, 34, 40-41, 45, 51, 59, 63, 74, 75, 101, 114-15, 125, 157; Mandatory Palestine, 56

Palestinian Authority, 68, 69, 75, 88

Palestinian press, 19

Palestinian Solidarity Movement, 126

Palestinian textbooks, 90

Palestinians, 13, 19, 20, 29, 30, 31, 34, 36, 39, 40-41, 45, 47, 55, 56, 58, 62-64, 70, 73, 75, 90, 100, 104, 112, 120, 122, 124-24, 130, 133-34, 144, 157, 159-60

Panama, 7

Paris, France, 2, 67, 70, 71, 77, 98-99, 146

Passion of the Christ, 107-09, 112

Passion Play, 108

Passover, 57

Penguin, Ltd., 85

Pennsylvania, 129, 153

Pentagon, 46, 52

Perle, Richard, 155

Pierce, William, 44

Pogroms, v, 11, 15, 108

Pohl, Oswald, 86

Poland, 85

Police training, 164

Political Research Associates (PRA), 40

Political science, 142

Pollock, Karen, 31

Pope John Paul II, 62-63

Portland, Oregon, v-vi
Posse Comitatus, v-vi, 44, 150
Powell, Colin, 2, 35, 38, 111, 155-56
Presbyterian Church USA, 32, 157-59
Press (as a group), 138
Princeton University, 119
Project Interchange, 134
Project Lemonade, 153-54
Prophet Muhammad, 56
Protocols of the Elders of Zion, The, 11, 26, 29, 31, 40, 52, 53, 58-62, 72, 73, 88, 155
Psychology, 142
Public Eye, The, 40

Qatar, 50, 58, 100
Quarantine Theory. *See* Antisemitism
Quotas (to exclude Jews), 118

Racial profiling, 46
Racism, 26, 111, 125, 137, 140; as having an impact on antisemitism, 20-21, 75
Radio Damascus, 24
Radio Islam, 60, 88
Rafsanjani, Ali Akbar Hashemi, 78
Rahowa (Racial Holy War), 43
Ramallah, 133
Rami, Ahmed, 88
Ramlawi, Rabil, 58
Raven, Greg, 87
Refuseniks, 133
Reinharz, Jehuda, 122
Religious right, 113-18
Respublika, 105
Resist, 45
Revolutionary Committees Movement in Libya, The, 31-32
Rifkind, Robert S., 73, 75
Riga, 86
Right of Return (Palestinian), 34
Righteous of the Nations, 144
Right-wing politics, 17, 22, 40, 48, 70, 72-73, 87, 89, 149-52; flirtation with left-wing, 155. *See also* Antisemitism
Roper survey, 137
Russia, 7, 15, 29, 33, 70, 120, 164, 166
Russian Orthodox Church, 166

Russian Revolution of 1905, 16
Rutgers University, 119, 126-27

Samoa, 100
San Francisco State University, 118, 120-22
Saqr, Turky Muhammad, 43, 49, 53
Satan, 149
Saudi Arabia, 47, 53, 58, 60, 63, 69, 110, 112, 166
Saudi Arabian textbooks, 110
Saut Al-Haqq Wa-Al-Hurriyya, 51
Scientific Creationism, 115
Secret Relationship between Blacks and Jews, The, 11, 91
Security (Jewish institutional), 161-62
Security (of Jews in Israel), 167-68
Segregationists, 39
Self-determination (right of), 24, 33-34, 101
Semitism, 1, 8; use of term to deny antisemitism, 26, 31, 36
Seotta, Spain, 70
Separation barrier, 159
September 11, 2001 attacks, 23, 43-69, 110, 119, 121, 124, 148, 151
    claim Israel carried out, 49-54, 58
    claim Jews did not show up for work, 42, 49, 50, 53
    claim Jews manipulated stocks in relation to, 50, 52, 53
    claim U.S. support for Israel was reason for, 43-44, 46-47
    left reaction to, 45, 48
Sexism, 111 *See also* Women's Rights
Sharon, Ariel, 4, 20, 53, 58, 63, 72, 114
Shepard, Matthew, 48
Shoah. *See* Holocaust
Sideman, Richard, 121
Sikhs, 46
Six-Day War, 56, 59, 156
Skinheads, vii, 4, 21, 29
Skokie, Illinois, 153
Slavery, 11, 26, 29, 32, 36, 37, 91, 92, 94, 114
Social psychology, 137, 142

Sociology, 142
South Africa, 7, 28-29, 36, 42, 118-19, 122, 157
Soviet Union, 16, 81, 85, 133, 160; Fall of, 17-19, 23, 24; Former, 113
Spain, 7, 70, 101, 164
Spanish-speaking Americans, 137
Spotlight, The, 17
St. Lawrence University, 119
Stalin, Josef, 16, 91
State University of New York at Stony Brook, 24
Statement of Jewish Caucus (United Nations World Conference Against Racism), 35
States' rights, 39
Stem-cell research, 115
Stereotypes of Jews
    as artful, 97
    as assimilationists, 75
    as capitalists, 75-76
    as cheats, 56
    as clannish, 136
    as communists, 76
    as connected with money, 97
    as corrupt, 97
    as deceitful, 97
    as foreign, 97
    as having too much power, 97, 137
    as hostile, 97
    as landless, 76
    as liars, 56
    as more loyal to Israel, 137, 144. See also Dual loyalty
    as nationalists, 76
    as part of a world conspiracy, 97
    as poor, 75
    as rich, 75, 77
    as separatists, 75
    as shrewd in business, 137
    as storm troopers, 76
    as traitors, 56
    as unclean, 56
    as wanting to be the head of things, 136
    as weak, 76

Stephan, Cookie, 140-41
Stern, Emily, 136
Stewart, Potter, 105
Sudan, genocide in, 74, 113
Suez Canal University, 52
Suhayda, Rocky, 45
Suicide bombers, 41, 68-69, 74, 125, 157, 159
Summers, Lawrence, 119
Surveys. See Attitudinal Surveys
Sweden, 7, 60, 69, 76, 96, 144-45
Switzerland, 7, 41, 71, 89
Syria, 36, 38, 43, 49, 51, 53, 58, 62-63, 69, 89, 168

Taliban, 35, 47
Talmud, 60
"Tear Down the Wall," 159
Technical University of Berlin, 96
Tehran, 25, 27, 43, 49, 53
Tel Aviv, 66-67
Temple Mount, 104
Terror and Liberalism, 47
Terrorism, 46, 63, 66-69, 77, 125-26, 146, 151-52, 156-57, 160, 162, 167
Textbooks. See individual countries. See also United Nations
"That is the fact ... Racism of Zionism & 'Israel,'" 28
Timmerman, Kenneth, 60
Tlass, Mustafa, 49, 58
Toole, Ken, 67-68, 150
Toulouse, France, 71
Treblinka, 3
Tufts University, 119
Tunisia, 72
Ture, Kwame (aka Stokely Carmichael), 24
Turkey, 61
Turks, 88
Turner Diaries, The, 44

Uganda, 66
Ukraine, 71, 164
United Church of Christ, 158-59
United Nations, 40-41, 156, 165; fund-

ing of antisemitic textbooks, 90
United Nations Charter, 23, 35
United Nations General Assembly Resolution 3379, 24-25, 33, 37, 38, 78. *See also* anti-Zionism
United Nations General Assembly, 66
United Nations Human Rights Commission, 41, 58
United Nations World Conference Against Racism, Racial Discrimination, Xenophobia and Related Intolerance, 3, 4, 7, 23-42, 45, 90, 109-10;
Youth Summit, 28, 30. *See also* Durban
United States, 13, 17, 18, 19, 22, 43-44, 45-46, 52, 53, 60, 62, 64, 69, 75, 82, 84, 109, 112, 115, 129, 138, 140, 143, 148-62, 164, 166
Arab land, charge that U.S. presence on is "blasphemy," 47
as "Great Satan," 18, 65
hate crimes in, 7, 71, 82
as imperialist power, 74
Israel, aid to (calls for end of), 43
Israel, as ally of, 74
Israel, claim "slavishly" pro, 43
United States campuses, 118-35, 154, 156. *See also* American Association of University Professors, and individual colleges and universities
United States Constitution, 39, 116, 149
First Amendment (free exercise of religion), 114-16
First Amendment (free speech), 126-27, 146, 152-54
Fourteenth Amendment, 150-51
Nineteenth Amendment, 150
United States Department of State, 1, 143
United States Global Anti-Semitism Act, 165-66
United States House of Representatives Appropriations Subcommittee, 156
United States State Department Report on Global Anti-Semitism, 1, 3, 44
Universal Declaration of Human Rights,

23, 35
University of California, 119, 126
University of Colorado at Boulder, 124
University of Haifa, 161
University of Illinois, 119
University of Maryland, 119
University of Massachusetts, 119
University of Michigan, 119, 126
University of North Carolina, 119
University of Pennsylvania, 119
University presidents' statement, 122-26
Uruguay, 31

Vatican II, 9, 108-09, 152
Victory of Judaism over Germanism, 26
Vienna, 164
Vietnam, 45
Villepin, Dominique, 72
Vilnius, 105
Voting Rights Act of 1965, 99

Walt, Stephen M., 156
Washington, D.C., 76
Washington, George, v
Wayne State University, 119
Weapons of Mass Destruction, 44, 66-69, 168. *See also* Israel and Jews, subcategories of calls for destruction of
Weber, Mark, 87
Weill, Jeffrey, 29-30
Weisskirchen, Gert, 164
Welfare Party (Turkey), 61
Wellesley College, 91
Western Europe, 70, 72, 76, 144. *See also* individual countries
Western Wall, 134
White Americans, 137, 148
White Aryan Resistance, 44
White Citizens Councils, 79
White Europeans, 97
White House, 46, 52, 66
White Nationalists, 22
White Supremacists, 11-13, 22, 40, 44-45, 48, 59, 60, 62, 65, 68, 80, 81, 87-89, 94-95, 112, 120, 146, 151, 153, 155. *See also* individual groups

Wistrich, Robert S., 58-59, 62, 78
Wolfowitz, Paul, 155
Women's rights, 47, 58, 113, 115-16, 125
Working definition of antisemitism. *See* European Monitoring Centre on Racism and Xenophobia
World Church of the Creator, 43
World Council of Churches, 32
World Trade Center, 43, 49-50, 52-53, 63
World War I, 15
World War II, 3, 14, 26, 37, 59, 80, 91-92, 101, 103, 105, 107, 163

Yad Vashem, 144
Yale University, 119
Yedid, Mordechai, 37
Yom Kippur War, 59
Youth Summit. *See* United Nations World Conference Against Racism, Racial Discrimination, Xenophobia and Related Intolerance

Zahran, Gamal, 52, 53
Zayid, Abu, 52
Zimbabwe, 36
Zionism, 12, 14, 23-42, 55, 57, 121, 131, 135, 160, 167
  calls for destruction of, 61 (*see also* Chapter 3)
  Zionism=racism charge, 14, 36, 45, 55, 66, 111
Zionist Occupied Government (ZOG), 12, 17, 65, 67, 156
Zionists, 19, 40, 122-23
  control of banks, charge that, 66, 160
  control of economies, charge that, 53
  control of media, charge that, 40, 50, 53, 66, 160
  control of manufacturing, charge that, 66
  control of politics, charge that, 53
  control of United States, charge that 66, 160
  death threats against, 123
  deaths of Jews in World War II, charge

  that responsible for, 90
  infiltrated CIA, charge that, 66
  invented Holocaust, charge that, 90, September 11 attacks, charge that responsible for, 43-54
  September 11, charge that actions of led to, 44
  Zionist "practice against Semitism" charge, 36
Zoloth, Laurie, 118, 120-21
Zündel, Ernst, 82-83, 89
Zyklon B gas, 81, 83